History as Romantic Art

DAVID LEVIN

HISTORY
AS ROMANTIC ART

Bancroft, Prescott,
Motley, and Parkman

A Harbinger Book
Harcourt, Brace & World, Inc.
NEW YORK AND BURLINGAME

Acknowledgments

In preparing this book I have received invaluable aid from a number of colleagues and former teachers. I owe an immense debt to Professor Perry Miller, whose criticism has helped me immeasurably since the time he was my tutor in Harvard College, and whose lectures on *Romanticism in American Literature* supplied me with essential insights to the period. I am grateful, also, to Professor Oscar Handlin for helpful criticisms, suggestions, and encouragement; and to my colleague Professor Yvor Winters and Professor Kenneth Murdock, both of whom graciously allowed me to audit their lectures on American historians as men of letters. Among other kind friends who read portions of the manuscript, Professors Charles A. Allen, Howard Mumford Jones, Thomas C. Moser, Thomas Pressly, and Henry Nash Smith should recognize their valuable suggestions in the text. I am deeply indebted to the Massachusetts Historical Society for permission to use the papers of George Bancroft, George E. Ellis, Edward Everett, Francis Parkman, and W. H. Prescott; to Mr. Stephen T. Riley, Director of the Society; to the editorial staff of the Stanford University Press; and to Mr. Walter W. Isle, who prepared the Index.

Chapter VII was published in substantially the same form in the Prescott memorial issue of *The Hispanic-American Historical Review* (February, 1959).

Preface

Historians and literary critics have always placed William Hickling Prescott, John Lothrop Motley, and Francis Parkman alongside Henry Adams as the giants of nineteenth-century American historical writing, and they have usually regarded George Bancroft as an important, if wayward, pioneer. Of the four older writers, however, only Parkman has received much critical attention during the last fifty years, and most studies of Parkman and the others have concentrated more on biography than on the historical works. The standard literary histories, moreover, recognize some affinity among the four historians, but then treat them separately, underscoring their individual differences.

There are good reasons, of course, for emphasizing biography. Bancroft the transcendental Democrat—who earned a German doctorate in philology, talked with Goethe about Byron and Coleridge, and then came home to found a progressive school and to enter politics as campaign biographer, Secretary of the Navy, diplomat—is an extremely attractive, difficult figure. Although his *History of the United States* expresses a notoriously effusive patriotism that he called "objective," he was capable of great shrewdness not only in political strategy but in perceiving the subjectivity of other historians.

Bancroft's close friend Prescott had a much less complex career and a much less puzzling personality. But his biography gains considerable interest from the collegiate injury that nearly blinded him and from the determination with which, though wealthy enough to live an easy life, he relied on one eye for his writing and the aid of an oral reader for his research. A bland, charming conservative, he seems no less different from the energetically Democratic Bancroft than from Parkman and Motley, both of whom seem to have suffered from neurotic anxieties.

Motley, too, was comfortably rich, and he spent most of his adult years traveling and writing in the high society of Boston, England, and the Continent: joining Thackeray and Macaulay at dinner; living as the guest, first, of the Queen of the Netherlands, and then, of his old friend Bismarck. But his career also had its gloomier drama. His passionate devotion to honor and justice spilled out not only onto the pages of his histories of the Netherlands, but into two diplomatic controversies that cost him his posts as Minister to Austria and then as Minister to Great Britain.

Parkman's life is surely the best known and the most pathetic of the four. The grim intensity with which he tracked down historical facts and vigorous experience in Nature makes a fine subject in itself. But his story becomes irresistible when one watches him work daily for only a few minutes, after a doctor has warned him that concentrated thought will drive him mad. His contempt for physical weakness, his passionate attacks on woman suffrage, and his heroic efforts to continue strenuous exercise after he had been crippled by arthritis give a peculiar interest to his historical achievement and his portraits of manly heroes.

These differences are important, and no critic of the histories can ignore them. But they can too easily tempt one to ignore even more relevant similarities. Although Prescott and Bancroft were students at Harvard before Motley and Parkman were born, it is more important to notice that all four went to Harvard; that Motley studied at Bancroft's Round Hill School; that Parkman read Bancroft's volume on La Salle and the Jesuits carefully in the year before he decided that he himself would write a history of France and England in North America. Both Motley and Parkman consulted Bancroft about various parts of their histories, and Bancroft and Prescott frequently consulted each other. All four historians, moreover, looked on the Past from a common geographical and cultural position.

Even if these biographical facts were not available, the massive evidence heaped up in the histories themselves and in the historians' journals and correspondence would make the relationship quite clear. In this book, therefore, I have declined to assume that the uniqueness of a writer's psychological experience or political ideas explains his most significant literary techniques. The evidence has forced me to ask instead whether other causes might not have been equally influential. If Bancroft's La Salle differs little from Parkman's, and if both La Salles resemble some characters of Byron's, then Parkman's battle with his own mysterious "Enemy" (his undiagnosed malady) does not necessarily explain his portrayal of La Salle.

For these reasons I have concentrated first on the histories and papers of all four men and on their relationship to other writers. One cannot understand the individual history without understanding its vocabulary and its context. In Parts 1 and 2 I have delineated the literary conventions that function in all these histories, and I have examined the relationship between the historian's assumptions and his literary techniques. In short, I have tried here to combine literary and intellectual history with literary criticism.

Clarifying the histories has also required me to answer some important questions about American versions of romantic thought. The common notion that Prescott, Motley, and Parkman sought some kind of escape from the Present into the Past is erroneous. Nor did Prescott try, as one critic has claimed, to put the Past safely away in a separate place. All three Brahmins sought as earnestly as Bancroft to give the meaning as well as the experience of history an immediacy in their own time. They all shared an "enthusiastic" attitude toward the Past, an affection for grand heroes, an affection for Nature and the "natural." But whether he approached the darker vision of Hawthorne and Melville or the expansive optimism of Whitman, every one of them saw history as a continuing development toward nineteenth-century America, the most "natural" of nations. Their histories tell a remarkably consistent, composite story of Western development from the Reformation through the American Revolution. They regarded romantic conventions not as meaningless stereotypes, but as effective ways of communicating a message that all their literate contemporaries would understand.

One of my major purposes, then, is to illuminate the individual histories by studying conventional themes, characters, and language in all of them. Yet this process of abstraction inevitably causes some distortion. When a conventional character is lifted out of the history in which he was originally placed, he may seem as lonely and unreal as the Byronic hero himself. For this reason, and because the evaluation of any work of art must consider it as a unit, I have devoted Part 3 to separate studies of the three best histories: Prescott's *The Conquest of Mexico,* Motley's *The Rise of the Dutch Republic,* and Parkman's *Montcalm and Wolfe.*

My judgment of these three masterpieces proceeds from a few convictions that can be stated briefly. I believe that the writing of history is a literary art, and that history is one of the most difficult of literary forms. However "scientific" the historian's preoccupations or research, he must eventually select the evidence that merits preservation in his work, and any principle of selection implies at least the quest for a coherent order, the choice of one or two major themes. If he believes that individual experience affects the development of history, he must find some convincing way of portraying human character, and he cannot avoid some evaluation of character. He must also arrange the events so that those which he considers most important appear to be the most important, while his narrative reveals a coherent relationship among events, between action and character, between particular fact and general principle.

These are literary problems, but one cannot divorce them from more narrowly "historical" questions without risking the absurdity that H. H. Brackenridge ridiculed when he wrote his model of pure form unencumbered by content. No serious student of history or literature will actually read Motley or Prescott "for his style," although some people talk of doing so. The judgment of a historian's characterization, his structure, and even his style must be based at least partly on his fidelity to the evidence and the validity of his interpretation. The history written by previous generations will always display interesting contemporary attitudes, but it can endure as literature only if it presents a defensible version, however liable to revision, of historical truth.

Clearly, then, the criticism of history, like the writing of history, demands more gifts than most men who attempt it can bring to it. The ideal critic of these four historians should know the literary materials on which I shall draw so heavily, and the historians' own sources as well: the records of fifteenth- and sixteenth-century Spain, France, England, Mexico, Peru, and the Netherlands; of seventeenth- and eighteenth-century France, England, and America. Since I cannot pretend to such erudition, I have had to rely on secondary materials for those periods, except for some random checking and the original research that I have done in American colonial history. The accuracy of particular statements of fact in the New England histories lies beyond my chief interest here and, with few exceptions, beyond my competence. I have assumed that transcriptions of documents in the histories are accurate, and my judgment of the historians' interpretations usually focuses on general questions or on those that can be discussed on the basis of internal evidence. One should understand, however, that although each of these historians has been criticized with varying severity for some faulty research, specialists in their different fields agree that most of their research was sound.

D. L.

Stanford University
July 10, 1959

Contents

1

ROMANTIC ATTITUDES

Themes and Judgment

CHAPTER I

The Historian as Romantic Man of Letters

In short, the true way of conceiving the subject is, not as a philosophical theme, but as an epic in prose, a romance of chivalry; as romantic and chivalrous as any which Boiardo or Ariosto ever fabled . . . ; and which, while it combines all the picturesque features of the romantic school, is borne onward on a tide of destiny, like that which broods over the fiction of the Grecian poets; for surely there is nothing in the compass of Grecian epic or tragic fable, in which the resistless march of destiny is more discernible, than in the sad fortunes of the dynasty of Montezuma. It is, without doubt, the most poetic subject ever offered to the pen of the historian.

PRESCOTT, Notebooks IX (MHS)

Before me lies a bundle of these sermons, rescued from six-score years of dust, scrawled on their title-pages with names of owners dead long ago, worm-eaten, dingy, stained with the damps of time, and uttering in quaint old letterpress the emotions of a buried and forgotten past.

PARKMAN, *Montcalm and Wolfe*

Behind all the histories of George Bancroft, William Prescott, John Motley, and Francis Parkman lies the conviction that the historian is a man of letters. Although their names dominated American historical writing for fifty years, every one of these men had established a place in the New England literary community before he wrote a word of history. Bancroft published a volume of poetry and wrote regularly for *The North American Review*; Prescott wrote a series of critical essays for the same journal; Motley published two historical novels, two essays on Goethe, and a long essay on Balzac for *The North American Review*; and before Parkman began his *France and England in North America*, he had written *The Oregon Trail*, a critical essay on Cooper, and his only novel. Of the four, only Parkman had decided in his earliest adult years to write a major history, but by the time he made that decision as a college freshman in 1841 he had the examples of Washington Irving, Jared Sparks, Prescott, and Bancroft.[1]

Membership in this literary aristocracy did not mean being a professional writer. The New England man of letters was a gentleman of letters, trained for some other, more "useful" profession and usually practicing it. Bancroft prepared for the ministry; Prescott, Motley, and Parkman made gestures toward the law. Both Motley and Bancroft tried to build careers in politics even after they had written their most successful histories, and Motley tried strenuously to get himself appointed to a Columbia professorship in history.[2] None of these men, moreover, had to write history for a living; they all considered some other useful occupation a duty, and Prescott and Parkman were prevented mainly by their physical disabilities from putting historiography in its "proper" place as an avocation.[3]

Thus the four historians typified the large community of men of letters that distinguished Unitarian Boston in the first four decades of the nineteenth century. They belonged to the world of the Everett brothers: Alexander, the diplomat, editor, essayist; and Edward, the minister, orator, politician, professor, college president. As a diplomat in Spain, Alexander served as Prescott's agent, document hunter, and overseer of copyists, and in England Edward performed the same favor—as well as some free copying himself—for Bancroft. As editors, at different times, of *The North American Review*, both brothers acted to introduce foreign literature to America and to encourage American writers. Motley's closest friend was Oliver Wendell Holmes, the doctor; Prescott's two confidential advisers were George Ticknor, a lawyer first and later a scholar, and William Howard Gardiner, another lawyer who revised Prescott's *Ferdinand and Isabella* for publication and then wrote a laudatory review of it.[4]

During the early years of Unitarianism, then, it was the Bostonian gentleman's duty to promote American letters, and the Unitarian ministers set the example. Perhaps O. B. Frothingham exaggerated when he defined the most conservative ministers' belief as "literary Unitarianism," but the phrase named a fundamental interest of the whole fraternity, conservatives and radicals alike. Joseph Buckminster, William Ellery Channing, Ralph Waldo Emerson, Theodore Parker, Jared Sparks, Andrews Norton, George Ripley, Charles W. Upham, John Gorham Palfrey, Edward Everett, George Bancroft—all were Unitarian ministers even more dedicated than their seventeenth-century predecessors to encouraging scholarship and good literature.

Indeed the reputations of Sparks and Bancroft did not suffer noticeably when the two young ministers decided to abandon the pulpit for scholarship, teaching, and letters. (As a new minister Sparks had been praised by his Boston friends for his delivery, but his style, one of them wrote, turned out to be "rather inferior to what we expected.")[5] Even Emerson was cherished in the fold until he was identified as archangel of "The Latest Form of Infidelity."

These Unitarian ministers also perpetuated their Puritan ancestors' strong interest in history. Whatever their allegiance in the Unitarian-Transcendentalist war, the question of the historicity of miracles engaged their attention.[6] For the rational, orthodox Unitarian, who had been repelled by trinitarian dogma, theology itself was a historical science, to be based on verifiable evidence. Andrews Norton, who had *not* gone to Germany to be corrupted by the most irreverent Biblical critics, wrote volumes emphasizing the historicity of miracles as the basis for Christian faith.[7] And Harvard sent young George Bancroft to study under Johann Eichhorn at Göttingen, there to be made into "an accomplished philologian and Biblical critic, able to expound and defend the oracles of God."[8] By thus pointedly reminding Eichhorn of the conclusions to which Bancroft's investigations were expected to lead, and by admonishing Bancroft to acquire Eichhorn's knowledge without catching his infidelity, Norton and President Kirkland made almost pathetically clear the orthodox Unitarian's belief in historical study. Although well aware that some German scholars liked to "scoff at the Bible and laugh at Christ,"[9] they sent this eighteen-year-old boy to learn the facts and methods which German scholars could teach. Eventually Kirkland advised Bancroft to give up Biblical criticism and German theology,[10] but he did not object to Bancroft's heavy concentration on historical study. Bancroft read all of Tacitus, Livy, Herodotus, and Thucydides in the original, and he studied under Heeren, whose *History of the Political Systems of Europe* he later translated.[11] This was part of the theologian's training.[12] At Bancroft's doctoral examination Eichhorn examined him in history; a decade later the young American followed Eichhorn's example, moving from theology and criticism to history.[13]

Without emulating Bancroft's apostasy to transcendentalism and Jacksonism, Jared Sparks took the same step from the ministry to history (becoming one of Parkman's Harvard teachers), and John Gorham Palfrey and Charles W. Upham combined preaching with diligent historical labor. Edward Everett, too, dabbled in the fashionable avocation by writing "The Life of John Stark" for Sparks's *Library of American Biography*.[14]

And in *Representative Men* Emerson himself, having rejected "historical Christianity," tried to write a new kind of history.

The Unitarian's religious inclination to historical study does not, of course, explain the strong general historical interest of this period, either in Boston or in the large world outside New England. If the Unitarian man of letters was interested in history because he was a Unitarian, he was interested also because he was a man of letters and an American. The patriotic call for a native literature had been reiterated since the days of the Connecticut Wits, and during the first thirty years of the new century Americans expressed the same growing desire to discover and preserve historical records that permeated Spain, France, Germany, and England during those years.[15] Municipal, state, and eventually federal appropriations encouraged the collection and publication of historical documents. In this atmosphere New England gentlemen considered it their patriotic duty to help the writers of their country's history, even those whose political bias offended them. Although Bancroft's activity for the Democratic party was regarded as apostasy,[16] and although it has been said that every page of his history voted for Andrew Jackson, his most determined political enemies considered him the historian of his country, and they helped him cordially when they could. Prescott's father, the old Federalist judge, "trembled with delight" when his son read him Bancroft's outline for the battle of Bunker Hill; Amos A. Lawrence, the pro-Bank, high-tariff Whig, sent Bancroft a cordial letter in 1842, offering him revolutionary documents; and Edward Everett continued to help him despite the political strains on their friendship.[17]

Important though this context is, however, the essential characteristic of the Unitarian's view of history was the kind of literature he had in mind when he referred to historical research as "literary research."[18] To the most conservative men of the older generation, the founders of Boston's Athenaeum, this expression meant simply that history was a branch of letters and that histories should be well written. Trained in the classics, they had read the Greek and Latin historians, and their affection for eighteenth-century English literature led them to think of Robertson and Gibbon when they thought of history. But to most New England men of letters after 1820 the expression carried new meanings suggested by the foreign books which the Athenaeum had been buying. They read not only Scott and Cooper but Wordsworth, Coleridge, and Byron. Those who had been to Göttingen read Schiller, Goethe, Herder, and perhaps Jacob Grimm; those who had not, read essays about them in *The North American Review*.[19]

Like so many lines in intellectual history, the lines leading to the sources of these historical ideas crossed in many directions, and different New Englanders held different lines. Some led directly to Germany, but more led to France and England: to Mably, Barante, Sismondi, Cousin; to Southey, Scott, Macaulay, and Carlyle. For all those minds informed by these lines the idea of "literary" history included new assumptions about the value and meaning of the Past, about the proper subjects for historical work, about the function of history, and about proper emphasis within the historical work. The historian was a romantic man of letters.

2

The New England historian was conditioned by the very attitude toward the Past that one can find in almost any literary young American's letters home from Europe during the early years of the nineteenth century—by the inclination to wallow in sentiment at the sight of ruins. The calm Prescott, whose prose and temperament were so stately in their balance, admitted that it was Gibbon's autobiography that had first moved him to consider becoming a historian;[20] and his susceptibility to Gibbon's account of inspiration among the ruins on Capitoline Hill seems unemotional in comparison with a letter he wrote his parents in 1816. "When I look into a Greek or Latin book," he said, "I experience much the same sensation one does who looks on the face of a dead friend, and the tears not infrequently steal into my eyes."[21] The extravagance of the comparison, the obvious posturing in the entire sentence, Prescott's confidence that his parents would know what the sensation was—these underscore the conventionality of the statement. One finds the same kind of prescribed sentiment in the awe with which he first viewed "the chaste Gothic" of Tintern Abbey, and in his "profound" emotion when he first saw some of England's other "venerable ruins."[22] Usually more extravagant than Prescott in both style and temperament, the young Bancroft told Andrews Norton that he was delighted to discover "how intimately" a learned man can "commune with antiquity," how "he rests upon her bosom as upon the bosom of a friend. He can hear the small feeble voice, that comes from remote ages, & which is lost in the distance to common ears."[23]

By the time Motley made his first trip to Europe one could even admit the self-consciousness of the conventional emotion in the same letter in which one expressed it. Having told his parents of two "complete and perfect ruins, but very well preserved," Motley apologized for his "very tame description"; "I shall undoubtedly see many a thousand times more interesting on the Rhine," he said, "but the effect which this first antiquity had upon my brain was so turbulent that it effervesced for some time, and at last evaporated in a disagreeably long ode in the German taste, which, however, I will not increase the postage of this letter with."[24] One might hear the "small feeble voice" of remote ages when contemplating a complete and perfect ruin or the site of any historic action. One might hear it speaking through a "barbaric" epic—not only Ossian's but the Spaniard Ercilla's as well[25]—or through the unruined architecture of Belgian cities, which Motley found just as picturesque as "the most striking and stirring tragedies" enacted there.[26]

Secure in the country of the future, the American writer could still lament conventionally, as Motley did on several occasions, the "naked and impoverished" appearance which the absence of a "pictured, illuminated Past" gave America.[27] But even in America Parkman heard the feeble voice from among the "blasted trunks," the "towering sentries" of the primeval forest.[28] And one could certainly hear it speaking from the authentic documents, the genuine private letters and diaries of historic figures. Wherever one heard the voice, one concentrated on responding emotionally to its sound, on putting oneself or one's reader in proper imaginative relation with it—with its reality as well as its message. To be thrilled with the idea of participating in a continuing history, to imagine the ruin in its former wholeness, and the life that it contained; to feel melancholy over, though seeing the moral in, those "silent Tadmors and Palmyras, where the fox dwells in the halls of forgotten princes"; to imagine oneself on the most familiar terms with "any ghost that ever flits by night across the moonlight air" of a historic city—this was the conventional experience of the literary observer.[29] In the ancient natural scenery, the vanished Aztec and Inca dynasties and architectural ruins, or the relics of French empire in North America, Bancroft, Prescott, and Parkman found the same opportunities for imaginative contemplation of the Past that Motley restricted to the Old World.

This romantic attitude toward the Past applied to human experience itself. The beauty in relics and scenes seemed less important than "their historic associations."[30] What thrilled the writer was his contact with the life, the vital feeling of the Past. To a group of men whose literary experience, however varied, hammered so consistently on the theme of *experiencing*, of the observer's responses to objects and ideas, no history could be valuable unless it brought the Past to life upon the printed page. Whether from Schiller and Goethe (whom Bancroft and Motley admired), from Wordsworth (whom all four historians read) or from Byron (whom all four read and admired), the New England man of letters acquired the habit not only of searching his own feelings when confronted with an affecting natural or historical scene, but of trying to share the felt experience of others. Not all these historians would have said with Keats, "According to my state of mind I am with Achilles shouting in the trenches, or with Theocritus in the vales of Sicily."[31] But they all tried to convey this sense of historical mobility to their readers by describing what some real Achilles in the trenches had felt. Nor would New England moralists have agreed with Carlyle that "the Dead are all holy, even they that were base and wicked when alive";[32] but they would have applauded his interpretation of the essential truth that Scott had taught "to writers of history and others":

. . . that bygone ages of the world were actually filled by living men, not by protocols, state-papers, controversies and abstractions of men. Not abstractions were they, not diagrams or theorems; but men, in buff or other coats and breeches, with colour in their cheeks, with passions in their stomach, and the idioms, features, and vitalities of very men. ["Men"] is a little word. . . . History will henceforth have to take thought of it. Her faint hearsays of "philosophy teaching by experience" will have to exchange themselves everywhere for direct inspection and embodiment: this, and this only, will be counted experience; and till once experience have got in, philosophy will reconcile herself to wait at the door. It is a great service, . . . this that Scott has done; a great truth laid open by him.[33]

Whether or not Scott laid open this great truth, the New England historians considered it a fundamental truth. They concentrated on literary technique, "interest," and effect not only because they had been literary men before they became historians, but also because they believed that the re-creation of the Past requires imaginative and literary skill. To give events their natural coloring, as Bancroft wanted to do,[34] to re-create men with passions in their stomach, one had to be "literary." The so-called philosophical historians were in disrepute.[35] The New England historians did not object primarily to their Toryism or to their writing (Prescott, for one, admired Hume's style);[36] the issue was the *kind* of experience that should be let in while philosophy waited at the door. Vitality, color, embodiment—these are the most important ideas in Carlyle's paragraph. The proper subject for the historian was one in which types of "very men" and ideas could be embodied. Prescott did not want to write as Hallam did, "like a technical Jurist."[37] Bancroft said he was unworried by the competition of Jared Sparks because *he* did not intend to write "a Mignet compendium"; "details," he added, "give life and charm."³⁸

Prescott's notebooks reveal how strongly the "literary attitude" could influence the choice of subjects. In his first written notice that he was considering a history of Ferdinand and Isabella, he said he preferred it "as more novel and entertaining" than any alternative topic. His recurrent doubts about the subject grew out of his dislike for "minute details," his desire to avoid "what I detest, hunting up latent barren antiquities."³⁹ When he confirmed his decision "finally, for the hundredth time," in 1828—after having long abandoned the subject for a study of English literature—he stressed again the idea that the narrative would be *interesting*; he reminded himself to "aim at wide rather than deep views, at a popular, rather than erudite compilation, avoiding intricate research, particularly in antiquities, and particularly too on topics relating to constitutions of Government, or economy." Such a history, he argued, "may be made novel, elegant, useful, and very entertaining. What more can I desire?"

But he needed still more convincing. "If I cannot *approfondir* an historical subject like Hume and Gibbon and such gentry," he wrote later on the page, "I can come nearer to the superficial merits of Roscoe and Watson; & is not this as well as to write like a technical Jurist, as Mr. Hallam does?" He warned himself to be scrupulous about "facts, facts," even to display this fidelity "a little ostentatiously." But again he came back to qualify, as he always did in these notes, in the name of interest: "Mem.: Never introduce what is irrelevant or superfluous, . . . for the sake of crowding in more facts. They injure yᵉ interest, and yᵉ effect."⁴⁰

This same refrain runs through the journal Prescott kept while writing *The Conquest of Mexico*. Despite its faults, he said, Voltaire's *Charles XII* had "the great requisite—in a work meant to be popular—of *interest*."⁴¹ "Interest, interest, interest," he commanded himself after he had finished the introduction to *The Conquest of Mexico*, "—I have given the reader, or at least myself—a sweat in the Introduction. The rest must be play for both of us." Preparing to write a few days later, he exhorted himself to "keep in view the most important, stirring, affecting incidents. . . . Above all, keep *character*,—& especially the pervading, dominant character of the hero in view. Omit no act or word of his that can illustrate it. Interest is created out of character. All other interest is not only inferior in kind, but in degree."⁴²

Prescott resolved, therefore, to follow Mably's method in *The Conquest of Mexico*: "sticking to the thread of the narrative," "approfondiring character," and giving the story a "dramatic interest" wherever possible. Although he remarked that this "unphilosophical plan" was not ideal for every historical subject,[43] the qualification seems unimportant when one remembers his comment on Hallam: Prescott never chose a subject that did not invite such an unphilosophical plan. Nor did Bancroft, Motley, or Parkman. Certainly the interest in human character was not new to historiography—Prescott reread Livy, "the greatest of painters," while writing *The Conquest of Mexico*[44]—but the complex of ideas and feelings to which this interest was central led the romantic historian to choose particular kinds of subjects and characters.

The subject had to be an interesting narrative, on a "grand theme," in which a varied group of remarkable, vigorous characters acted heroically on the largest possible stage. The grand theme involved the origins of a nation (preferably, in some way, America), the progress of Liberty in her battle against Absolutism, the conquest of a continent, or all of these. It included, if possible, some "poetic"—that is, melancholy—incidents. The scenery had to include something of the picturesque, and as much of the sublime as possible.

Interest and character, stirring incidents, variety of characters—these terms recur endlessly in the historians' notebooks and journals, in their letters of congratulation, and in their literary criticism. They all knew Mably's *Sur l'étude de l'histoire*, which Prescott said he read "for the tenth time" while writing *The Conquest of Mexico*;[45] they all knew and used Barante and Macaulay, both of whom Prescott paraphrased in his review of Irving's *Conquest of Granada*.[46] From some of their critical remarks, however, and especially from their presentation of character, scene, and incident, it seems clear that they also found useful models in historical fiction. They distinguished, of course, between history and historical romance; although they often compared the two genres, they were always careful on such occasions to boast of their restraint in avoiding "imaginary" conversations, of their fidelity to the documents.[47] But while they respected the theories and techniques of the French and English historians, they admired no historian more than they admired Sir Walter Scott.

Parkman, then, does Cooper a great honor when he says that the American novelist sometimes "approaches" Scott, and his reason for placing both writers at the head of English literature echoes the very language of Carlyle. "Their conceptions of character," Parkman declares, "were no mere abstract ideas, or unsubstantial images, but solid embodiments in living flesh and blood." Here again, embodiment, the external re-creation, represents essential character, and when Parkman chooses Natty Bumppo as his finest example of Cooper's "breathing men,"[48] he reserves his highest praise for externals: "The tall, gaunt form of Leatherstocking, the weather-beaten face, the bony hand, the cap and foxskin, and the old hunting-frock, polished with long service, seem so palpable and real that in some moods of mind one may easily confound them with the memories of his own experiences." It is no accident that Parkman refers to Cooper's characters as "portraitures," or that he says Cooper's "reputation must . . . rest upon three or four finely conceived and admirably executed portraits."

3

This analogy to portraiture appears so frequently in the letters and histories of the four historians that one might easily dismiss it as a cliché. Like many conventional metaphors, however, it deserves careful attention. Behind all the allusions to historical painting and broad canvases lie significant assumptions about historical technique. The romantic historian considered himself a painter.

Motley revealed the basis of this comparison when he praised Rubens' *Descent from the Cross* in the same rhetoric that Parkman chose to praise Scott and Cooper:

It seems to me as if I had really stood at the Cross, and seen Mary weeping on John's shoulder, and Magdalen receiving the dead body of the Saviour in her arms. Never was the grand tragedy presented in so profound and dramatic a manner. For it is not only his colour, in which this man so easily surpasses the world, but in his *life-like flesh and blood action*, the tragic power of his composition. And is it not appalling to think of the large constitution of this man, when you reflect on the acres of canvas which he has covered? How inspiriting to see with what *muscular masculine vigor* this splendid Fleming rushed in and plucked up drowning Art by the locks. . . . Well might Guido exclaim, "The fellow mixes blood with his colours!"

He is certainly the Shakespeare of painting. . . . How providentially did the man come in and invoke *living, breathing, moving men and women* out of his canvas![49]

Rubens was the "Shakespeare of painting"; Scott, Prescott said, "Shakespeare in prose."[50] The qualities admired in both, and the qualities Parkman praised in Cooper, were the same: energy, masculine vigor, flesh-and-blood action, stirring movement, color, the illusion of participation. In the essay on Cooper and the essay on Scott, moreover, Parkman and Prescott admired the vigor and energy of the authors themselves, just as Motley admired Rubens. How valuable these qualities seemed, one can infer from the critics' pleasure in finding them not only in the novelists' work but in their personal character.[51] They were qualities that could be suggested pictorially, on canvas or on the printed page.

The habit of conceiving the subject pictorially had many important effects on the histories. The most obvious was the convention of writing "portraits" or "sketches" of characters as they appeared—and even, sometimes, as they died. The term "sketch" was not simply a metaphor, for a character sketch usually began with a careful description based on a contemporary portrait. These historians agreed with Carlyle (and with Hawthorne) that a portrait reveals the essential character of the subject;[52] indeed, some of their verbal portraits show the influence of phrenology. Motley's description of two sons of William the Silent demonstrates how literally the analogy could be applied. The stock figure of the "Jesuitical" conspirator (exemplified by Scott's Rashleigh Osbaldistone)[53] appears in William's oldest son and namesake, whom Philip II had carried off to Spain when William fled the Netherlands.

He had already become so thoroughly Hispaniolized under the masterly treatment of the King and the Jesuits, that even his face had lost all resemblance to the type of his heroic family, and had acquired a sinister, gloomy, forbidding expression, most painful to contemplate. All of the good that he had retained was a reverence for his father's name.

The next son was Maurice, then seventeen years of age, a handsome youth, with dark-blue eyes, well-chiseled features, and full red lips, who had already manifested a courage and concentration of character beyond his years.[54]

In such a contrast, the conventional juxtaposition of dark and fair symbolizes the antithesis of the sinister Jesuit "treatment" and the candid, manly heritage of Nassau. But Maurice of Nassau lived to become the arch-enemy and "judicial murderer" of another of Motley's heroes, the Arminian Barneveld. The portraits of Maurice in *John of Barneveld* retain some traces of the frank Nassauvian face depicted above; but a phrenological blight has afflicted the lower half of the face, and the color of the eyes has changed:

The face, although unquestionably handsome, offered a sharp contrast within itself; the upper half all intellect, the lower half quite sensual. Fair hair growing thin, but hardly tinged with grey, a bright, cheerful and thoughtful forehead, large hazel eyes within a singularly large orbit of brow; a straight, thin, slightly aquiline, well-cut nose—such features were at open variance with the broad, thick-lipped, sensual mouth, the heavy pendant jowl, the sparse beard on the glistening cheek, and the mole-skin-like moustachio and chin tuft.[55]

One sees the full implication of this change when Motley paints the two enemies at their final confrontation; by that time all the honorific color has disappeared from Maurice's face and eyes:

The Advocate, with long grey beard and stern blue eyes, haggard with illness and anxiety, tall but bent with age, leaning on his staff and wrapped in black velvet cloak—an imposing magisterial figure; the *florid, plethoric* Prince in brown doublet, big russet boots, narrow ruff, and shabby felt hat with its string of diamonds, with hand clutched on sword-hilt, and *eyes full of angry menace,* the very type of the high-born, imperious soldier—thus they surveyed each other as men, once friends, between whom a gulf had opened.[56]

However strongly one might object to this manipulation of rhetoric to praise and then condemn the same person, one must notice that these are three portraits of a man at different stages of his life, and in different moods. Rightly or wrongly, Motley is using a portrait in the same way in which Hawthorne used his portrait of Judge Pyncheon in *The House of the Seven Gables*: to reveal pictorially the character of the subject. It is only fair to remember that the Prince in the last portrait is a jealous Prince who has been described through allusions to Othello.[57]

Usually, of course, the successive portraits of a major figure were more consistent with each other than these three portraits of Maurice. Once the portrait of a major character had been presented, the writer might use it frequently, keeping before the reader a visual idea of the character's nature. Motley's sketches of Philip II leaning over his desk in the Escorial, and of the dark Henry, Duke of Guise; Prescott's gloomy Ferdinand, darker than the fair Isabella; Parkman's stern but passionate Pontiac, who was "darker than is usual with his race"[58]—these reiterated images are only a few of the most striking examples. Although Motley's repetitiousness eventually becomes tiresome, such an image as that of Philip bending over his desk is, as Macaulay felt historical pictures should be, "not merely traced on the mind, but branded into it."[59]

These examples demonstrate that the romantic historians often dealt in character types. "The types are various," Bancroft wrote to Edward Everett, "grand in their character, and capable of being arranged in an interesting narrative."[60] The "arrangement" of types was often an arrangement of pictures. Whenever clear historical evidence did not contradict the convention, a villain, for example, was painted in colors and lines much the same as those Motley used for the "Hispaniolized" son of William the Silent. Looking at an "engraved portrait" before writing about Father Olier, founder of the Sulpitian Seminary, Parkman said that "his countenance, though marked both with energy and intellect, was anything but prepossessing. Every lineament proclaims the priest."[61]

Despite the strong temptation to do so, one would be unwise to conclude from this statement alone that Parkman was anti-Catholic; the description itself indicates that Parkman, like Motley, was consciously writing within a phrenological context and a strict literary convention. When the details of Maurice's historical face do not support the emotion Motley wants to suggest, he abstracts "floridity," takes the color from the eyes, substitutes the phrase "eyes full of angry menace," and relies lamely on the abstraction "the very type of the high-born, imperious soldier"; in the portrait of Olier, who is not a major figure in his history, Parkman abstracts all the qualities from the engraved portrait: he gives no details at all.

In a multivolume history that emphasized individual characters, the resources of the palette were bound to be quickly exhausted in the pictorial suggestion of emotion and temperament. By the time the writer had described a dozen faces and forms, he would have found it difficult to keep from repeating himself even if he had determined to avoid "types." But these writers considered the types an advantage. Like Cooper and Scott, they were interested in generalizing about such subjects as "national character," and in illustrating through minor characters such abstracted traits as "remarkable resolution," "intrepidity" (especially the intrepidity of an occasional woman), and chivalric generosity. They seemed pleased, too, to be able to show at times that a genuine historical character resembled the fictitious creations of a Scott or a Cooper. When Prescott, for example, sent Bancroft a list of episodes in *Ferdinand and Isabella* from which Democratic reviewers might want to quote, he emphasized a moving scene that was "very like the scene described by Scott, of Louis XI and the Astrologer, in Quentin Durward, vol. III., chap. 6. Eng. ed."[62] And he pointed out the same connection in the text of his history.

In using the conventional character the historian had whatever advantage came from his reader's familiarity with the convention; but at the same time he knew that the historicity of the character would impart at least some individuality even to an embodied cliché. Except on rare occasions when the writer had perfect material for the portrait of a unique figure, a character's pictorial features identified the type to which he belonged, and his actions individualized him. Even when a character's actions were completely stylized, he had at least his own name, his actions had specific dates and localities, and the events had really happened. "Strange power of *Reality*!" Carlyle exclaimed when he praised an anecdote in Boswell's *Johnson*. ". . . Do but consider that it is true; that it did in very deed occur!"[63]

The use of conventional characters does not necessarily weaken the histories. When a character had "lineaments" appropriate to the desired moral effect, a writer as skillful as Motley needed no more than convention offered. Lacking a dominant hero for his *United Netherlands*, Motley lavished as much emphasis and "natural coloring" on Queen Elizabeth as the documents would allow. She appears in these pages as a coy, vain, niggardly, sometimes heroic, and always petulant woman. Pausing several times to paint his fascinating subject, Motley gives this picture of her at fifty-three, when "she considered herself in the full bloom of her beauty":

Her garments were of satin and velvet, with fringes of pearl as big as beans. A small gold crown was upon her head, and her red hair, throughout its multiplicity of curls, blazed with diamonds and emeralds. Her forehead was tall, her face long, her complexion fair, her eyes small, dark, and glittering, her nose high and hooked, her lips thin, her teeth black, her bosom white and liberally exposed.[64]

The grotesque incongruity of the red, black, and white in this picture does much more than the heavy satire of Motley's narrative and his indignant moral judgments to achieve the effect he wants. This picture and others of Elizabeth seem to answer Macaulay's promise that "a great artist could produce a portrait" of Elizabeth "at least as striking as that in the novel of Kenilworth, without employing a single trait not authenticated by ample testimony."[65]

The analogy to painting applied also to natural scenery. Through his landscapes, too, the historian wanted to communicate not merely external features but essential significance. In romantic history as in historical romance—in historical "painting" as in the canvases of Thomas Cole—one had to convey the emotional impact of Nature. Parkman praised *The Deerslayer's* scenery for its "genuine game flavor":

It exhales the odors of the pine-woods and the freshness of the mountain-wind. Its dark and rugged scenery rises as distinctly on the eye as the images of the painter's canvas, or rather as the reflection of Nature herself. But it is not as the mere rendering of material forms that these wood-paintings are most highly to be esteemed; they breathe the somber poetry of solitude and danger.[66]

Parkman, of course, attributed his choice of the French-Canadian sub-ject to his "taste for the woods and the Indians."[67] Throughout his journals and his published works he reveals an unusually intense appetite for physi-cal activity, especially among wild natural scenes. But although Bancroft's adolescent letters about "regaining [his] youth on Nature's bosom" seem amusingly self-conscious when placed against Parkman's intense revela-tions, the contrast demonstrates the conventionality of the attitude.[68] Mot-ley alone chose a subject that could not always be "ennobled" by "primeval" natural scenery; but in his volumes on the Netherlands he used the wild ocean when he could, and when he argued that Peter the Great's action in "the Northern war" was "a magnificent subject for the historical painter," he included the scenery as an essential advantage: "What imposing per-sonages," he exclaimed,

what dramatic catastrophes, what sudden and bewildering reverses, what wild scenery, what Salvator-like *chiaroscuro*—dark Sarmatian forests enveloping the actors in mystery and obscurity, with flashes of light breaking upon the anxious suspense of Europe, and revealing portentous battles, sieges, and hair-breadth escapes—what "dreadful marches" through the wilderness.[69]

In order to exploit the locale in this way, the historian felt obliged to know it personally. The fame of Parkman's thorough explorations has obscured the importance of Bancroft's, made when Parkman was only four-teen years old. "I marked as near as I could the spot where Jacques Cartier may have landed," Bancroft wrote from Montreal in 1837; at "sublime" Quebec he "trod the soil where Wolfe landed" and "marked the very hill-side" Wolfe had climbed.[70] Motley, of course, knew thoroughly the Dutch and Belgian cities that he had to describe, and he relied on historic asso-ciation or the "wild ocean" when he wanted to achieve a sublime effect.[71] Prescott, though unable to travel very often, recognized the importance of knowing the natural scenery through which his characters moved. Rely-ing on the eyes of others, especially Humboldt and Malte Brun, for the details of his scenery, he believed that his description in *The Conquest of Mexico* ought to emphasize the "sublime scenery." He realized that his description, though "full of the picturesque," read "very much like Miss Porter—rather boarding-schoolish finery. . . . But the tierra caliente with-out flowers," he knew, "would be like a garden without roses."[72]

Landscape was not mere ornament in these histories. It was intended as an integral part of the historic action. Whatever the historians' indebted-ness to the geopolitical theories of Montesquieu and Herder, they were happiest when they could emulate Scott and Cooper by staging a battle on a sublime natural scene. If the action revealed sublime—that is, awe-inspiring—character or produced such important results as the battle on the Heights of Abraham, the historian had his perfect subject. His purpose was to bring the reader, "as it were, to play a part in the scene."

When Parkman praised Cooper for achieving this effect in *The Deerslayer*, he distinguished sharply between the effect of a "great battle" and that of a skirmish. One reads of a battle, he said, with "the same kind of interest with which he beholds the grand destructive phenomena of nature"—although one's "feeling" is "far more intense" here because the forces are "living tides of human wrath and valor." In well-described skirmishes or single combats, however, "the reader is enlisted in the fray"; he shares the feelings of the participants and, instead of imagining a picture, seems actually to feel the spray of the "foaming cataract," and "the tangible presence of rock, river, and forest."[73] Parkman's control of point of view in his own histories reveals the importance of this paragraph: again and again he tries to put the reader on the scene—inside a small stockade attacked by Iroquois, bivouacking with a French and Indian war party, trying to sleep in a reeking Indian hut.

Parkman's distinction between the effect of a great battle and that of a skirmish helps to explain the abundance of detailed anecdotes, the episodic quality of most of these histories. The description of a great battle is almost always generalized; the writer does describe it as he describes a tempest at sea; he does keep the general scene before the reader's eye, emphasizing tides of wrath and valor, masses of foot and horse, until the conventional climax, when the quick eye of the successful leader or the heroic action of a small group capitalizes on the chance for victory.[74] This kind of description might illustrate national character, as Prescott's accounts of French impetuosity, Motley's anecdotes of Spanish endurance, or Parkman's criticisms of Indian hit-and-run tactics are intended to do; but except for the hero's quick decision or the losing general's indecision, it rarely particularizes a character.

To achieve that effect, each of the historians pauses frequently to tell an anecdote involving one or very few characters—often minor characters. Many of these episodes describe what Cotton Mather called "Remarkables" and Motley, "hair-breadth escapes"; almost all of them reveal unusual devotion, courage, cowardice, cruelty, or generosity. Most of them, moreover, depict some individual in the face of unusual danger. A generous chevalier in single combat against a more powerful Spanish knight; a lone woman calling out to an imaginary garrison in her house, and thus scaring off an Indian war party; a Jesuit missionary tortured and maimed by the Indians but rescued by a Dutch minister; an envoy from the Low Countries, but a man loyal to the Spanish crown, secretly murdered in a Spanish prison by order of Philip II—these particular experiences dramatize the chivalrous spirit of some men in a barbarous age, individual resourcefulness among the terrors of the frontier, a priest's devotion and a Protestant minister's charity, and the courage and piety of a man who trusted the "diabolical" Philip too far.[75] No matter what the justification given for such an anecdote, whether or not it was meant to reveal the character of the times, the writer almost always tried to paint this picture in greater detail than the panorama of a great battle, and to give the reader the illusion of participation.

Too often, however, he failed. Such episodes as that of the intrepid woman or the hero's hairbreadth escape from the enemy became conventionalized: Prescott's injunction to "omit no act or word that can illustrate" character seems at times a self-inflicted curse on his own writing. If many of these anecdotes do justify Parkman's evaluation of the "petty" skirmish, the reason is not that the writer evokes the tangible presence of rock, river, and forest, but only that (again) the dreadful or affecting experiences were real experiences. The trouble is that the foaming cataract had itself become a cliché, and none of these writers could do with a foaming cataract what Motley had done with Elizabeth's black teeth. For a writer committed to "vigorous," "colorful" language, moreover, and limited besides in the number of documented details, the rhetoric available for describing a skirmish did not differ very much from that used to describe a great battle. The conventional scene was particularized by the same kind of quality that particularized the conventional character: its location and its reality. For the reader familiar with Scott and Cooper the cliff did not need to be described in great detail. The writer had only to announce that the skirmish had occurred on a "rocky eminence" or a towering height and then to suggest the danger or the aptness of the setting. By addressing the reader in the second person or using the historical present, by controlling the point of view at a moment of crisis, he could sometimes achieve the illusion of participation.[76]

4

Since this illusion implies a dramatic technique, it is not surprising that in their remarks about history these writers compared history to drama almost as often as they compared it to painting. Macaulay had declared that the difference between history and drama lay more in conception than

in execution,[77] and Barante and the New England historians agreed with
him. Writers preoccupied with recreating historical experience and with
portraying vigorous character were bound to use dramatic methods when
they could. It was the dramatic effect of Rubens' *Descent from the Cross*
that Motley praised, a dramatic interest that Prescott hoped to achieve in
The Conquest of Mexico. As my discussion of their best histories will
demonstrate, Prescott, Motley, and Parkman gave their individual histories a dramatic structure. History was moral drama.

Bancroft, especially, received critical praise for his dramatic ability.
Prescott told him he admired "your original & very effective way of a dramatic form of writing, by making the parties not only act but speak for
themselves." When Bancroft's next volume appeared four years later,
Prescott admired the "greater reality" which Bancroft had given the story
by "making actors tell it with their own mouths."[78] This greater reality
was the main purpose of making the actors speak for themselves, but it did
not mean only the more impressive effect that dialogue gave to a narrative. It meant exemplifying the peculiar language of a nation or an age.
If the historian was lucky enough to find a reasonably important character
whose language was "colorful," his use of the character's own words would
add the "natural coloring" that he wanted in his history. In his essay on
history Macaulay had complained of having "to look for the wars and
votes of the Puritans in Clarendon and for their phraseology in Old Mortality."[79] One can find the Puritans' phraseology and at least the translated
phraseology of the Indians in Bancroft and Parkman, along with the wars
and the votes.

The historian did not always apportion his quotations according to their
dramatic importance in the over-all plan of his history. He gave a special
hearing to the eloquent and the colorful speaker. Parkman quoted speech
after speech in the style of Indian metaphor, whether the speaker was a
European or an Indian. In *A Half-Century of Conflict* and *Montcalm and
Wolfe* he repeatedly used the diaries of unlettered New England soldiers,
of a chaplain, of a doctor, making the most of their concrete language.[80]
Bancroft, by making the actors throughout the colonies speak for themselves just before the Revolution, brought "all the various phases of sentiment in a flash as it were before the eye of the reader."[81] In the *United Netherlands,* however, Motley outdid all the others—primarily, it would seem,
because he had Elizabethan characters to portray and meant to use their
prose for all the color it could provide. With excellent material to choose
from in the letters of Elizabeth, Leicester, and other Englishmen of high

and low degree, he filled the first two volumes of this history with long letters, pithy fragments, and, wherever possible, scenes in which Englishmen could speak their vigorous language. He used a character's style to reinforce his emphasis in the moral portrait; and he often picked up a characteristic phrase from the documents to use ironically in his own commentary.[82]

Colorful as Indian eloquence or Puritan diaries could be, Elizabethan language was incomparable for writers who admired both a "flowing," "ornate," and "aphoristical"[83] style and men of frankness, independence, and action. The conceit, the striking epithet, the alliteration, and the stirring rhythms seemed to exemplify the vigor of honest Englishmen during Elizabeth's reign: " 'Rob,' " Elizabeth writes to Leicester in the Netherlands,

"I am afraid you will suppose, by my wandering writings, that a midsummer's moon hath taken large possession of my brains this month; but you must needs take things as they come in my head, though order be left behind me. . . . It frets me not a little that the poor soldiers that hourly venture life should want their due, that well deserve rather reward; and look, in whom the thought may truly be proved, let them smart therefore. And if the treasurer be found untrue or negligent, according to desert he shall be used. . . .

"Now will I end, that do imagine I still talk with you, and therefore loathly say farewell one hundred thousand times; though ever I pray God bless you from all harm, and save you from all foes."

When Leicester complains of dissension among his officers, who Motley says "were all at daggers drawn," Motley lets him speak: " 'Would God I were rid of this place!' he exclaimed. 'What man living would go to the field and have his officers divided almost into mortal quarrel? One blow, but by any of their lackeys brings us altogether by the ears.' "[84]

Such language as this suggests the heroic, flesh-and-blood action that Motley found in Rubens' painting. The dramatic method gave muscular vigor a value that is reflected in the historians' criticism of historical language as well as their choice of subjects. It was Bancroft's "crisp, nervous style" that Motley admired, his ability, "by a few sudden strokes, to reveal startling and brilliant pictures."[85] Washington Irving praised Bancroft's accounts of Lexington and Bunker Hill because "a vigorous fire runs through the language and flashes out occasionally in epithets and phrases that startle";[86] Prescott, whose style was anything but "nervous," admired Motley's *Rise of the Dutch Republic* because "y^r portraiture of character is vigorous and animated."[87]

5

Committed to the idea of re-creating the Past, and considering himself a man of letters, the romantic historian did not think about a historical controversy or a historical period and then say, "I shall investigate this subject and find out what happened." He was more likely to say, "No history (or no good history) exists in English on this subject. The theme is grand, interesting, novel." He searched earnestly for the truth, but in discussing his subject he usually emphasized questions of presentation or the value of the subject as historical reading. This emphasis appears in his attitude toward facts, toward research, as well as in his critical comments. Whatever value facts had for their own sake, it was the story, and the kind of story, that counted. Reviewing *Ferdinand and Isabella,* Bancroft says that even after Irving's "historic romance," Prescott's "story" of the conquest of Granada "loses nothing of its charm in the accurate narration, which is confirmed by sober criticism, and gains a new and a deeper interest from its authenticity."[88] When Motley boasts that he is giving the *"ipsissima verba"* of Elizabethan characters,[89] that no "imaginary conversations" occur in his work, he not only reminds the reader of his scrupulous accuracy; he implies the same judgment Bancroft expressed in comparing Irving and Prescott on Granada: that however great Scott's conversations are in *Kenilworth, he* cannot provide what appears in this history—the very words, just as colorful as those in romance, but words of a deeper interest because they are authentic. Motley adds interest to his history by reminding the reader that he is reading "the secret never published correspondence" of royalty; Parkman insists repeatedly that he has actually studied the historic scenes, that he has painted his picture of Indians "from life"; Prescott defends *Ferdinand and Isabella* as "an honest record, from rare and authentic sources, of a period, rich in circumstance, of personages most remarkable in their character."[90] Authentic sources provide the pleasure of picking from "the dressing-gown folds of the stealthy, softly-gliding Walsingham the last secret which he has picked from . . . the Pope's pocket," the pleasure of sitting "invisible at the most secret councils of the Nassaus and Barneveldt and Buys."[91] "It may seem dreary work," Prescott says, "to plod through barbarous old MS. chronicles, of monks and pedants, but this takes up but a small portion of the time."[92]

The fact that the stories of Cortés and Pizarro were well known was a distinct advantage, Prescott remarked in his journal—provided he could get original documents.[93] The major events of every one of the histories these men chose to write were well known by the time they started writing.

But even though the "judicious selection" of documents in foreign archives often had to be made by hired agents or literary friends, the authenticity which these documents gave to a familiar story added authority to the historian's portraits of the major characters. If the story he had to tell had been well told by someone else, as Schiller had narrated the Dutch rebellion, it had not been based on the documents newly available to the man of letters. The romantic historian's job was to find documents that would enable him to paint an authentic and colorful picture, that would add detail and correct earlier errors in detail.

Thus the New England historians shared a romantic attitude toward the Past and toward the historian's aesthetic problems. But their interest in ruins, in vital experience, in portraits, conventional characters, and Nature has a far greater significance than the merely technical aspects of the literary attitude can indicate. History, like all literature, had more important purposes than entertainment. The New England Unitarian's version of romanticism included important assumptions about the meaning of history, and he adapted romantic literary conventions to communicate that meaning.

CHAPTER II

Nature, Progress, and Moral Judgment

The history of the world, like the laws of nature, is consistent with itself, and simple as the soul of man. Like conditions produce like phenomena.

J. C. F. Schiller, "The Revolt of the Netherlands"
(from the Boston edition of 1847)

The minute and unwearied research, the scrupulous fidelity and impartial justice with which you execute your task, prove to me that you are properly sensible of the high calling of the American press—that rising tribunal before which the whole world is to be summoned, its history to be revised and rewritten, and the judgment of past ages to be cancelled or confirmed.

Letter from Washington Irving to Motley

In his severely critical essay "Prescott as an Historian" Theodore Parker insisted that the New England historian, because of his unique moral advantages, had unique responsibilities. A Turk or a Russian, he said, might be excused for failing to give us the philosophy of history: "But when a man of New England undertakes to write a history, there is less excuse if his book should be wanting in philosophy and in humanity; less merit if it abound therewith."[1] Although Prescott might have questioned Parker's interpretation of "philosophy" and "humanity," he certainly would have denied the charge that he had omitted either, for he, too, accepted the obligation. Believing that the American writer looked on the Past from the highest station reached in human progress, each of the romantic historians felt obligated to reflect this viewpoint in his sympathies and in his judgments. The idea of a special New England mission was as old as New England itself, and the Jeffersonian philosophers had extended the obligation to the whole country.[2] In nineteenth-century America as in seventeenth-century New England the writer's duty was based on the unusual moral purity of his country, on its unique situation as the country most nearly in harmony with divine (or natural) laws.

The historians based this appraisal of America's moral condition partly on their own experience. Bancroft wrote repeatedly from Germany in praise of German scholarship and literature, but in letter after letter he deplored its immorality, the motives of the scholars (who looked on scholarship "as a trade"), their irreligion. He wished that German literature and scholarship could be transplanted to the United States, where they could be enriched by that purity which was the only quality they lacked in Germany. When traveling through Europe with some other young men, he discovered that his Polish companion had "a great deal of moral principle for an European"! Motley, who had already spent several years in Europe before writing his essay on Balzac, did admit that Balzac was neither moral nor immoral, that he was simply an artist dedicated to anatomizing French society. But in this estimate, which anticipated William Dean Howells' comment on Dostoyevsky and Zola, Motley left no doubt either that he believed an American writer was obligated to a higher purpose or that the same kind of analysis would be impossible in the healthy society here. He declared that he could not recommend Balzac for "general circulation" in America. Parkman and Prescott, in their journals of trips to Europe, recorded with a disgust that approaches Mark Twain's the corruption, the moral degradation of southern European peasantry and the "hypocrisy" of Catholicism in Europe.[3]

As young men, then, all four historians were prepared to accept the judicial responsibility that Washington Irving said Motley discharged so well in *The Rise of the Dutch Republic*. The romantic historian was not only an artist but a judge. Obliged to judge nations as well as men, he based his decisions on a loose system of "natural" laws that grew out of a clear, though largely implicit theory of history. Both the theory and the laws demand close attention, for they often determined the historian's literary techniques as well as his judgments, and they expressed the historical views of many more Americans than those in Unitarian Boston.

Despite the peculiarities of his transcendental and Democratic ideas, it was Bancroft who stated the fundamental theory most clearly. He believed in a dynamic Providence whose infinite wisdom had established the laws of the moral world and controlled the direction of history; he declared that "the moral world is swayed by general laws," each acting in harmony with all the others, and that "event succeeds event according to their influence." Every event, therefore, reflected one of these laws, and since no general law—no truth—could contradict another, there was an essential harmony among the separate incidents of history. History was the unfolding of a vast Providential plan, and the laws of the moral world were the links between the ages, forming "the guiding principle of civilization, which marshals incongrous incidents into their just places and arranges checkered groups in clear and harmonious order." The historian had a didactic as well as artistic duty to arrange apparently disconnected events in their proper order. Facts were, as Macaulay had said, "the mere dross of history," but the historian could achieve the proper rearrangement of historical facts only by reducing "historic truth" to "a science." Just as Thoreau the transcendental naturalist examined his specimens, so the transcendental historian had to "compare document with document" and then to refer each fact to the general laws that it represented. He could check his arrangement by applying his intuitive reasoning to the mass of facts and by remembering that "every false statement contains a contradiction," that "truth alone possesses harmony." Having put himself in tune with divine reason by consulting the known general laws of the moral world, he could, then, say that he was an impartial, an "indifferent" historian who abhorred that history which takes its bias from "the selfish passions of a party." When Ranke said Bancroft's history was the best history written "from the democratic point of view," Bancroft was hurt; the democracy in his history was not subjective, he said, but objective.[4]

Although Parkman scorned "the she-philosophers" of Brook Farm and Prescott and Motley had little more respect for them, all three emphasized eternal moral laws and the causative power of principles. Unchanging moral laws seemed as self-evident to the "understanding" and "common sense" of a conservative Unitarian as they were to the "reason" of the tran-scendentalist.* Motley was the closest of the three to Bancroft in the frequency and flamboyance of his allusions to these laws and to Providence. He often reminded his readers that certain characters had violated "elemental laws," he summarized the lessons of his history frequently, and he stressed the importance of finding in history "general rules for the infinite

---

* Bancroft (who called his daughter Susan his "transcendental baby") distinguished "reason" from "understanding." By "reason" he meant "not that faculty which deduces inferences from the experiences of the senses, but that higher faculty, which from the infinite treasures of its own consciousness, originates truth, and assents to it by the force of intuitive evidence; that faculty which raises us beyond the control of time and space, and gives us faith in things eternal and invisible." See "The Office of the People in Art, Government, and Religion," in *Literary and Historical Miscellanies* (New York, 1855), p. 409. Theodore Parker to Bancroft, September 2, 1846, Bancroft Papers, MHS.

future." Prescott and Parkman were less explicitly didactic, but they, too, wrote many pointed judgments into the narrative and "reflective" parts of their works.[5]

Recognizing these temperamental differences, one can ask what the law was that these judges administered. The "eternal dictates" were "simple,"[6] and perhaps because they were both simple and self-evident nobody bothered to transcribe all of them in one place. One finds them written in the decisions of the judges.

2

The basic assumption was human progress. Motley went so far as to say that were it not for progress, history would be the most "contemptible" subject to study.[7] Human progress had proceeded westward, from the Middle East to North America. And all along the way, whether they knew it or not, the people of the vanguard had carried with them a new principle: Christianity in the "German woods," nationality in the Iberian peninsula, the Reformation in the Netherlands and England, Democracy (or Liberty) in the American colonies. In the grand design of Providence the victories of these principles were the most meaningful advances in history; moreover, a nation owed her successes to her adherence to the progressive principle—a principle which, by definition (had there been a definition), agreed with natural law.

Recognizing the continuity in history, the historian then had to discover and communicate "the spirit of the age" that he was bringing to life. His highest responsibility was to recognize and abstract the principle that lay behind every major action. His portraits were designed to convey individual character through "lineaments" and actions; his description of a nation was meant to delineate national character and the principles motivating the nation at a certain time, for national "institutions are the result . . . of the national character";[8] his history of an age was meant to bring its spirit before the reader.

This obligation was both literary and moral. In his reviews of both Irving and Bancroft, Prescott insisted that the historian must find a "pervading" principle or moral to keep constantly before the reader. Without the pervading principle a history would have no unity; without proper morality its style could not be properly "elevating." Bancroft's pervading principle was the American colonies' "tendency toward independence."[9] Motley told his readers to find in his history of the Netherlands "the creative power of civil and religious freedom."[10] Parkman kept the large issue, the battle of Liberty and Absolutism for North America, always before the reader.

Like other natural laws, the law of progress was incontrovertible; progress was inevitable. Wrong principles could not, in the long run, triumph. The battle between French Absolutism and Anglo-American Liberty could have been protracted, Parkman said, if the French government had used better political and military strategy. But the result would have been the same.[11] Bancroft said that Lord Baltimore and Shaftesbury could have brought "the oldest oaks in Windsor forest" to America more easily than the "antiquated and rotten" social forms that they had actually tried to transplant.[12] Prescott endorsed this idea in his review of Bancroft's *History*,[13] and in the best of his own histories he saw "the resistless march of *destiny*" in "the sad fortunes of the dynasty of Montezuma." Motley, in criticizing Bancroft's assignment of democratic motives to the authors of the Mayflower Compact, said that if John Carver had been elected "Grand Duke of Moratiggan" for all time instead of Governor of Plymouth for a year, "these United States would have been a democracy notwithstanding." And Philip II, he wrote in his own history, was sure to fail because he was swimming against "the great current of events" which bore on "the great moral principles by which human affairs in the long run are invariably governed."[14]

The irresistible advance of progress might have held little interest for the historian if its direction had been a straight line. But it rose, these historians believed, in a spiral.[15] From the altitude of the nineteenth century the historian could see that the movement had always been upward, but without this perspective the unaided reader, when dropped onto the level of a lower curve, might lose the sense of upward motion.[16] The spiral figure explained the temporary triumphs of wrong principles, the sufferings of the progressive leader, and the strange moral vehicles into which Providence or historical fate had sometimes chosen to drop the burden of libertarian progress. For these "seeds" or "germs"[17] had sometimes been carried by people who would have tried to destroy them had they known what fruit they were to bear.

According to an elaborate natural analogy that Bancroft used, the party of the Past helps to achieve natural progress, because its conservatism provokes the reform party to action and its resistance prevents excessive reform. In the conflict of central power with individuality, Bancroft said, the law of "attraction" and "repulsion" works constantly, "in every country, in every stage of existence." If this law is not respected, "society will perish in chaotic confusion or stagnant calm." The reformers, who strive constantly to enact "the eternal law of justice," must avoid an unnatural push for which the whole society is not prepared; but the resultant of the two opposing forces must point toward progress. Necessary though it is, the party that clings to the Past opposes Nature and Providence when it tries to block a reasonable progressive movement.[18]

Since each of these parties "in its proper proportion is essential to the wellbeing of society," and since only excess is unnatural, Bancroft insisted that it was easy for the historian to be impartial. Historical "crimes" were to be judged according to the eternal law of virtue written in "the depths" of every man's "consciousness," but Bancroft did not define either political excess or proper proportion. He apparently felt that anyone looking back into history could see which actions had conformed to the will of Providence. For since Providence was supreme, the proper rate of progress was clear in the actual rate of progress! John Winthrop had prevented "chaos" when he opposed "the popular party"; Cotton Mather had held for "stagnation" when he tried to maintain the old religious regime.[19]

Despite Bancroft's and Motley's insistence that the eternal laws of the moral world were simple, not all of them seem to have been either eternal or simple. The law of progress committed the historian to a relative standard of judgment. As the sole standard, it was simple enough: the historian studied the age, looked for the banner of progress in any conflict, and supported the side fighting under it. When he had no heroes who completely understood their progressive mission, he might have to praise the unwitting bearer of the progressive banner by comparing him with his more reactionary antagonists. Bancroft, for example, saw the flag of Progress flying in England when she denied the supremacy of the Pope and, in developing her commerce and her navy, fought against the reactionary forces of France and Spain. But almost immediately the moral laws seem to have grown more complex. Religious authority was "allied with avarice" in Spain; and in Elizabethan England it joined with monarchy to organize a united national front. "Elizabeth reformed the court"; but it was "the ministers, whom she persecuted, [who] reformed the commons."[20] From the time of Archbishop Laud's first persecutions the situation was much more complex than it had been before the Establishment. Still the chief liberal foe of the Catholic powers, England had become a reactionary force in her relations with the Puritans and then with all the colonies.

Such ambiguities could be explained by an appeal to the pervading principles of the age. In the period from the Reformation through the first half of the eighteenth century, Bancroft believed, the main issue had been the struggle of Protestantism and intellectual freedom against Catholic reaction. Therefore, although England's rulers had generally been linked with France and Spain in the seventeenth century as opponents of political freedom, Bancroft's (and Parkman's) English _people_ suddenly rose,[21] at the lowest point of English fortunes in the Seven Years' War, to carry on the fight against infallible prelacy. By 1763 Protestantism had won its battle, "had fulfilled its political end, and was never again to convulse the world."[22] Bancroft's analysis explained the new alignment of principles and powers in the war of the American Revolution. France, having fought for the supremacy of a Catholic empire until 1763, could fight for the principle of Liberty in 1778; and England, her duty as the chief defender of Protestant freedom accomplished, could be led by a Parliament that was "fretting itself into a frenzy at the denial of its unlimited dominion."[23]

Although Motley's portrait of Elizabeth is far from flattering, he follows the same rule used by Bancroft. In her relations with her own people and the Dutch she is not progressive, libertarian, or heroic; both the English people and the Dutch people walk ahead of her in the progressive march of humanity. Against Philip II, however, she stands for the English nation—for Protestantism, independent nationality, and the spirit of commerce. The fundamental question that the judge had to answer in applying the law of progress was how closely a given character conformed to "the spirit of the age"—that is, the most progressive ideas of the age. Thus Motley can admit Elizabeth's and Henry IV's similarity to Philip II without condemning them; for although they virtually agreed with Philip on "the right divine and the right of the people," they came closer than he did to understanding the spirit of the age, and they had "the keenest instinct to keep themselves in the advance in the direction whither [history] was marshalling all men."[24]

The involuntary agents of progress were not always those who, like Elizabeth, Henry IV, and intolerant Calvinists, had kept themselves "in the advance." Nor was it only the good acts of these agents that had contributed to the advance. Elizabeth's disingenuousness, her selfishness, her "niggardliness," and her jealousy of Leicester's possible power in the Netherlands—the delay caused by these "follies," Motley said, had carried the Netherlands through a dangerous period when even the people had wanted a monarchy. Even the assassination of William the Silent, committed by order of the "monstrous" Philip II, had produced the same kind of effect some years earlier; had William not been assassinated, Motley assured the reader, he would have become a king.[25] Moral and progressive law functioned so smoothly that reactionary evil itself worked for progress. "How happy for a nation," Theodore Parker exclaimed ironically, "that, when brought to the brink of ruin, it has a perennial inexhaustible fountain of salvation in the follies, vices, and crimes of its rulers!"[26]

In very similar language Parkman reminded his readers of the debt liberty owed to the "fatuity of Louis XV. and his Pompadour." The outrages committed by Prescott's Pope Alexander VI made an essential contribution to the Reformation. The moral, in Bancroft's words, was that "evil when it comes is intermixed with good; the ill is evanescent, the good endures." England's long-range policy of "oppression" from 1660 to 1775 had given the American colonists the very experience they needed in order to appreciate the value of liberty; indeed George III was "the instrument chosen by Heaven to accelerate [the] movement of the age."[27]

The determinism implicit in this view of progress did not trouble these historians. Despite his involuntary contributions to progress, the evil agent was no more immune to damnation than the Devil whom Calvinist historians had said God used for similar purposes. The irony of his occasional utility in the Providential plan was, in a sense, a part of his punishment: his very crimes accelerated the progress that he hoped they would halt. The historian never questioned the free will of such an agent, although Motley, oppressed by Philip's massive record of evil, did argue that Providence tolerated evil only as a "stormy" background for the "spotless marble" character of such heroes as William the Silent.[28] The historian's major concern was with the motives, the morality, and the results of the evil agent's behavior; he did not pretend to debate the evil agent's freedom of choice or his utility, but was satisfied to demonstrate them—the first repeatedly and the second on strategic occasions. In discussing evil characters he concentrated on moral judgment and instruction and on the operation of natural law. Virtue, of course, was morally instructive, but the results of evil were more so.[29]

In his moral drama, then, the romantic historian recorded the operation of a natural law, "the inexorable law of Freedom and Progress."[30] In nearly all his histories he took the point of view of the nation that illustrated the law at a given period. Whatever the faults of Ferdinand and Isabella, Cortés, or Pizarro, all helped to lead the upward march of humanity; all acted against opponents standing obstinately, whether from necessity or evil motives, in the path of progress. It is true that Parkman said his "point of view" was "within the French lines" in the war for North America,[31]

but in both *A Half-Century of Conflict* and *Montcalm and Wolfe* he stands
just as often within the English lines, and his allegiance is always there.
In the earlier volumes, moreover, his French heroes, from Champlain to
La Salle, serve as agents of progress. Parkman's *The Old Régime in Canada* and Prescott's *Philip II* are the major exceptions, but the first is not a
narrative history and the second, a logical successor to Prescott's earlier
volumes on Spanish achievements, presents the culmination of Spain's
material glory as well as the unmistakable symptoms of her decline.

3

But what did "progress" mean? Except for a few minor variations,
all of these histories narrate a consistent story of political and religious
change from the fifteenth century through the American Revolution; both
the terminology and the substance of the story are romantic. Although
material progress had made civilization more complex, this progressive
movement had always led toward greater simplicity in ideas, toward a
clearer perception of a few truths that were "devoid of mystery."[32] In
religion, progress had moved toward nineteenth-century Unitarianism; in
politics, toward American democracy. It had been a movement from the
"artificial" toward the "natural." The man who clung to his artificial
principles after humanity had discarded them had inevitably slipped off
the spiral highway of progress. He had suffered materially as well as
spiritually, for in the long march material success depended directly on
right, "natural" principles.

The story begins in Spain. Temporarily in the vanguard of political
and geographic progress, and elevated by Isabella's "exalted" religious
fervor,[33] Spain opened the way to the New World and set new standards
of national unity, royal justice, and efficiency. Having defeated the self-
indulgent Moors, Ferdinand stood firm against the Pope for the principle
of national integrity. His armies succeeded in driving the French from
Spain because of "the glorious *union*, which brought together the petty and
hitherto discordant tribes of the peninsula under the same rule and, by
creating common interests and an harmonious principle of action, was
silently preparing them for constituting one great nation,—one and indi-
visible, as intended by nature."[34] The principles of nationalism and religious
enthusiasm gave the Spaniards an energy that could not fail against the
demoralized Italian states. Gonsalvo de Cordova's Spaniards were crude,
and the Italians were handicapped by an over-refined culture. Because
they depended so much on "intellect," deceit, "the subtle webs of policy,"

and "the refinements of the cabinet," they had lost the principle of physical courage, of nationality, of straightforward action. They lacked that precious quality which would have saved them: "an invigorating national feeling."[35] Corrupt, spiritless intellect led to self-indulgent effeminacy, materialism, cowardice, "torpor." These qualities could not stand against the Spaniard's rugged natural energy and disciplined self-denial.

But Spain's virtue gave way to "mad schemes of ambition," to avarice and bigotry, to indolence and pride, and these eventually threw her into a "paralytic torpor" that allowed her to be stripped of her wealth and shoved aside by smaller nations moving more energetically up the spiral path of progress. Under the emperor Charles V Spain made greater conquests, but his success only demonstrated that "the seed sown under a good system continues to yield fruit in a bad one." Charles's "golden age," Prescott said, would not seem golden to the true Spanish patriot; its "outward show of glory will seem to his penetrating eye only the hectic brilliancy of decay." Charles and his successors forgot the ancient liberties that Ferdinand and Isabella had respected, and the Inquisition settled "like a foul mist" on the national character.[36]

The Netherlands rose to defend against Spain the principle of nationality that Ferdinand and Isabella had asserted. But the Dutch were more natural than the Spaniards; their leader saw clearly the natural law that demanded freedom of conscience, and "the untaught impulses of the great popular heart" told them that theirs was a struggle not only for Dutch liberty but for world liberty.[37] As the hardiest Moors fighting against Ferdinand and Isabella had been nurtured in the rugged mountain country of the Alpuxarras, as the seaboard was the "natural seat" of Spanish liberty,[38] so the Dutch had been trained to adversity, and to an understanding of Nature, through their experience of the wild ocean that so often threatened to destroy them.[39] They carried not only the seed of religious liberty, encased in the hard shell of Calvinism, but also the spirit of commerce, the principles of industry and self-reliance. They were interested, Motley said, in facts rather than theories;[40] they had comparatively little use for man-made superstitions and divine-right theories of monarchy. By following the natural laws of commerce these "hardy mariners," whose "moral sense" (Bancroft said) rebelled against Spanish mercantile avarice, turned the stupid, contrived theory of Spanish colonial trade to their own advantage—bleeding Philip's treasury as well as his army.[41]

Again true principles and raw energy overthrew unnatural laws; again intrigue, materialism, self-indulgence, unfeeling intellect, and torpor were defeated. Motley emphasizes this contrast by a variety of devices. Although forced to admire the skill and courage of several energetic Spanish military leaders, he focuses on the contrast between the artful deceit of Philip and his servants, and the natural straightforwardness of the Dutch and later the English. The greatest Spanish military figures reflect the worst characteristics of their declining nation: Alva in camp, refusing to be drawn into a battle, is the counterpart of the "sluggish" Philip leaning over his desk and writing interminable messages. Alexander Farnese, though a great soldier, personifies military falsehood. And in his insincere negotiations for peace with Queen Elizabeth, she, who has been "disingenuous" at times in her treatment of the Dutch, behaves with "confiding simplicity and truthfulness"—traits which make the Englishman incapable of even conceiving Mediterranean deceit.[42]

The most successful figure of this kind, embodying the opposing qualities in this long war of principles, is Motley's description of the Spanish galley, an unmaneuverable hulk, a lumbering monster symbolizing Spanish pride and stupidity. Motley's objection to it is both moral and aesthetic; he condemns its use of "slave labor," and he remarks that any "true lover of the sea" must regard it as

. . . about as clumsy and amphibious a production as could be hoped of human perverseness. High where it should be low—exposed, flat, and fragile, where elevation and strength were indispensable—encumbered and top-heavy where it should be level and compact, weak in the waist, broad in the stem and stern, awkward in manoeuvre, helpless in rough weather, sluggish under sail, although possessing the single advantage of being able to crawl over a smooth sea when better and faster ships were made stationary by absolute calm, the galley was no match for the Dutch galleot, either at close quarters or in a breeze.[43]

The more natural productions of self-reliant Englishmen and Dutchmen sailed circles around this freak of the Spanish brain. The sluggishness of the galley and its commanders could not stand against the natural storm that destroyed the Spanish Armada or against the quick native intelligence of free sailors. The Spanish and Portuguese in the galleys showed a sluggishness of mind appropriate to the "top-heavy," "sluggish marine castles" in which they sailed.[44]

Natural vigor, instinct, and energy belonged to the people who followed the law of progress. The Puritans who fled Archbishop Laud carried into the wilderness a simpler and more natural system than that top-heavy construction of man, the Anglican Church. The "simple" farmers of Bancroft's Connecticut, where "there was . . . hardly a lawyer in the land,"[45] and the merchants and "mechanics" up and down the coast protested for over a century against the impediments placed in the way of natural law by English political and mercantile theorists and by royal authority.

In America as in the Netherlands the influence of Nature helped true principles to give comparatively crude men vigor in their struggle against more sophisticated, less natural Europeans. Parkman repeatedly contrasts the rugged French-Canadian with the less vigorous Frenchman who stayed at home, the Frenchman in the wilderness with the Frenchman who stayed at Quebec. Both Parkman and Bancroft, moreover, contrast the British colonial troops with the English regulars; Rogers' Rangers win more glory than Braddock's Redcoats. The self-reliant amateur who adjusts to the conditions imposed on him by Nature often excels the professional who fights by the book. As Motley's Dutch "militia of the sea" defeated Spanish professionals, so Bancroft's New England militia defeats British regulars.[46]

It is no mere coincidence, then, that in the controlling image of the Introduction to his first volume Parkman pictured New England as "a body without a head" and New France as "all head."[47] The New England colonies won because of their raw energy, which overcame faults of organization. But they would not have had this energetic superiority had they been based on "absolutist" religious, political, and economic principles, the very principles that produced New France's more grotesque and eventually fatal deformity. Despite the "peculiar crop of faults" borne by "New England Puritanism," Parkman insisted that "it produced also many good and sound fruits":

An uncommon vigor, joined to the hardy virtues of a masculine race, marked the New England type. The sinews, it is true, were hardened at the expense of blood and flesh,—and this literally as well as figuratively; but the staple of character was a sturdy conscientiousness, an undespairing courage, patriotism, public spirit, sagacity, and a strong good sense.

The Seven Years' War was "the strife of a united and concentered few against divided and discordant many. It was the strife, too, of the past against the future; of the old against the new; of moral and intellectual torpor against moral and intellectual life; of barren absolutism against a liberty, crude, incoherent, and chaotic, yet full of prolific vitality."[48]

Thus the historians described the fundamental conflicts of their histories in familiar terms. The American appeal to simplicity was as old as the Puritan Thomas Hooker's announcement that he did not expect his plain style to please those who "covet more sauce than meat"; but when

Francis Parkman set the New England body against the Canadian head he gave a political extension to the nineteenth-century romantic conflict between heart and head. All four of the historians used this terminology, and they all characterized the "natural" in rhetoric that emphasized ruggedness and hardihood. Even intellectual and moral progress accompanied physical, instinctive energy and deep feeling; "torpor" was a condition induced by excesses of the "head." The progressive man was usually an energetic, warm-hearted protestant cutting through the layers of artificial forms that unnatural intellects had wrapped around the simple truths of politics and religion. The natural man was an active man, usually taught as much by experience as by books; the reactionary forces that opposed him often included "theorists," "casuists," "philosophers."

4

Although the precise origins of these ideas, if they can be determined at all, are beyond the range of this study, it is important to understand that these historians did not consider themselves indebted to what Bancroft called "eighteenth century philosophy" or to its idea of progress. Bancroft was proud that he had leveled his guns against Locke himself, the originator of eighteenth-century "materialism." And in their historical narratives about mid-eighteenth-century Europe, both Bancroft and Parkman deplored the spiritual barrenness of the whole continent. "The latter half of the reign of George II.," Parkman wrote, "was one of the most prosaic periods in English history." Even the enthusiastic loyalty which some people had felt toward the fallacious "divine right of kings" had, he said, disappeared with the theory itself. Politics, morals, and religion "had run to commonplace." The Whig aristocracy, having "done its great work when it expelled the Stuarts," was now occupied mainly with minor issues and squabbles over offices. Underneath the surface, forces eventually led by Whitefield, Wesley, and Pitt were stirring, but the surface itself was "dull and languid." Indeed, "over all the Continent the aspect of the times was the same. . . . No great idea stirred the nations to their depths."[49]

Bancroft pronounced the same judgments even more vehemently. The Twelfth Parliament "was corrupt, and it knew itself to be corrupt, and it made a jest of its own corruption." The fundamental evil, Bancroft believed, was a philosophy of materialism. Locke, Voltaire, Dr. Johnson— he contrasted them all with the "spiritual" John Wesley and George Fox. He did not once mention Locke's reason, but allowed him only "a mighty understanding." He condemned the pretentiousness of Locke's and Shaftesbury's effort to impose an aristocratic political system on the Carolinas; true philosophy had come to government in Carolina only when George Fox, who had acquired his wisdom largely "by deep feeling," had helped the Friends at Albemarle to write their natural laws. In a letter to Emerson about this volume, Bancroft boasted that he had put Locke in his place.[50]

Eighteenth-century philosophy, as Bancroft read it, led directly to the "despotism of the senses." "George Fox and Voltaire," he said, "both protested against priestcraft; Voltaire in behalf of the senses, Fox in behalf of the soul."[51] The man who submitted to this despotism could not be honored in history. Despite the "ostentatious pomp" of Samuel Johnson's morality, Bancroft concluded, "his own heart was riveted to the earth." Even at the moment of death Johnson was unable "to fix his eye on God, or to grasp eternity," and he lay in terror, "scarifying his limbs in the vain hope of breathing though but a few hours more." This dying "materialist" Bancroft called "the emblem of the old political system, which also lay on its deathbed, helplessly longing to live on." But even the "new" political system planned by the rebels for France could not succeed; "the [French] philosophy could not guide a revolution, for it professed to receive no truth but through the senses, denied the moral government of the world, and derided the possibility of disinterested goodness." The whole century, Bancroft charged in his largest generalization, "refused to look for anything better" than man; "the belief in the divine reason was derided like the cowering at spectres and hobgoblins; and the worship of humanity became the prevailing idolatry."[52]

Motley laughed at "his serene highness, philosopher Locke," and he expressed the conventional judgment of Hume in a letter recommending reading for his daughter. Advising her to read Lingard's *History of England,* he observed that Lingard "is a Roman Catholic, but honest enough, and at any rate more respectable than Hume"![53] Prescott did not condemn Gibbon's deathbed behavior, but his judgment of the spiritual weakness in Gibbon and Voltaire is as severe in its way as Bancroft's condemnation of Dr. Johnson. Voltaire's style was graceful and witty, but his "pernicious philosophy" prevented him from elevating his reader; he could never "kindle into high and generous emotion the glow of patriotism, or moral and religious enthusiasm." Gibbon's writings were "nowhere warmed with a generous moral sentiment." By sneering at the Christian martyrs' self-sacrifice, he was "not only in bad taste, as he is addressing a Christian audience, but he thus voluntarily relinquishes one of the most powerful engines for the movement of human passion, which is never so easily excited as by deeds of suffering, self-devoted heroism."[54]

This view of eighteenth-century thought helps to explain one of the most important standards of judgment in the romantic histories. Although the Unitarian historian himself was more strongly committed to morality than to piety, he could rarely tolerate what he called religious skepticism. "Materialism," or unfeeling intellect, was even worse, for it ignored "enthusiasm," the energetic force of spirit, the causative power of principles. The formal thinker who did not act warmly for humanity was liable to this charge. Whether as a transcendentalist or as a Unitarian believer in "common sense," as a lover of Nature or as a hard-headed American advocate of self-reliance, the romantic historian expressed little respect for theorists, for theological argument, or for metaphysical speculation.

Despite his admiration for "the sublime lessons of Kant,"[55] Bancroft repeatedly underscored the superiority of less intellectual, progressive groups to learned philosophers. George Fox towered over Descartes, although their method "coincided."[56] Tennessee frontiersmen proved what Frederick Jackson Turner later asserted in language surprisingly similar to Bancroft's: that "political wisdom is not sealed up in rolls and parchments. It welled up in the forest, like the waters from the hillside." Just as there were no lawyers in early Connecticut, so there were no ministers or priests in the Quaker colony at Albemarle, no newspapers or churches on the Virginia frontier in 1674.[57] At Concord in 1775, the "humble trainbands acted" when prudent statesmen would have "lost from hesitation the glory of opening a new era on mankind."[58] And even Kant's ideas had little effect on mankind until William Pitt answered a sound legal argument of Mansfield's by proclaiming his "distrust" in "the refinements of learning." Only when Pitt appealed to "the simplicity of Common Sense," were the theories of "Scotland" and of Kant "translated into the Halls of legislation."[59]

When Bancroft said, then, that "mind rules the world," he did not necessarily mean the mind of the learned man. He referred to the true principles that any intelligent man might perceive. The Whigs of his own day, he said, were materialists; the Democrats, the party of "morality and mind."[60] None of the romantic historians was opposed to learning; what they deplored was learning without natural enthusiasm, without humanity—the sort of learning that had led to the "monstrous" doctrine of the Trinity, the doctrine of predestination, Catholic casuistry. Motley did not let his reader forget that Philip II had "had daily discussions . . . on abstruse theological points," or that James I had had an unhealthy interest in theology and had taken a ridiculous pride in his learning.[61]

This kind of emphasis placed a premium on the virtues of active experience. The man suffering in the trenches knew more of war and patriotism than "grave-visaged statesmen, in comfortable cabinets," who "exchanged grimaces and protocols which nobody heeded";[62] Prescott's Gonsalvo de Cordova was a forthright, honorable soldier until he asked the advice of "casuists" on an ambiguous problem of moral duty;[63] Parkman's frontiersmen knew more about Indian character than theoretical pacifists meeting in sheltered Philadelphia;[64] Dutch and English merchant sailors knew more about economic law than mercantile theorists. Even when natural men did not know the ultimate principles toward which their actions led, "the creative power of civil and religious freedom"[65] was working through them; natural behavior eventually led to good results. Thus Motley's Netherlanders created a republic in spite of themselves, beginning to build it before they knew that they wanted it; and Bancroft's Americans were unwittingly building a democracy as early as the seventeenth century.[66]

In private morals, too, the "artificial" was materialistic. Spirituality came from the heart, the affections, the conscience. Physical hardship and endurance usually helped to preserve spirituality; for however strongly interested in profit, the rugged man was used to self-denial. The vices of the frontier or the merchant service were neither so unnatural nor so enervating as those of the French, Spanish, and Italian courts. Bancroft asserted that "despotism favors the liberty of the senses; and popular freedom rests on sanctity of morals."[67] The first half of this statement, at least, seemed to be borne out by history, and all four historians took full advantage of the evidence. As they portrayed him, the authoritarian opponent of progress always fought for selfish ends—always to preserve his own power and often to preserve his sophisticated vices. Sixteenth-century Italians, Moorish leaders, Montezuma and the Incas, the Valois, Philip II, James I, Louis XIV, Louis XV, several of the corrupt Canadian officials—all were called sensual, self-indulgent. Intellectual subtlety often worked together with "effeminacy."[68]

What was effeminate in the materialist was his self-indulgence, his use of subtlety and deceit, his "languor" or "torpor." The masculine virtues were courage, self-reliance, self-denial, endurance, candor, and vigorous activity. These were chivalric virtues, and in the code dramatized in the romantic histories the lie, the sacrifice of honor, takes on chivalric importance. The most degrading sacrifice a character could make to selfish or unnatural purposes was the abdication of his manhood by deceitful practices. Bancroft, as historical judge, was careful to give the name of an otherwise unimportant British officer who had violated his parole during the Revolution. Prescott did not criticize Gonsalvo de Cordova for his immediate execution of an officer who had made a lewd joke about Cordova's daughter; but he deplored as "the one foul reproach" on Cordova's character his breach of a promise to a captured commander—even though the promise had been countermanded by the Spanish king.[69]

The importance of this code is most clearly illustrated by Motley's treatment of William of Orange. For Motley, every kind of deceit was unmanly. Since he believed that governments must be judged by the same moral laws that govern individual men, he considered it almost as reprehensible to employ spies as to break one's word of honor. He wandered through a maze of private casuistry in order to explain William's use of spies against Philip II. In the end he could not wholly exonerate William, and his apology led him to imply that the end justifies the means—a doctrine he loathed.[70] Later on in *The Rise of the Dutch Republic* and again in the *United Netherlands,* Motley, apparently forgetting both William's and Elizabeth's excursions into intrigue, excused their failure to detect Franco-Spanish trickery by emphasizing their personal honor: William would have needed "malignity" even to suspect the St. Bartholomew massacre; and Elizabeth simply was not "base enough" to suspect the Duke of Parma of duplicity.[71]

Thus romantic admiration for honor and masculine vigor merged with bourgeois admiration for industry. The inactive person, the torpid society, could not progress. To a nineteenth-century American who knew that his continent had to be "improved," torpor and languor seemed subversive. Provided one could find historical evidence for them, they were the very faults to emphasize in the opponent of progress. The warm-hearted, self-denying man progressed in spite of cold theorists and self-indulgent materialists.

5

Because so many of their unnatural antiprogressives were motivated by greed, because the historians scorned materialism, one might expect them to be suspicious of the profit motive and its results. Parkman and Motley, at least, saw the problem: How could one find lofty heroism in merchants? When Parkman deplored the absence in America of a gentlemanly corps of officers devoted to principles of honor and valor, he recognized the faults encouraged by such a corps; but he was even more distressed by the pettiness, the sordidness, of a merely commercial society.[72] Motley felt that there was something "almost vulgar" about commerce, and in his account of the last Dutch failure to relieve Antwerp he complained: "It was a city where there was much love of money, and where commerce—always timid by nature, particularly when controlled by alien residents—was often the cause of almost abject cowardice."[73]

The romantic historian rarely attributed the profit motive to a specific character without making it an unseemly motive, but commerce in general was another matter. The commercial peoples in these histories are not materialists but agents for "the spirit of commerce." They escape the stigma of materialism because they defend other natural principles— Protestantism, nationality, free thought, republicanism—or the natural economic principles of free trade, "enterprise" or industry, and self-reliance. If a Drake, a Frobisher, a Heemskerk, is a pirate and a profiteer, he is also a "Puritan" and a nationalist.[74] The desire to profit from an investment is materialistic, but self-reliance is admirably "natural"; when one acts for the spirit of commerce, one adheres to a progressive principle.

All of these historians saw something of that connection between Protestantism and capitalism which Weber and Tawney have more recently established; but in the romantic histories the connection often serves to elevate the economic motive rather than to lower the religious one.[75] In describing the transition from a chivalric age to an age of commerce, Motley seeks to equate the virtues of the old period with those of the new. Here he comments on an English officer's lament that long years of peace, encouraging a commercial attitude, had weakened England:

He was wrong in his views of the leading tendencies of his age. Holland and England, self-helping, self-moving, were already inaugurating a new era in the history of the world. The spirit of commercial maritime enterprise—then expanding rapidly into large proportions—was to be matched against the religious and knightly enthusiasm which had accomplished such wonders in an age that was passing away. Spain still personified . . . chivalry, loyalty, piety; but its chivalry, loyalty, and piety, were now in a corrupted condition. The form was hollow, and the sacred spark had fled. In Holland and England intelligent enterprise had not yet degenerated into mere greed for material prosperity. The love of danger, the thirst for adventure, the thrilling sense of personal responsibility and human dignity—not the base love of land and lucre—were the governing sentiments which led those bold Dutch and English rovers to circumnavigate the world in cockle-shells, and to beard the most potent monarch on the earth, both at home and abroad, with a handful of volunteers.[76]

It was a struggle, Motley adds in the next paragraph, "for national independence, liberty of conscience, freedom of the seas, against sacerdotal and world-absorbing tyranny"; it was "the battle of Protestantism on sea and

shore." Motley recurs often to this theme, praising the "rhythm and romance" and the "genial poetic essence" of the early Dutch expeditions to
"the flaming lands of the equator."[77]

By frequently considering commerce as a spiritual endeavor, and by
connecting it when he could with other principles and with deeds of
courage and endurance, the romantic historian was able to maintain a
convenient distinction between materialism and natural principles—but
often at the cost of serious inconsistency. For Bancroft Spanish mercan-
tilism was "a system as old as colonies and the spirit of commercial gain
and political oppression"; that system was created by greed; but it was "the
moral sense" of Dutch "mariners" that "revolted against the extravagance."
Under Bancroft's George III the crown acted always "from love of authority," and in Parliament "the administration of public affairs had degenerated into a system of patronage, which had money for its object"; Boston's
merchants, mechanics, and laborers, however, struck for world liberty.[78]
Prescott, after noting that an adviser wanted Queen Isabella to release a
captured Moorish prince because freeing him would accelerate Granada's
dissolution, said that Isabella "decided for the release of Abdallah, as a
measure best reconciling sound policy with generosity to the vanquished."[79]

Motley always combined Spanish motives of religion and material gain
ironically when he was able to combine them, but he treated the same
combination of Dutch motives quite differently. Among some nobles, he
confessed, the motives for the Dutch rebellion were partly economic; but
he insisted that the rebellion was essentially a "popular" movement and
that its real force was religious. In the very paragraph justifying this argument he returned, however, to economic motives in different language.
The remarkable sixteenth century, he argued, could not allow the Inquisition to "reign undisturbed over the fairest portion of the earth, and char-
tered hypocrisy [to] fatten upon its richest lands." Four times in two
paragraphs he mentioned the energy and industry of the Netherlanders,
contrasting these traits with the greed and corruption of the clergy, who not
only produced little, but refused to pay taxes. It was here, too, that he named
commerce as "the mother" of Flemish freedom.[80]

Materialistic motives, then, were suspect; but although the historian
believed that the motivating principle made the result inevitable, he often
tested the principle by its results. Seeing a decadent country, he could look
for the false principles that had caused its decay; examining those principles
in his history, he might point to their results as proof of their falsity. Since
the "eternal laws" were not systematically defined, the moral value of his-

tory lay in demonstrating them through the material fate of nations. Commerce, industry, and prosperity were the natural nation's reward as well as the cause of its success. Just as Motley pointed with pride to the United Provinces and with pain to the "obedient provinces," so Parkman and Bancroft contrasted the material condition of New France with the teeming vitality and prosperity of New England. Prescott deplored the fact that Spanish overseas conquests had "seduced" the Spanish people "from the humble paths of domestic industry,"[81] and he concluded that the Inquisition and the expulsion of the Moors and Jews had also helped to sink Spain into economic misery. Commerce was not only the mother, but the child of freedom.

6

The administration of undefined natural law through historical judgment allowed the judge a good deal of discretion. As it was applied in the romantic histories the law cannot be codified consistently, but its most prominent features can be briefly restated. The law of progress was supreme; it was by this law that the historian could determine how stringently to apply the "eternal" laws governing private and political behavior. Progress meant an increase in political and intellectual liberty, a movement toward what Theodore Parker called "humanity," a movement away from artificiality or formality toward simplicity, away from torpor and disease toward vigor and health. Natural principles produced health; therefore, although materialism itself was unnatural, the historian could look at the material health of a nineteenth-century country as a test of its earlier principles. In these terms the largest lesson of history was that unmaterialistic freedom was fertile; materialistic despotism, barren.

No method of illustrating this barrenness was more impressive than a contrast between heroic efforts and disastrous results. By treating Spain and New France as ruins which had once been inhabited by "a giant race," Prescott and Parkman added moral force as well as melancholy sentiment to their subjects. The vast accomplishments of Spanish heroes had their monument in Spain's grass-grown streets and crumbling palaces and bridges, "the tokens of [the] nation's degeneracy."[82] New France's records shone "with glorious deeds, the self-devotion of heroes and martyrs; and the result of all is disorder, imbecility, ruin."[83] In the same way, Motley painted into one large Gothic picture a symbol of the "prize" won by all the disciplined energy of thousands of Spanish soldiers. When the daughter of Philip II took possession of her inheritance at Ostend after having besieged it for three years, she received the portion she deserved. The ruins and the gloomy forces of Nature give the picture a power which shows that

Motley, despite his inconsistencies, was a master of the specific moral painting:

The Archduke Albert and the Infanta Isabella entered the place in triumph, if triumph it could be called. It would be difficult to imagine a more desolate scene. . . . There were no churches, no houses, no redoubts, no bastions, no walls, nothing but a vague and confused mass of ruin. Spinola conducted his imperial guests along the edge of extinct volcanoes, amid upturned cemeteries, through quagmires which once were moats, over huge mounds of sand, and vast shapeless masses of bricks and masonry, which had been forts. He endeavoured to point out places where mines had been exploded, where ravelins had been stormed, where the assailants had been successful, and where they had been bloodily repulsed. But it was all loathsome, hideous rubbish. There were no human habitations, no hovels, no casemates. The inhabitants had burrowed at last in the earth, like the dumb creatures of the swamps and forests. In every direction the dykes had burst, and the sullen wash of the liberated waves, bearing hither and thither the floating wreck of fascines and machinery, of planks and building materials, sounded far and wide over what should have been dry land. The great ship channel, with the unconquered Half-moon upon one side and the incomplete batteries and platforms of Bucquoy on the other, still defiantly opened its passage to the sea, and the retiring fleets of the garrison were white in the offing. All around was the grey expanse of stormy ocean, without a cape or a headland to break its monotony, as the surges rolled mournfully in upon a desolation more dreary than their own. The atmosphere was mirky and surcharged with rain, for the wild equinoctial storm which had held Maurice spellbound had been raging over land and sea for many days. At every step the unburied skulls of brave soldiers who had died in the cause of freedom grinned their welcome to the conquerors. Isabella wept at the sight. She had cause to weep. Upon that miserable sandbank more than a hundred thousand men had laid down their lives by her decree, in order that she and her husband might at last take possession of a most barren prize. This insignificant fragment of a sovereignty which her wicked old father had presented her on his deathbed—a sovereignty which he had no more moral right or actual power to confer than if it had been in the planet Saturn—had at last been appropriated at the cost of all this misery. It was of no great value, although its acquisition had caused the expenditure of at least eight millions of florins, divided in nearly equal proportions between the two belligerents. It was in vain that great immunities were offered to those who would remain, or who would consent to settle in the foul Golgotha. The original population left the place in mass. No human creatures were left save the wife of a freebooter and her paramour, a journeyman blacksmith. This unsavoury couple, to whom entrance into the purer atmosphere of Zeeland was denied, thenceforth shared with the carrion crows the amenities of Ostend.[84]

Thus the moral view of history had important advantages, despite the inconsistencies and oversimplifications that it encouraged. The "pervading principle" that Prescott demanded could indeed supply a unity indispensable to literary art. Although the historians often abused the opportunity, the moral emphasis could also add a meaning and interest beyond the merely anecdotal to exciting individual tales—as in Motley's brilliant narrative of Montigny's secret execution in *The Rise of the Dutch Republic*.[85] In the discussion of nations the moral attitude enabled the historian to demonstrate the ironies of Providential justice (or historical fate) in a way much more impressive than that of an amoral economic historian. Prescott summed up the moral of Spain's disastrous colonial policy by alluding to King Midas. Using the conventional "health" rhetoric, he said that her colonies "were miserably dwarfed" because they were "condemned to look for supplies to an incompetent source"; Spain herself, meanwhile,

contrived to convert the nutriment which she extorted from the colonies into a fatal poison. . . . The golden tide, which, permitted a free vent, would have fertilized the region, through which it poured, now buried the land under a deluge which blighted every green and living thing. Agriculture, commerce, manufactures, every branch of national industry and improvement, languished and fell to decay; and the nation, like the Phrygian monarch, who turned all that he touched to gold, cursed by the very consummation of its wishes, was poor in the midst of its treasures.[86]

Motley's account of the proud Portuguese begging the "untiring Hollanders" for a chance to buy spices that had once been controlled by Portuguese monopoly;[87] Bancroft's demonstration, through the "avaricious" bickering of the three great powers while the American colonies grew in vitality, that "the selfishness of evil defeats itself"[88]—these, with their Old Testament quality, are effective moral judgments.

As the historians themselves recognized, however, their moral drama was least effective when it depended solely on nations, or characters less than heroic, as vehicles for the warring principles of history. Their method was most effective when they could embody the principles in heroic flesh-and-blood characters.

2

CONVENTIONAL CHARACTERS

Individuals and Races

CHAPTER III

Representative Men

---

*The genius of humanity is the right point of view of history.
The qualities abide; the men who exhibit them have now more,
now less, and pass away; the qualities remain on another brow.*

EMERSON, "History"

In order to understand the romantic historians' heroes, their solid embodiments in living flesh and blood, one must begin with what the heroes
embodied: with what Motley called "this abstraction," the People. From
the rhetoric in which the historians discussed the more "natural" peoples,
one can see that all four—the Whig-Republicans and the lone Democrat—
agreed on the vitality of the middle class, on defining progress as movement
toward popular liberty. Their belief in the causative power of principles
led them to emphasize the force of national character in progressive advances. "In Netherland story," Motley wrote, "the people is ever the true
hero"; and when he continued his history beyond the death of William the
Silent he boasted of "the hero-people and the people-King."[1] Bancroft's
Americans, Parkman's Englishmen and Yankees, and Prescott's Spaniards
were similarly influential and sometimes equally exalted. In contemporary
politics, too, whether he demanded as Bancroft did that the People be
allowed to defend their government against predatory businessmen, or
whether he denied with Motley and Daniel Webster that there were in
America any classes at all, each of the historians expressed serious interest
in the character of the People, because he considered it the key to the
nation's future. Progress depended on "the genius of the People."[2]

But even in the work of Bancroft, the most aggressively "popular" of
the historians, the common people—though always present, though second
in creative power only to Providence—remained, like Providence, in the
background. They were a perceptible force only in crises. In crises, too,
they acted, more often than not, through their agent: the great man. The
People were always present; the great man stepped forward only in mo-

ments of emergency. He could appear as Roger Williams, "one of those clear minds, which sometimes bless the world by their power of receiving moral truth in its purer light";[3] or, in answer to a more urgent need, as the great political or military leader, as Pitt or Washington. Bancroft agreed with Emerson's theory that "if Napoleon is France, if Napoleon is Europe, it is because the people whom he sways are little Napoleons."[4] Conversely, if the People lived in harmony with Nature and were ruled by moral laws, their best leaders—their Pitts and Washingtons—had to live the same way, under the same laws, at one with the People. Thus Bancroft said that Oliver Cromwell had failed "from the inherent impossibility growing out of the origin of his power," which he had derived "from the submission, not from the will of the people."[5]

Each of the four historians presented at least one hero who perfectly represented his people. Even in a representative government such as that of England, the Netherlands, or the United States during the Revolution, it was natural that in times of great stress "the spirit of the people far outran conventions and congresses." Newly aware, at such moments, of some general truth—"the controlling principle of the age"—the People asserted it through the one man who was their direct representative. At the moment of decision for the Netherlands, William of Orange took the lead, and "the whole nation thought with his thoughts, and spoke with his words." The ideal of virtue, courage, and good sense, Bancroft's Washington sometimes knew better than the People themselves what was good for them. Motley's William "never followed the nation, but always led her in the path of duty and honor"; Washington was "a ruler over the willing." The most important fact about the authority of Prescott's Queen Isabella was that it derived from "the hearts" of the People. The ideal relationship stands forth most clearly in Parkman's evaluation of William Pitt, whom the British people elevated despite his lack of "strong connections" or wealth:

The middle class, as yet almost voiceless, looked to him as its champion; but he was not the champion of a class. His patriotism was as comprehensive as it was haughty and unbending. He lived for England, loved her with intense devotion, knew her, believed in her, and made her greatness his own; or rather, he was himself England incarnate.[6]

The ideally representative man, then, was the incarnation of the People. He represented national ideals. He acted in the name of the People, and they acted through him. The relationship was emotional, often almost mystical. However lofty the leader was, he loved the People. When he had to, he reprimanded them, and he often rejuvenated them in a moment of peril. Every one of the historians iterated a cliché that dramatizes this relationship: in battle after battle the leader "infused his spirit" into his men, or "animated them with his own spirit," or "inspired them with his own energy," or "breathed his own spirit into them." This respiratory influx of grace was nearly irresistible; having received it, the People almost always won the battle.[7]

The representative man was both a historical phenomenon and a literary device. For an age that glorified individualism, for historians who emphasized individual moral responsibility and to whom self-reliance was a moral duty, the historical character had to be influential. Happily, the historical subject often justifies the representative man's importance in the histories; it is not inaccurate to focus attention on La Salle in a history of the discovery of the Great West, on Washington in the American Revolution, on William the Silent in his great conflict or on Cortés in his. Motley frankly admitted the literary value of the device at the same time that he emphasized its historical validity. He regretted that in his *United Netherlands* he had no hero, no William, "to impersonate the great struggle with Spain and Rome, and to concentrate upon his own head a poetical, dramatic, and most legitimate interest."[8]

But the representative man represented more than his nation. In the struggle against antiprogress he represented the progressive principle; and when he was the true hero he stood for great moral principles, represented ideal virtues. Appearing "on the brows" of many characters in the romantic histories, the virtues did, as Emerson said, abide in men from different centuries, and on different continents.

2

The representative hero's first characteristic was naturalness. Bancroft and Parkman, writing about their wild native country, were able to display a kind of correspondence between the scene of the hero's activities and his natural character. The knowledge of Nature, and early training in Nature, were assets hoarded by the historian and entered in heavy black ink at proper places on the ledger of history. Bancroft, as a transcendentalist who believed that the idea of right arises "from the depths of man's consciousness," that evil comes from without, was the most explicit in recording the influence of nature on his heroes.[9]

Although not a major hero in Bancroft's *History,* Daniel Boone has an important representative place: he is "the woodsman," the type of those self-reliant Kentuckians so important to American independence and virtue. His traits are those of Cooper's Natty Bumppo:

[Boone was] the cheerful, meditative man, careless of wealth, knowing the use of the rifle, not the plough, of a strong, robust frame, in the vigorous health of early manhood, ignorant of books, but versed in the forest and forest life, ever fond of tracking the deer on foot, away from men, yet in his disposition humane, generous, and gentle. . . . Nature was his intimate, and as the roving woodsman leaned confidingly on her bosom, she responded to his intelligence. . . . Triumphing over danger, he knew no fear. . . . He loved the solitude better than the towered city or the hum of business.[10]

Bancroft ignored Boone's connection with the intrigues of Richard Henderson; it was Boone's proficiency in woodcraft that had "led him to love solitude and habitually to hover on the frontier with no abiding place." The roving woodsman, the intimate of Nature, could have no material motive for emigrating to Missouri. What is important here, however, is not the idealization of American motives, but the portrait of a man who possessed "every natural virtue," who "never wronged a human being, not even an Indian, nor, indeed, animal life of any kind."[11]

A perfect type for the common man, and in this sense ideally representative, Boone had neither enough education nor enough historical importance to be a hero. Thus, the same kind of conventional limitation that Henry Nash Smith has explained in his discussion of the woodsman in American fiction restricted the woodsman in Bancroft's history and in Parkman's. But the type was important in the history and mythology of the country, and the counterpart of Parkman's natural guide, Henri Châtillot, appears in the histories of both.[12]

Parkman's woodsman is no Natty Bumppo, no Filsonian Boone. From his own experience, Parkman wrote of the frontiersman as "a distinct, peculiar class, marked with striking contrasts of good and evil." Admitting that "many, though by no means all, were coarse, audacious, and unscrupulous," Parkman nevertheless stressed their "warlike virtues, an iron endurance, an undespairing courage, a wondrous sagacity, and singular fertility of resource." "The nursling of civilization," he said, ". . . is helpless as an infant" in the woods. But "Not so the woodsman. To him, the forest is a home." Often, like Natty Bumppo, he outlearned his Indian tutor. His representative in Parkman's histories is Major Robert Rogers, who appears as the natural man—"a strong, well-knit figure, in dress and appearance more woodsman than soldier, with a clear, bold eye, and features that would have been good but for the ungainly proportions of the nose." Although Parkman points out that Rogers was something of a scoundrel, he portrays him consistently in the favorable rhetoric reserved for the virtues of the woodsman.[13] In the romantic histories the "clear, bold eye" never appears in the head of a character who is not admired for his energy and skill, whatever his morals.

Just as the tutored white man excels the Indian despite the Indian's slight advantage in sensory perception, so the cultivated hero who has been trained in the wilderness is superior to the mere woodsman. Here again the historians respect the hierarchy described in conventional fiction. In George Washington, who appears in Parkman's history of the Seven Years' War and dominates Bancroft's history of the Revolution, one can see the natural virtues, and the lessons of the wilderness at work in the genuine hero. "At sixteen," Bancroft wrote, Washington "went into the wilderness as a surveyor, and for three years continued the pursuit, where the forests trained him, in meditative solitude, to freedom and largeness of mind; and nature revealed to him her obedience to serene and silent laws." From Nature and from the immortal spirit infused in him, Washington acquired "a divine and animating virtue." He was modest, pious, and so humane that in 1753 he refused to let his men kill an Indian who had tried to murder him. Parkman, too, believed that Washington's fine mastery of his "proud and passionate" nature resulted from his early natural training on the frontier. His vain effort to control a pack of unruly soldiers suffering from hit-and-run attacks over a 300-mile frontier was perfect training for his later duties.[14]

Although Motley and Prescott had less opportunity to emphasize the natural schooling of their heroes, Europe, too, had its wild natural scenes. However unlikely a royal hero might be to live the life of a frontiersman, each of the historians seized on the natural training when he could, and treated it in the manner of Cooper, Scott, Bancroft, and Parkman. At the beginning and the end of *Ferdinand and Isabella,* Prescott insisted that Isabella had spent her early years under the tutelage of a careful mother, far from the corrupt influences of the Castilian court:

far from the voice of flattery and falsehood, she had been permitted to unfold the natural graces of mind and person, which might have been blighted in the pestilent atmosphere of a court. Here, under the maternal eye, she was carefully instructed in those lessons of practical piety, and in the deep reverence for religion, which distinguished her maturer years.

Once she was brought to court, to "this abode of pleasure," although "surrounded by all the seductions most dazzling to youth, she did not forget the early lessons, that she had imbibed; and the blameless purity of her conduct shone with additional lustre amid the scenes of levity and licentiousness by which she was surrounded."[15]

Motley uses the same technique in describing the virtues of Henry of Navarre. When Henry is a progressive soldier, he appears on Motley's pages as manly and natural; when he fights on the wrong side, he is corrupt. Henry's "sensible grandfather" ordered "the boy taught to run about bareheaded and bare-footed, like a peasant, among the mountains and rocks of Béarn, till he became as rugged as a young bear, and as nimble as a kid. Black bread, and beef, and garlic, were his simple fare; and he was taught by his mother and his grandfather to hate lies and liars, and to read the Bible." This natural morality causes some confusion in Motley's treatment of Henry, as it does in his moral judgments of William the Silent. He condemns Henry for forgetting the simple virtues of his education and keeping a harem at Pau; soon afterward, however, when describing Henry's refusal of a bribe offered by Philip II, he writes proudly: "But Henry—no longer the unsophisticated youth who had been used to run barefoot among the cliffs of Coarasse—was grown too crafty a politician to be entangled by Spanish or Medicean wiles." Still natural enough to remember "some of his old love of truth, of his hatred for liars," Henry is at this point just sophisticated enough to be too shrewd for Philip II.[16]

The character whose unfortunate youth had not included the joys of running barefoot through Nature or of tracking the deer on foot was, of course, none the less natural for his misfortune. The epithet "natural" denoted a wide range of virtuous traits in the romantic histories. First among these was simplicity. In the judgment of individuals as well as of nations, the simpler was usually the better. The self-denying man, straightforward and, however conscious of his own ability, unencumbered by ostentation— this man was the ideal. William the Silent may have been a prince, and a rich, pleasure-loving one, but Motley makes much of his modest dress when he can, and of his "simple and sublime expression." Isabella's simple, austere frugality in matters of dress wins Prescott's special attention. And all four historians praise military leaders for their willingness to share the hardships which their men must suffer.[17] The true hero could not be so simple as Daniel Boone or Bancroft's Connecticut farmers. But, as in Cooper's novels, he had to retain a relative simplicity which, despite his occasional ability to confound practitioners of "Medicean" or "Machiavellian" deceit, could be contrasted with the corrupt artificiality of his enemies.

By far the most important natural quality, however, was a moderate amount of passion. The natural hero had to have warm emotions, a quick sympathy, a delicately balanced sensibility. As Scott, Cooper, and Hawthorne often did in their fiction, Prescott found it most convenient to embody these qualities in a beautiful young woman. He discovered in Queen Isabella the perfect fair heroine of romantic fiction.

Besides fair hair and blue eyes (features unusual to the Spanish type), Isabella has a warm heart. Her shy nature recoils conventionally from the idea of marrying the corrupt old master of Calatrava, to whom she has been betrothed; to describe her behavior in this predicament, Prescott relies heavily on "tradition"—and on tradition appropriate to the conventions of contemporary fiction. With perfect propriety, Isabella fasts in order to win God's help in preventing the marriage; her "faithful friend" Beatriz is ready, meanwhile, to use other means: impulsively taking a dagger "from her bosom," she "vowed to plunge it into the heart of the master of Calatrava, as soon as he appeared!" After the master, with equal respect for convention, dies "with imprecations on his lips," Isabella is in due time betrothed to Ferdinand. Prescott gives the prudent, political reasons for this choice, but he is careful to add, too, that Isabella "was not insensible to those [arguments] which most powerfully affect the female heart."[18]

In her royal decisions, moreover, Isabella often consulted her own heart rather than the heads of the wise. Her response to Columbus' plea for sponsorship was dictated, Prescott says, by the "natural impulses of her own noble and generous heart," after she had refused "to hearken any longer to the suggestions of cold and timid counsellors."[19] Even her mistakes, Prescott serenely implies—with a circular logic that infuriated Theodore Parker—even the few stains on her administrative record resulted directly from her virtues. Her piety and natural humility led her to trust her "ghostly advisers" in religious matters, when her own "natural kindness of heart" would have dictated different policies. In the ominous position of the innocent young girl's confessor, the insidious Torquemada gained an influence that persuaded her, in her maturity, to establish the modern Inquisition. Her pious, humble heart trusted this priest, and he abused the trust by making her vow that she would extirpate heresy. In this description Prescott takes advantage of the conventional romantic device, used in *Rob Roy* and Hawthorne's *Blithedale Romance,* of having a shrewd or fanatical counsellor try to poison an innocent girl's mind and soul. What saved Isabella, although she could not escape all the consequences of such subtle misuse of a sacred trust, was "her sound understanding and natural kindness of heart."[20]

Having established that natural kindness as a fact—by assertion and a few examples of kindness, but mostly by painting Isabella as the conventional fair heroine—Prescott uses it to demonstrate the subtle intellectual power of her advisers. The fact that they could convince her to cheat the Moors of their property (a decision which "was obviously most repugnant to Isabella's natural disposition") proves, Prescott says, that before the Reformation the clergy had an overpowering influence on even the best minds. He offers no evidence that Isabella made this decision on the advice of others; in view of her "natural kindness," no evidence is necessary.[21] However "indelible" the "stain" left "on her memory" by this decision, he tries to scrub some of it off by reminding the reader of her "unfeigned humility," of her "natural distrust of herself" in religious matters, and of her refusal to accept the advice of those who urged her to *kill* all the Moors. Within a few pages Isabella is pawning the crown jewels and her own jewels for patriotic reasons, and then appearing "as some celestial visitant" among her troops, "to inspire them with her own energy" before a battle.[22]

Having endured successes and trials through a long reign, Isabella's "tender heart," grieving over the madness and the suffering of her daughter Joanna, leads her eventually to her deathbed. And to that deathbed she carries all her virtues, including a natural propriety so delicate that she will not allow her feet to be exposed even while she is receiving the last rites of the Church. The virtues that Prescott summarizes in his long obituary include temperance, simplicity, sedateness, magnanimity, a hatred of artifice and duplicity, unfeigned humility, and tenderness and benevolence of "heart."[23]

The conventionality of Prescott's fair Isabella serves a further purpose than the depiction of a virtuous woman. It epitomizes the representative. Not only was the rhetoric of Prescott's portrait familiar to the novel reader, but the qualities highlighted by that rhetoric explained her hold on her people; Prescott demonstrated that both the rhetoric and the qualities were peculiarly appropriate to the representative of Spain. Describing her appearance in the field when she encouraged her armies, he declared that "the attachment to Isabella seemed to be a pervading principle, which animated the whole nation by one common impulse, impressing a unity of design on all its movements."[24] "Pervading principle," one should remember, is the very phrase that Prescott used when arguing that the historian ought to keep a moral theme before his reader. Isabella's character is the pervading principle of his three-volume work, and Prescott makes it clear that "attachment" to her was a pervading principle because it revealed the character of the Spanish people. Throughout his histories the Spanish character appears as romantically religious and chivalrous. It is perfectly appropriate, then, that the "attachment" to Isabella

was imputable to her sex as well as her character. The sympathy, and tender care, with which she regarded her people, naturally raised a reciprocal sentiment in their bosoms. . . . The chivalrous heart of the Spaniard did homage to her, as to his tutelar saint; and she held a control over her people, such as no man could have acquired in any age,—and probably no woman, in an age and country less romantic.[25]

Two extended contrasts—with Ferdinand and with Elizabeth—accent the importance of Isabella's sentimental qualities. The regency of Ferdinand after her death, the subject of the last section of the history, undid many of the good deeds of Isabella's reign. The fact that Ferdinand arranged another marriage soon after Isabella's death—in the very place where he had married her—emphasizes the fair qualities of Isabella. His disloyalty to her memory and to Columbus and Gonsalvo de Cordova, the noblest subjects she had sponsored, demonstrates his coldness. But this fault has been foreshadowed even before Isabella's death. Saddened by Joanna's madness and then by the infidelity of Joanna's husband, Isabella was stricken with fever. When Prescott remarks that Ferdinand, who had also caught a fever, unwittingly added to the Queen's fatal worries and then recovered, he seems to make physical recovery itself a fault in Ferdinand! Isabella's "tender heart," he says, "was more keenly sensible than his to the unhappy condition of their child, and to the gloomy prospects, which awaited her beloved Castile."[26]

Both in public and in private, Ferdinand shows an "impenetrable frigidity." Even his religion is closer to "superstition" than to Isabella's "piety." Because of his coldness and because only innocent girls seem to be excusable for accepting the evil ideas of sly confessors, he is condemned as a bigot; "for he cooperated with Isabella in all her exceptionable measures in Castile, and spared no effort to fasten the yoke of the Inquisition on Aragon."

While Isabella's character is "all magnanimity," Ferdinand is "the spirit of egotism." As "a shrewd and politic prince," Prescott concludes, Ferdinand represents "the peculiar genius of the age"—a genius described as Machiavellian. But Isabella, "discarding all the petty artifices of state policy, and pursuing the noblest ends by the noblest means, stands far above her age."[27]

The second contrast is gratuitous. In his obituary essay on Isabella, Prescott compares her at length to Elizabeth of England, with whose reign and character he assumes his readers to be familiar. In this essay Elizabeth resembles the dark heroine of romantic fiction, the *belle dame sans merci*.[28] Both great queens, Prescott says, were reforming administrators; both, women of unusual courage. Their experiences before coming to the throne and the "inconsolable melancholy" that each suffered in her last years can be readily compared.[29] In all else they were black and white.

Against Isabella's gentle qualities Prescott places Elizabeth's darker passions. Elizabeth, like many an unfortunate dark heroine, had no mother to teach what Isabella's mother had taught; and many of her passions were those of her father. She "was haughty, arrogant, coarse, and irascible; while with these fiercer qualities she mingled deep dissimulation and strange irresolution." She was "desperately selfish," and unable to forgive "the slightest affront to her vanity." Whereas Elizabeth was "merciless in exacting retribution," Isabella "sought every means" to be lenient, "even toward the guilty." And Elizabeth stepped beyond the bounds of fictional propriety in another way common to heroines of her type: she was more learned than Isabella. But although she was "better educated, and every way more highly accomplished than Isabella," the latter "knew enough" to patronize learning very generously. It is this difference that leads Prescott to contrast most clearly the kinds of feeling expressed by the two heroines:

The masculine powers and passions of Elizabeth seemed to divorce her in great measure from the peculiar attributes of her sex; at least from those which constitute its peculiar charm; for she had abundance of its foibles,—a coquetry and love of admiration, which age could not chill; a levity, most careless, if not criminal; and a fondness for dress and tawdry magnificence of ornament, which was ridiculous, or disgusting, according to the different periods of life in which it was indulged.[30]

Although the accessibility of the hero's heart could not be so repeatedly demonstrated as the heroine's sensibility, each of the representative heroes had his share of natural passion. Bancroft was careful to remove the immobile mask that Stuart had painted on the portrait of Washington. As Parkman was later to emphasize Washington's "proud and passionate" temperament, Bancroft explained away Washington's external impassiveness as the consequence of his tremendous responsibilities: "[his] joyousness of disposition remained to the last, though the vastness of his responsibilities was soon to take from him the right of displaying the impulsive qualities of his nature." Indeed, joyousness was one of Washington's most valuable traits, for it carried him through the most severe trials suffered by virtuous men in Bancroft's *History*: "Hope and zeal illuminated his grief. His emotions come to us across the century like strains from that eternity which repairs all losses and rights all wrongs; in his untold sorrows, his trust in Providence kept up in his heart an undersong of wonderful sweetness." His impetuous courage and quick indignation could lead him to chastise his army when it failed him, and to dare to face an enemy force alone—until convinced by his officers that he was too valuable to take such a risk.[31]

The hero's sensibility could also be accented by contrast with the corrupt man's frigidity. Just as Prescott's Isabella overruled her "cold and timid counsellors" when her heart responded to the grandeur of Columbus' plans, so Bancroft's William Pitt overruled Lord Mansfield; "cautious even to timidity," Bancroft said of Mansfield, "his understanding was clear, but his heart was cold." Pitt, who had risen to authority from the ranks of the People, was a man of passion both in *Montcalm and Wolfe* and in Bancroft's *History*. Bancroft praised not only his courage and his strong faith in Providence, but what Parkman called his "domestic virtues," by painting a sentimental picture of the affectionate man at home.[32]

Pitt's emotional nature shone most clearly, however, in his eloquence. The romantic historians' idea of eloquence was naturally very close to that of Emerson and Whitman.[33] The eloquent man could establish that "electric," "impulsive" rapport with the People on which successful leadership so often depended. In the conventional description of a crucial battle it is usually by a few eloquent words at the moment of crisis that the great leader "breathes his own spirit" into his men and moves them to the successful charge. In the legislature, too, eloquence is an essential heroic trait, and the historians rarely fail to stress its emotional quality or its emotional effect. When Bancroft's Patrick Henry, who hated "the black-letter of the law-books," made his most famous speech, "his transfigured features glowed as he spoke, and his words fell like a doom of fate." And when William Pitt spoke to the House of Commons on the Treaty of Paris, he inspired every member: "At the word," Bancroft wrote, "the whole house started as though their hands had been joined, and an electric spark had darted through them all." Parkman called Pitt's eloquence "fiery and passionate"; Motley called William's "simple and sublime."[34]

In the military hero domestic tenderness seems to be nearly as important as more energetic passion. In General James Wolfe, for example, both Bancroft and Parkman not only stress "ardor and daring," or contempt for book soldiery; both historians also insist that "one sees him most closely in the intimacies of domestic life."[35] Parkman underscores the same qualities in Montcalm; and Motley dramatizes parental sympathy in his Prince of Orange, who risks his life in order to carry the body of a ten-year-old girl to her "unhappy parents."[36]

This delicate balance of emotions, though often described in merely sentimental situations, was essential for the popular or military leader. If he was "the soul" of his army or nation, he had to know his people perfectly, had to feel with them, in order to be able to inspire them at just the right moment. Bancroft, for example, insisting that the Declaration of Independence was not the product of "the prevalent freethinking of [eighteenth-century] Englishmen," said that the decision arose not from the "intellect" but from "the heart" of the People. The agent best qualified to express the People's will in writing was Thomas Jefferson, who was qualified because of his feelings rather than by any ideas he had learned from Locke, Pufendorf, or Montesquieu. What Bancroft admired most was "the sympathetic character of his nature, by which he was able with instinctive perception to read the soul of the nation, and having collected in himself its best thoughts and noblest feelings, to give them out in bold and clear words." By drawing his opinions from those of Jefferson's writings that expressed tender emotions, love of Nature, and faith in the People, Bancroft painted him as one of the finest examples of the natural man. Faced with concrete evidence that Jefferson was "indifferent to religion," he insisted that Jefferson's "instincts" nevertheless "inclined him to trace every effect to a general law, and to put faith in ideal truth." Although Jefferson had told John Adams that "once we quit the basis of sensation, all is in the wind," Bancroft said that "the world of the senses did not bound his aspirations, and *he believed more than he himself was aware of.* He was an idealist in his habits of thought and life, as indeed is every one who has an abiding and thorough confidence in the people."[37]

The true hero, the hero for all ages, was not, of course, a slave to his emotional nature. Even though the two greatest heroes in the histories, William the Silent and Washington, led rebel armies, neither general was wholly or even largely destructive. Both were "chosen" to overthrow usurpers in the name of higher laws, the laws of the moral world. In this sense, and even in a more practical political sense, both were conservative. Motley presents William as the defender not only of eternal laws but of the Netherlands' ancient charters and liberties. Bancroft argues that Washington and his followers defended a constitutional as well as a natural right. Like Isabella, moreover, both leaders knew where to stop. William had come "to maintain, not to overthrow." Providence had elected Bancroft's Washington not only "to guide the fiery coursers of revolution along untried paths," but also "to check them firmly at the goal." Both leaders rebuked extremists, showing a prudence and self-control as essential to greatness as the "practical good sense" that balanced Isabella's sensibility. William disagreed with the "hot Calvinists" on toleration; Washington and the People distinguished more clearly than the congress between a tyrannical royal governor and an efficient democratic executive. William's patriotism was not that of the demagogic "beggars," of Nicholas de Hammes or the rash and drunken Count Brederode; Washington's courage was not the arrogant bullheadedness of General Braddock.[38]

It is true, though, that William's "heart" led him to make the only mistakes which Motley is willing to call mistakes. Throughout *The Rise of the Dutch Republic,* and in the face of evidence that he himself must present, Motley refers to William as "the first statesman of the age." This primacy includes, as Motley makes very clear in his conclusion, "profound" dexterity in the use of "the subtleties of Italian statesmanship, which he had learned as a youth at the Imperial court, and which he employed in his manhood in the service, not of tyranny, but of liberty." Despite William's inexplicable decision to leave his eldest son behind, at the mercy of Philip, when he fled the Netherlands; despite his many costly, if often understandable, political and military mistakes; Motley says twice that he was "never . . . outwitted by his enemies." The only men who did manage to "overreach" William were "those to whom he gave his heart."[39] If these men were agents of Philip, one might conclude that Philip had outwitted the Prince, but this reasoning goes one step further than Motley wanted to go. Unable to admit that the great leader was inferior to his corrupt enemies in any branch of statesmanship, he tried to show that William's mistakes were the results of his virtues. One could forgive the errors of a noble heart.

3

Despite his natural simplicity, the representative hero had to achieve a certain "loftiness." Every major hero in the histories has a grandeur, and some of them have an *hauteur,* that the historians considered worthy of serious contemplation. In different characters they created this effect in different ways, but it always emphasizes the hero's isolation from the rest of humanity, even though he remains representative. Bancroft's Washington and Motley's William were set apart by their vast responsibilities as well as by their characteristic reticence, their suffering, and their endurance. The effect might be created by the physical portrait, too: by a suggestion of commanding presence, as in Motley's favorite comment that "there was something in his brow . . . which men willingly call master";[40] by an emphasis on the subject's eyes as reflecting "the spirit within"; or, when the evidence permitted, by an emphasis on the subject's physical size. The grandeur of the hero's "vision," the tenacity and transcendent power of his will, and his unconquerable resolution were other qualities accented for the same purpose.

The very nature of the great man's mission helped to produce this effect of lofty isolation. Every progressive hero had to remain "true to himself" when others could not understand him; and when he pursued his own ambitions, he followed "not so much his own wish as a necessary law of his being."[41] In obeying this law he sometimes displayed a singular haughtiness as he brooded over his difficult plans or stood off an angry mob to prevent them from damaging the common cause.

The perfect hero was isolated even by his representativeness, for he suffered for a whole nation. "The trials of Washington," Bancroft wrote, "are the dark, solemn ground on which the beautiful work of his country's salvation was embroidered." In Bancroft's volumes on the Revolution, and even more clearly in the first two parts of *The Rise of the Dutch Republic,* the pathetic sufferings of the hero became a major theme. Washington endures trial after trial, defeat after defeat, desertion after desertion; William loses his possessions, his friends, his trustiest lieutenants; when he is finally forced to make his decision, William can "find no one to comprehend his views."[42]

Motley saw at least temporarily the danger of distorting the history of so great a man as William. Although this perception did not save him from repeated inconsistency in his moral judgment of William, it helps to explain the importance of adversity in these histories—perhaps the very reason for Motley's inconsistencies. Anyone, Motley wrote, must find it very difficult "coldly to analyse" such a "self-sacrificing and heroic" character as William's; should the historian express "the emotions which naturally swell the heart at the contemplation of so much active virtue," he would probably be "liable to the charge of excessive admiration." Then, in an image that cannot be overemphasized, Motley revealed the effect of adversity:

Through the mists of adversity, a human form may dilate into proportions which are colossal and deceptive. Our judgment may thus be led captive, but at any rate the sentiment excited is more healthful than that inspired by the mere shedder of blood, by the merely selfish conqueror.[43]

In all the histories, then, the great man suffers, and the extent of his suffering "dilates" him. However sure the long-range advantage of his alliance with inevitable progress, he struggles against almost overwhelming power. Sometimes he must work against the follies or shortsightedness of his own people or their legal representatives. If he is a pathfinder—a Columbus, Cortés, Pizarro, or La Salle—he must overcome not only men of smaller vision, but also the vast forces of Nature, the numerical power of savages, and the frustrating distances from civilization, from the source of his supplies, and from the scenes of his enemies' machinations.

Each of the historians pauses frequently to contemplate such a hero in the depths of his suffering. The pathos of his misery is intended to move the reader; his "sublime" endurance and constancy, to "swell the heart." Motley admits that his purpose is to describe William as "a statue of spotless marble against a stormy sky."[44] Through failure after failure the perfect hero (William or Washington) may feel somewhat melancholy, but he must not despair. Often when it seems, because of Motley's emphasis, that the Prince has at last reached his nadir, Motley must recount a catastrophe that produces even greater suffering. Having lost two armies without a battle; having been surprised and nearly murdered in his tent by a force of 600 Spaniards, although his own army numbered 15,000; having been unable to force Alva into battle; William reaches the nadir of misery at the terrible siege of Harlem.

Motley's attempt, in describing this siege, to keep his great leader in control of his destiny is almost ludicrous. After the besieged inhabitants have been starving for several weeks, William begs them to hold out a while longer because he will soon do something—what, one never learns. He can do nothing. After a long delay, he finally decides to send a small relieving force, and he sends word to the besieged by carrier pigeon. The Spaniards shoot down the pigeons, discover the plan, ambush and destroy the relievers, and then, after taking Harlem, slaughter the remaining 2,300 inhabitants. On hearing the news, Motley says, the Prince "was neither dismayed nor despondent." William is a man who goes "through life bearing the load of a people's sorrows on his shoulders with a smiling face." His "joyousness" and endurance are even greater than Washington's. After twelve years of costly fighting, Philip II, the Spanish people, and the Dutch people have tired of the war, but not so the Prince. "Prerogative was weary—Romanism was weary—Conscience was weary—the Spirit of Freedom was weary—but the Prince of Orange was not weary. Blood and treas-

ure had been pouring forth so profusely during twelve flaming years that
all but one tranquil spirit had begun to flag."[45]

Neither this kind of character nor the kind of scene in which he revealed
his titanic quality originated solely in the historical documents. Nor do the
afflictions of Prescott and Parkman entirely explain their attraction to characters whose gigantic wills had overcome severe physical handicaps. Historical evidence often justifies the historians' emphasis and it always justifies
their scenes, but one can also find the counterparts of both in Carlyle, in
Byron, and in contemporary fiction. When Motley's William, for example,
rode unarmed to the Red Gate of Antwerp to quiet "as formidable a mob
as ever man has faced," he reenacted an almost identical scene that Motley
himself had written into a novel sixteen years earlier.[46]

As for Parkman, it seems true that his personal troubles led him to emphasize Byronic characters more strongly than any of the other historians—
and, indeed, more intensely than any other American writer except Herman
Melville. But one must recognize that every one of the romantic historians
portrayed similar characters in the same rhetoric that Parkman used. Long
before Parkman was either a sick man or a writer, Bancroft, who remained
healthy and energetic for ninety years, had packed his eleven pages on La
Salle with praise for La Salle's "immense power of . . . will"; for his "sublime magnanimity," his "constancy," and his dependence "on himself"; for
"the giant energy of his indomitable will"; for his ability, despite "the terrible energy of his grief," to display "the powerful activity of his will"; for
his "constancy and elastic genius" when "Heaven and man seemed his
enemies"; and, finally, for his ability to conquer "affliction by energy of
purpose and unfaltering hope."[47] Parkman read Bancroft's volume carefully in 1840. It is in this context, beside Cooper's John Paul Jones and
Prescott's Columbus and Cortés, that one should consider Parkman's La
Salle.

What is different in Parkman's *La Salle* is the oppressive atmosphere of
gloom, an effect increased by the large scale of the study and the relentless
intensity with which Parkman focuses on the single character. La Salle's
faults and virtues resemble those of Prescott's Columbus; his endurance and
his difficulties, those of Cortés. But this man has no eloquence. His profound loneliness, his inability to communicate, and the complete wreck of
his final plans make him a much more pathetic figure than any of Prescott's
heroes, despite the trite language in which his suffering and his character
are often described. In *La Salle*, moreover, there are no Aztecs, no Montezuma, to relieve the concentration on the one man's endurance. Although

others share his traits, La Salle is the grand type of the historians' isolated man.

A reticent, distant man, of "reserved and seemingly cold pride," Parkman's La Salle loves both solitude and power. He is so transcendently self-reliant that he asks "counsel of no man." Committed from the beginning to vast plans of discovery and colonization, he tries to counteract in Illinois the intrigues of enemies in Montreal and of equally malicious conspirators in Paris. Suffering disaster in the wilderness, he walks back a thousand miles to Fort Frontenac. While he works desperately there to save his plans, his men in the West betray him, and the Iroquois slaughter his Indian friends. The ship carrying the furs to finance his next expedition is destroyed by some unknown catastrophe. "Man and Nature," Parkman says, "seemed in arms against him; for him there was neither rest nor peace." But La Salle is a man of "iron-hearted constancy," and he loses "neither heart nor hope" in the ruins of his plans. "Calm, impenetrable," as he marches across the country, he deserves Parkman's entire chapter on his "hardihood," for both his spiritual and physical endurance are prodigious. After describing the loss of his ship, Parkman asks rhetorically, "Did he bend before the storm?" The answer comes in more description of his incredible resolution. After a series of still greater misfortunes, La Salle (in a chapter called "La Salle Begins Anew") refuses to despair: "He had no thought but to grapple with adversity, and out of the fragments of his ruin to build up the fabric of his success."[48] This is the achievement of William after Harlem and of Washington after Valley Forge, the achievement of Cortés after the *Noche Triste*.

Because of his magnificent will La Salle did navigate the Mississippi, but his success was only "the prelude of a harder task." Attacked by illness, "a foe against which the boldest heart avails nothing," he continued to fight both the Iroquois and his enemies in Montreal and Paris, and his reserve deepened, making him "a sealed book to those about him." Even after his return to Paris he "still thirsted after greatness." He had the basic fault of Prescott's Columbus: "he dared too much, and often dared unwisely; attempted more than he could grasp; and forgot, in his sanguine anticipations, to reckon with enormous and incalculable risks."[49]

As La Salle moves closer to his final, mad scheme for colonization at the mouth of the Mississippi, Parkman reemphasizes his unbearable loneliness as well as his madness. Friendless and unable to communicate with lesser beings, he lacks "that sympathetic power, the inestimable gift of the true leader of men, in which lies the difference between a willing and a constrained obedience. This solitary being, hiding his shyness under a cold reserve, could rouse no enthusiasm in his followers." Rather than the treachery of his friends and his enemies or the misfortunes resulting from the grandeur of his plans, it is this "fatal flaw" that causes his downfall. Resolutely carrying out his wild plan—still "impenetrable" and now paranoically suspicious not only of all his men but even of the naval commander on whose good will his success depends—La Salle is presented toward the end as a nobly pathetic, Byronic figure: oppressed by his worrisome responsibilities after his ships are wrecked, "pale and haggard with recent illness, *wrapped within his own thoughts, and seeking sympathy from none.*" Now, as he tries to recover from the last series of catastrophes, he must face again the same multiple sources of opposition: natural catastrophe, a troop of Indians trying to loot the wreckage, his own inability either to be everywhere at once or to delegate authority, the faults of his men, the enmity of his associates. Amid the wreckage, Parkman says, "the fate-hunted chief" keeps his drearier vigil, "encompassed with treachery, darkness, and the storm." Despite his noble resolution, the scene of the ruin of his last hopes is pathetically comic:

. . . and here, among tents and hovels, bales, boxes, casks, spars, dismounted cannon, and pens for fowls and swine, were gathered the dejected men and homesick women who were to seize New Biscay, and hold for France a region large as half Europe. The Spaniards, whom they were to conquer, were they knew not where. They knew not where they were themselves; and, for the fifteen thousand Indian allies who were to have joined them, they found two hundred squalid savages, more like enemies than friends.

La Salle has become indecisive; his grandiose plans have given way to fretting about the smallness of a meat cellar built at the new fort. As he leaves in search of the Mississippi, he is still devising plans for a meat cellar "on a grand scale." All he has left at the time of his death are his "haughty reserve," his resolution, and his hardihood.[50]

In almost all of the romantic histories one sees the image of this lofty type, of a large, strong man standing resolute or moving with frenetic energy as the crushing force of his enemies, and other misfortunes beyond one man's control, try to bend or destroy him. He rarely rolls on, as the star of Byron's Manfred does,

> Without a sphere, without a course,

but he is always depicted as

> . . . rolling on with innate force.

His triumph, when it comes, is a spiritual triumph, a triumph of will. Columbus, Cortés, and Pizarro, like Bancroft's and Parkman's La Salle, face the impossible task of fighting simultaneous battles against enemies thousands of miles apart. Although the distances are less astounding, William the Silent, Henry IV (at the end, in "pathetic isolation"), Maurice of Nassau, Alexander Farnese, Wolfe, Washington, and Frederick the Great—all face the same gigantic problem. The great military leader is the man who, in battle, can be "everywhere at once." With his army in panic or hesitating around him, he rushes here and there, or stands firm, seizes the one opportunity for success, and produces victory by the force of his will over his men. He, too, often creates "the fabric of success" from "the fragments of his ruin"—a heroic achievement in which William, Maurice, Alexander Farnese, and Cortés impress even the enemy.[51]

Parkman was fascinated by the type. His William Pitt is haughty and inordinately vain. But that vanity proceeds from his virtue, and his disdainful character—which enables him to "blast the labored argument of an adversary with a look of scorn or a contemptuous wave of the hand"— forces even the men who have served shamefully under Newcastle to serve "manfully" under his "robust impulsion." His love of power equals La Salle's; but this "British Roman" has complete control of himself. Parkman sees the type even more clearly in Frederick the Great, a military as well as a political genius. Through both the early pages and the final pages of *Montcalm and Wolfe* Parkman sends the almost oppressively energetic image of Frederick, scornful of his enemies, scornful of peace ("for him," as for La Salle, "there was no peace"). Frederick, too, is deserted by all his allies, and one sees him standing in sublime isolation, erect and defiant. Having "passed between the upper and nether millstones of paternal discipline," Parkman says, "he came at last out of purgatory; and Europe felt him to her farthest bounds." A collection of contradictions whose coherent center is an indomitable will, Parkman's Frederick resembles the equally paradoxical Henry IV, who typifies energetic kingliness in Motley's *United Netherlands*. "Surrounded by enemies, in the jaws of destruction, hoping for little but to die in battle," Frederick "solaced himself with an exhaustless effusion of bad verses . . . till, when his hour came, he threw down his pen to achieve those feats of arms which stamp him one of the foremost soldiers of the world."[52]

Bancroft's Pitt, though not at first so clearly "patrician" as Parkman's more aristocratic figure, is also haughty, proud, and grand. Bancroft makes his ambition a fault, as Parkman criticizes his vanity. By accepting an

earldom, Bancroft says, Pitt succumbed to material temptation, thus for-
feiting his true claim to nobility as the champion of the British people:

The lion had left the forest, where he roamed as the undisputed monarch, and
of himself had walked into a cage. His popularity vanished, and with it the
terror of his name. He was but an English Earl and the shadow of a Prime
Minister; he no longer represented the enthusiastic nationality of the English
people.

This weakness Bancroft attributes partly to Pitt's age and physical infirm-
ity; had the lion been well, he might have stayed on to rule in the forest.
But even in his physical and spiritual decline Bancroft's Pitt is still a lion,
a lofty leader far above the party bickering of the day: "Transmitting to
his substitute every question of domestic, foreign, and colonial policy un-
settled, the British Agamemnon retired to his tent, leaving the subordinate
chiefs to quarrel for the direction." And in the hour of England's need,
though suffering severely from gout, he calls on his mighty will to deliver
a final, eloquent speech to Parliament. Both Bancroft and Parkman present the scene, the effort, and the eloquence as characteristic of Pitt's grandeur.[53]

When they were contemporaries, it seems, there was a sympathetic
bond among such titans. Count Frontenac, an old man with "unconquerable vitality" and the "elastic vigor of youth" who was "representative"
of the best in French aristocracy, understood La Salle very clearly. The
understanding between them was "the sympathetic attraction of two bold
and energetic spirits," Parkman said; and the similarity of their traits—
energy and fire, imprudence, self-reliance and resolution, "unshaken will
and unbending pride"—makes of Frontenac an octogenarian La Salle. The
relationship was even clearer between two greater men, Pitt and Frederick.
Describing them on consecutive pages, Parkman used Frederick's famous
statement that England, long in labor, had at last "brought forth a man,"
to conclude his own description of Pitt, the man who for four important
years "towers supreme in British history."[54]

Bancroft extended the relationship to include George Washington, who
kept in his home the bust "of one only among living men, the king of
Prussia, whose struggles he watched with painful sympathy. Thus Washington had ever before his eyes the image of Frederic. Both were eminently
founders of nations, childless heroes, fathers only to their countries." Later,
Bancroft wrote proudly that after Pitt came to power "England, and

Prussia, and the embryon United States,—Pitt, Frederic, and Washington,—worked together for human freedom."[55]

Endurance and constancy, then, were so important that Parkman did not misrepresent the other historians when he placed those qualities at the center of his definition of manhood. In his novel, *Vassal Morton*, written at a time when he suffered intensely,[56] he allowed his dark heroine to define the term. While her speech illuminates Parkman's own psychology, it also describes the manhood of Prescott's Columbus and Cortés, of Motley's William and Bancroft's Washington. After Parkman has alluded to Byron in describing her, Edith defines "manhood" as

that unflinching quality which, strong in generous thought and high purpose, bears onward toward its goal, knowing no fear but the fear of God; wise, prudent, calm, yet daring and hoping all things; not dismayed by reverses, nor elated by success; never bending nor receding; wearying out ill fortune by undespairing constancy; unconquered by pain or sorrow, or deferred hope; fiery in attack, unshaken in the front of death; and when courage is vain, and hope seems folly, when crushing calamity presses it to the earth, and the exhausted body will no longer obey the still undaunted mind, then putting forth its hardest, saddest heroism, the unlaurelled heroism of endurance, patiently biding its time.[57]

In many of the romantic histories, moreover, these traits even go far toward saving a few reactionary characters and some others whose relation to progress is ambiguous. Although Parkman was disposed to "smile at the futility" of the Jesuits' aims,[58] and although he could not even smile at their morality, he found their courage and their endurance sublime. It was not their piety so much as their self-sacrifice, their perseverance, and their endurance that compelled his admiration. Indeed, the sole reservation that Parkman expressed when he praised their physical endurance concerned the supernatural sources from which they drew their strength. Despite the doubt which this aid threw on their self-reliance, his actual descriptions of the suffering of Brébeuf, Jogues, and the frail Garnier place these Jesuits clearly in the category of manly heroes. Their willingness "to suffer and to die" belongs to the hardest, saddest heroism.[59]

Endurance also helps to dignify Prescott's "stern and lofty" Cardinal Ximenes, a man so sublime that one's "admiration" for him must be "akin to terror." Although the Cardinal was "merciless," Prescott admired not only his intellectual ability, but his resolution, his love of the smell of gunpowder, his superiority to adversity, his unbending will, and his "heart-

stirring eloquence." Confronted with the opposition of Ferdinand and of
the nobles, Ximenes proved by his behavior that "the storm, which pros-
trates the weaker spirit, serves only to root the stronger more firmly in its
purpose"; and his genius, "rising with the obstacles it had to encounter,
finally succeeded in triumphing over all."[60] Motley, faced with the brilliantly resourceful, resolute character of Alexander Farnese during a period
when no single Englishman or Netherlander could excel him, had to warn
the reader of the danger of admiring the wrong side's hero, the reactionary
hero. The admonition appears after a passage of high praise for Alexander's
heroic endurance and constancy.[61]

His duplicity temporarily muted, Alexander's endurance becomes the
theme of a section of the *United Netherlands*. Here Motley writes from
this "heroic general's" point of view. Alexander's "almost poetic intellect"
and his "iron nature that never knew fatigue or fear" prove that "he deserved to be a patriot and a champion of right rather than an instrument
of despotism." At this point Motley pauses to contemplate Alexander's
portrait, which reveals clearly both his resemblance and his unlikeness to
the progressive hero. The lighting effects are the same as those in the image
of William against the stormy sky; but although he stands in the sunlight,
Alexander's coloring is not that of spotless marble:

And thus he paused for a moment—with much work already accomplished, but
his hardest life-task before him; still in the noon of manhood, a fine martial
figure, standing, spear in hand, full in the sunlight, though all the scene around
him was wrapped in gloom—a noble, commanding shape, entitled to the admiration which the energetic display of great powers, however unscrupulous, must
always command. A dark, meridional physiognomy, a quick, alert, imposing
head; jet-black, close-clipped hair; a bold eagle's face, with full, bright, restless
eye; a man rarely reposing, always ready, never alarmed; living in the saddle,
with harness on his back—such was the Prince of Parma; matured and mellowed,
but still unharmed by time.[62]

As in *The Rise of the Dutch Republic* the repeated disappointments of
William and his people were an almost oppressive theme, so too in the first
volume of the *United Netherlands*—especially in the 130-page chapter on
the fall of Antwerp—the recurrent theme is the suffering, endurance, and
ingenuity of Alexander. Here it is the *anti*-progressive leader who is everywhere at once, who overcomes poverty and inadequate supplies, and whose
timely heroism saves his army when it seems certain that the Dutch have
relieved Antwerp. The page headings for this chapter reflect Motley's
repeated emphasis in the text. Among them are "Energy of Farnese with

Sword and Pen," "Impoverished Condition of Parma," "[Critical] Position of Alexander and his Army," "Perpetual Anxiety of Farnese," "Impoverished State of the Spaniards," "The Dyke Pierced [by the Dutch]," "Parma Comes to the Rescue," "Fierce Struggle on the Dyke," "The Spaniards Successful," "Premature Triumph at Antwerp," "The Defeat of the Patriots," and "Triumphal Entry of Alexander."[63]

Like American antislavery forces during the years when Motley wrote this volume, the Dutch patriots have the superior strength during most of this battle; but they lack the leadership that Alexander gives the enemy. They make inexcusable mistakes because they have no William—a moral that Motley points in his introduction to the chapter. Alexander's victory is a victory for heroic, enduring, resourceful leadership. Motley deplores the bungling progressives' leadership, pauses repeatedly to observe the condition of Alexander, and even apologizes for admiring the "wrong" leader:

It is impossible not to admire the steadiness and ingenuity with which the prince persisted in his plans, the courage with which he bore up against the parsimony and neglect of his sovereign, the compassionate tenderness which he manifested for his patient little army. So much intellectual energy commands enthusiasm, while the supineness on the other side sometimes excites indignation. There is even a danger of being entrapped into sympathy with tyranny, when the cause of tyranny is maintained by genius; and of being surprised into indifference for human liberty, when the sacred interests of liberty are endangered by self-interest, perverseness, and folly.[64]

Like "full, bright, restless eye," "patient little army" is the kind of honorific phrase usually reserved for the forces of progress.

4

This massive emphasis on constancy and endurance reveals the indomitable perseverance epitomized in Longfellow's *Excelsior*, the qualities of Emerson's "Self-Reliance," as well as the isolation of a Byronic hero. In the romantic vocabulary the extreme sufferings of a majestic man were, like the terrible violence of a thunderstorm or a wild, overpowering natural scene, "sublime"; in the vocabulary of an aggressive society bent on progress, expansion, and production, perseverance was an exalted virtue. Adversity not only creates a mist through which the figures of heroes seem, as Motley said, to dilate; it is also the best training for the natural, progressive man or nation. Motley's image of the "spotless marble [statue] against a stormy sky" is itself extremely close to the romantic painter's idea of the sublime. But to understand his conception of William one must set beside the statue the image of a prudent William, not merely enduring but acting resolutely, with proper attention to detail—a William who learns from his suffering. Don John of Austria, Motley said, was the romantic hero; William, the real hero.[65]

For Motley and Parkman (as for Emerson) there was something of the lament in this portrayal of the titans of the Past. But they did not retreat into the Past with "a happy sense of escape" from nineteenth-century America. Like Emerson and Bancroft, though with different political standards, they used their conventional heroes to appeal for individual heroism in democratic America. Bourgeois democracy, Parkman said, had failed to produce a race of heroes; and in the last lines of his history he challenged democracy to produce them. The United States of 1884, he said, had to "rally her powers from the race for gold and the delirium of prosperity," to turn some of her energy away from "material progress and the game of party politics." She had to "prove, if she can, that the rule of the masses is consistent with the highest growth of the individual; that democracy can give the world a civilization as mature and pregnant, ideas as energetic and vitalizing, and types of manhood as lofty and strong, as any of the systems it boasts to supplant."

In all the romantic histories, the loftiest, strongest types of manhood were usually defined through the portrayal of physical endurance and military virtues. Except when he defended "the spirit of commerce" by braving natural dangers and imperial monopoly, the businessman did not qualify. Once the principles of natural commerce had been established as law, Parkman saw the greatest danger in "the excess and perversion" of democracy and materialism. Other writers, in portraying their "Captains of Industry," their Curtis Jadwins, might borrow the military virtues; the romantic historians were not interested in business as business.[66]

Motley was frankly embarrassed at having to make John of Barneveld a protagonist, for Barneveld was a "burgher-statesman," not a genuine hero. Even though the historian could emphasize such a character's "patrician" lineage and his noble death, there was no denying his lack of heroic dimensions. One could be the *heroic* representative of a nation's "corporations"[67] only in a mighty struggle against tyranny. After the Civil War, which destroyed the only American institution that was "more accursed than the Spanish Inquisition,"[68] America offered little opportunity for such heroism. The hero's occupation was gone.

During the war, it is true, both Parkman and Motley had found the essential qualities in young Oliver Wendell Holmes, and in the campaign of 1868 Motley had tried gamely to make a grand hero of Ulysses S. Grant; but he seemed more confident, less shrill, when he applied the heroic rhetoric to Bismarck.[69] Although Lincoln qualified on the grounds of simplicity and martyrdom in a great cause—although he had represented "all that is most noble in the American character"—he had not belonged to the type of the grand man of action. After the anger of the war years had left him, Motley confessed that "the valor, the endurance, and the self-sacrifice [had been] equal on both sides"; that the Southern soldiers could not have been defeated if their cause had been just.[70] The country soon came to believe that the most colorful generals had been Southern generals, the products of a chivalrous rather than a commercial society. In literature, the virtues of resolution, quick action, and endurance were transferred to the Southern generals; the virtues of the Drakes and the Heemskerks, to the Curtis Jadwins.

5

Thus the device of representativeness allowed the historian to focus on individual characters as the organizational center of his work. The history of the rise of the Dutch Republic was "the biography of William the Silent"; the battle between liberty and despotism was the battle between William and Philip II, who represented "Spanish chivalry . . . in its late and corrupted form"; the factional war of Dutch Remonstrants and Contra-Remonstrants was a war between John of Barneveld, the representative "burgher-statesman," and Maurice of Nassau, the representative "soldier." In *Montcalm and Wolfe* Parkman made "the names on the titlepage stand as representative" of France and England. Bancroft's Jefferson and Washington were representative Americans; George III, representative of "king-craft." Every one of Prescott's histories was based on the activities of a representative figure.[71]

The representative technique applied as well to minor characters. If Daniel Boone was the representative woodsman, Benjamin Franklin—"the sublime of common-sense"—represented the middle class. The representative French chevalier appeared as Bayard in Prescott's *Ferdinand and Isabella*; the English "incarnation of martial valour, poetic genius, and purity of heart" appeared in Motley's *United Netherlands* as Sir Philip Sidney. As the Franklin of Bancroft and Parkman represented one facet of the New England character, Bancroft's Jonathan Edwards represented "the New England mind." Bancroft's and Parkman's Pontiac and Prescott's Montezuma were representative Indians.[72]

In the long march of progress, moreover, certain countries seemed to have been peculiarly apt representatives of the natural virtues.

CHAPTER IV

Teutonic Germs

---

*To all who speak the English language, the history of the
great agony through which the Republic of Holland was
ushered into life must have peculiar interest, for it is a portion
of the records of the Anglo-Saxon race—essentially the same,
whether in Friesland, England, or Massachusetts.*

MOTLEY, *The Rise of the Dutch Republic*

The idea of representativeness was based on a belief in national character. The Frenchman was mercurial; the Spaniard, romantic, haughty,
sometimes chivalrous, often cruel, fanatical; the Italian, subtle and crafty;
the Dutchman and the Englishman, frank and manly, self-reliant, enter-
prising, vigorous. The conventional coloring in the historians' portraiture,
which placed fair against dark; the qualities of "self-help," frankness, and
"enterprise" that they so often praised; and the alignment of powers in
the wars between Liberty and Absolutism after the Reformation—all
demonstrate that in the histories the enduring progressive traits belong to
Dutchmen, Englishmen, and Americans rather than to Frenchmen, Spaniards, or Italians. Principles, the historians believed, were important causes
of the differences. But behind the principles lay the answer to a question
that Theodore Parker asked in his essay on Buckle's "History of Civilization":

If, in the middle ages, the Angles, Saxons, Danes, and Norsemen had settled in
France instead of England, and there mixed their blood, does anyone think this
Teutonic people would have now the same character which marks the Celtic
French? What a difference between the Spanish and English settlements in
America! Is there no odds in the blood?[1]

Each of the romantic historians thought he saw odds in the blood. Although none of them went to the theoretical source of the assumption, they
all believed that the essential libertarian gene was Teutonic. Two kinds of
evidence seemed to support this conclusion: the kind that Parker cited, the

seemingly overwhelming evidence of historical results; and certain eighteenth-century European studies of the primitive origins of Western liberty. The basic assumption was expressed by several English historians in the latter half of the eighteenth century: a clear division between the traits of the Gothic and Celtic, the Northern and Southern "races." As Montesquieu had said that the British constitution originated in the German woods, so John Pinkerton argued that the Goths were the ancestors of all the great peoples, and he and others supported the corollary that the Celts were naturally inferior.[2] All four New England historians accepted this genealogy.

In the romantic histories this broad racial distinction functioned largely in discussions of the origins of liberty and of the spirit of nationality. Despite the importance of "sticking to the thread of the narrative," discussion of these origins had several important literary advantages. It could demonstrate the "continuity" that Motley believed one must recognize in order to understand history. If the great men of different times could be connected not only by their perception of the eternal moral laws that link the ages, but also by a genealogical relationship, then the epic meaning of an important narrative would be intensified, and the sense of constant progress according to Providential plan would be sharpened. The "clear and harmonious order" in history would be clearer and more harmonious.[3] Discussions of the origins of liberty also added the dimension of depth to panoramic narrative history. Both Prescott and Motley set their energetic narratives against a background filled in by long introductory chapters on the origins and development of the people in whose country the action occurred; and Bancroft made his comparisons of this kind in the body of the narrative itself, at moments when the analogy might be most effective. Finally, concern with the origins of liberty had its nationalistic value: Americans were descendants of a "race" that had long been fated to carry liberty across the earth. The historian of other countries and of his own was a more useful teacher when he showed this relationship to his American readers.

Although Prescott wrote about a Southern, Catholic country, he found some opportunity to apply the basic Teutonic theory to Spanish history. In his preparation for historical writing during the 1820's, he had read and admired not only Montesquieu but Sharon Turner, who insisted that historians should pay less attention to Indians and other savages and more to the "infancy of celebrated nations," especially "our Saxon ancestors." Prescott justified his choice of a subject partly by noting its connection with the infancy of America; and once at work on *Ferdinand and Isabella*, he went back dutifully to the infancy of Spain and the origins of her liberty.[4]

Given to presenting much of what he called the "philosophical" material in his long introductions, Prescott emphasized the Visigothic ancestry of the Castilians and attributed largely to this lineage the early Castilian traditions of constitutional liberty. When he praised the comparative liberalism of the Visigoths' institutions, he was careful to relate them to "their Teutonic brethren," assuming that his reader already knew of the Teutonic tribes' libertarian reputation. Summarizing the liberal policies of these fifth-century conquerors, he noted their willingness to intermarry with the "Roman inhabitants of the country," and he often referred to the Castilians thereafter as "the Goths."[5]

The language in which Prescott commended the Visigoths' liberalism is especially interesting. "In short," he said, "their simple polity exhibited the germ of some of those institutions, which, with other nations, and under happier auspices, have formed the basis of a well-regulated constitutional liberty." Not only the idea but the image of the "germ" shows Prescott's awareness of what later became popular among American historians as "the germ theory" of history. The work of Bancroft and Motley as well as Prescott demonstrates that this interest in finding the germs of Western liberty in the customs of Teutonic tribes and in Anglo-Saxon towns was common among American historians at least a generation before the students of Henry Adams' Harvard seminar published a book on the Anglo-Saxon towns.[6]

More important than dating the early germs of the germ theory is Prescott's reference to the Goths' "simple polity." The romantic historian, it seems, felt obliged to seek *primitive* origins of liberty, among "barbaric" or "simple" people. The theory of racial distinction was thus merged with the prevailing faith in "natural" peoples. Prescott's chapter on Castile is a good example. He turned from the polity of the Goths to the apparently calamitous Saracen invasion of the eighth century, an invasion which, he argued, had greatly "accelerated" the development of liberal principles in Spain. For the best Castilians—the nobles "of more generous sentiments"—had retreated to "natural fortresses" in the northern mountains, and in that natural setting their society had lost all its "artificial distinctions" and returned "at once to its primitive equality."[7] The experience had also revived "the moral energies of the nation, which had been corrupted in the long enjoyment of uninterrupted prosperity." Thus the advantages of natural simplicity had combined with those of adversity to condition "a sober, hardy, and independent race . . . , prepared to assert their ancient inheritance, and to lay the foundations of far more liberal and equitable forms of government, than were known to their ancestors." The heirs of the Goths had progressed by going back to the woods. However slow the progress of their battle to regain the country, "it was easy to foresee" that such a people must eventually defeat "a nation oppressed by despotism," by the "effeminate indulgence" usually found in "a sensual religion and a voluptuous climate."[8]

Consistent in this interpretation of prenational Spanish history was the superiority of the northern people. Tribes of Germanic origin had conquered Castile, had imposed their principles on her government, and, when corrupted by uninterrupted prosperity, had been driven into the "barren mountains," there to recover their primitive physical and moral energy. In the next few centuries they demonstrated their superiority to the southern Moors, and later to the Latins of Italy. In *The Conquest of Mexico* the mountain-dwelling Tlascalans were similarly superior to their southern countrymen.[9]

My discussion of principles has already shown the value that Prescott placed on national unity as a natural principle; he insisted that Spain was "intended by nature" to be "one great nation," and he remarked that only "an invigorating national feeling" could have saved the Italians from Spanish conquest. In the Introduction to *Ferdinand and Isabella* he sought to explain the origins of this essential feeling among the Castilian Goths, whose descendants were destined to unite the whole Peninsula. The patriotic spirit was, of course, closely allied with religion, for the usurpers were not only foreigners but infidels. Since the Castilians of the twelfth century were still "a simple people," the "religious fervor" that "exalted" their patriotism was tainted with superstition, but it had not yet become the "fierce fanaticism" of later days.[10]

Next in importance to religion was the influence of patriotic minstrelsy. The historian of Spain did not need to "discover" an Ossian, for he could praise the author of *The Cid*. To emphasize the effect of "such popular compositions on a simple people," Prescott cited the conventional example of Homer, referring the reader to Bancroft's translation of Heeren's *Politics of Ancient Greece*. Although Prescott denied Heeren's contention that Homer's poems had been "the principal bond which united the Grecian states," he insisted that *The Cid*, "by calling up the most inspiring national recollections in connexion with their favorite hero, must have operated powerfully on the moral sensibilities of the people."[11]

The very fact that Germanic "blood" is so difficult to recognize in the main arteries of Spanish history makes Prescott's allusions to its importance all the more significant. He discussed it in his history of the rise of Spain to national unity, to world power, to a political position more advanced than that of countries which eventually passed her.[12] But he believed that in her conflict with the superior principles and vigor of the more northern peoples, Spain's defeat had been inevitable. Describing the beginnings of Spanish decline in the Dutch rebellion, Prescott observed that the Inquisition, which could not survive in the Netherlands because it was repulsive to the Dutch character, had "succeeded in Spain, for it was suited to the character of the Spaniard." The "oppressive policy and fanaticism of the Austrian dynasty" had overshadowed the early Castilian's "proud sense of independence," and in the nineteenth century all that was left of this Gothic inheritance resided in "that erect, high-minded peasantry" who were not yet wholly subdued.[13]

2

When a scholar went off in search of the germs of liberty, he could not return without a sample of Germanic blood. No admirer of the Spanish heritage, Motley himself admitted that before the Moorish invasion Spain had been blessed with "Germanic institutions." Theodore Parker "traced" the origins of democracy to "the wilds of Germany," where "the idea of individual liberty" existed as "a dim sentiment in the breast of the German in the Hiercynian forest." Emerson endorsed the theory in *English Traits*, where he announced that "the Teutonic tribes have a national singleness of heart, which contrasts with the Latin races. The German name," he added, "has a proverbial significance of sincerity and honest meaning." Speaking on "Historic Progress and American Democracy" during Bismarck's campaign to unify Germany, Motley made perhaps the most inclusive American statement of the theory. After calling Germany "the political and social heart of Europe" and the main source of European and American culture since the Reformation, he turned to genealogy: "The common mother of nations and empires—alma mater felix prole—she still rules the thought of her vast brood of children; Franks, Goths, Saxons, Lombards, Normans, Netherlanders, Americans—Germans all."[14]

The Teutonic germ was most virulent in the histories of Bancroft and Motley. Both wrote histories of "Germanic" nations that had accelerated "the march of humanity"; both felt obliged to describe regularly the grand upward curves of the progressive spiral and to acknowledge repeatedly the heroism of the People; and in their correspondence, their speeches, and their histories both expressed an exhilarated conviction that democracy was advancing faster than ever to the American West and eastward to Europe. Both men, too, had studied in Germany, and both renewed old friendships there when sent abroad on diplomatic missions. Their friendship with Bismarck—Motley's had begun during his student days in Berlin—encouraged both men to connect his successes directly with the dim sentiment in the primitive German's breast. Under the influence of this magnetic leader, both men reinforced their emphasis on the Germanic theme in the 1860's and 1870's. Both men, finally, were enthusiastic nationalists whose patriotism was intensified by the American Civil War.

Bancroft, one must remember, worked from a major premise that asserted the unity of all moral truths in the infinite mind of Providence. The highest function of the historian was to find in events evidence of that unity. For him there were no chance coincidences in history; it was "useless to ask what would have happened if the eternal providence had for the moment suspended its rule." The fundamental cause behind all events, Providence was never at rest. Since Providence worked through principles, which "gain the mastery over events," Bancroft found the continuity of history not in chronological dates and incidents, but in the relation of men in different ages to eternal principles. From this viewpoint he saw a clear relationship between Martin Luther and Thomas Jefferson, between Kant and Franklin, and between Washington and Frederick the Great.[15]

There is no doubt that the unity of the human race was one of Bancroft's universal truths, or that he looked forward to the day when humanity, "growing conscious of its unity," would snap "the bonds of nationality" and "know itself to be the spirit of the world."[16] But he also believed that the conscious unity of one race, one segment of the whole, was a step toward that higher unity. The achievement of national integrity was a step toward the unity of all nations.

The Providential historical plan had assigned to each division of humanity a function in human progress; even George III and Philip II had unwillingly done their part. But to Bancroft, as to the other historians, it seemed that Providence had chosen the members of one race as "the apostles of the people's liberty." The banner of truth had passed from nation to nation, but some branch of the Teutonic race had always helped to carry it forward. Besides securing Protestantism and freedom of mind in America, the Seven Years' War had decided "what race, the Romanic or Teutonic, shall form the seed" of the American people. To Bancroft the answer was a foregone conclusion; even when describing Britain's "frenzied" opposition to the Revolution, he admitted that "Britain was the mighty mother who bred and formed men capable of laying the foundations of so noble an empire; and she alone could have formed them."[17]

But Bancroft, like Prescott, went back to the origins of liberty, to a time, long before "the mighty mother's" birth, when Providence had anointed the original apostles of Western liberty. The motto that appeared on Bancroft's volumes, "Westward the star of empire takes its way," was the key to his interpretation of progress. Before Christianity had been established in the Roman Empire, it had "found its way, as if by instinct, into the minds of the Goths." The northern Teutonic tribes had then become "the intrepid messengers" of the faith and of personal liberty, and they had carried their system "out of their forests to the councils of Saxon England." In the westward movement of freedom the Teutonic tribes—especially the Anglo-Saxons, "that Germanic race most famed for the love of personal independence"—had served as the missionaries of truth. Freedom was a seed. The Teutonic tribes, "emerging freshly from the wild nurseries of nations," had planted it on the continent and later in England; the German Luther had cut out a weed that threatened to smother it; the Puritans had transplanted it to America, and Washington had harvested its fruit.[18]

Bancroft was no nativist. But although he boasted that the United States stood, "more than any other [country], as the realization of the unity of the race," his America nevertheless inherited the traditions of the "Teutonic race, with its strong tendency to individuality and freedom"; and the American people succeeded the early Teutons as "the intrepid messengers" of freedom. Though proud that America had welcomed all races, he emphasized repeatedly the predominance of Anglo-Saxons:

The immense majority of American families were not of "the high folk of Normandie," but were of "the low men," who were Saxons. This is true of New England; it is true of the south. Shall the Virginians be described in a word? They were Anglo-Saxons in the woods again, with the inherited culture and intelligence of the seventeenth century. . . . The Anglo-Saxon mind, in its serenest nationality, neither distorted by fanaticism, nor subdued by superstition, nor wounded by persecution, nor excited by new ideas, but fondly cherishing the active instinct for personal freedom, secure possession, and legislative power, such as belonged to it before the reformation, and existed independent of the reformation, had made its dwelling-place in the empire of Powhatan.

Other minds had been liberated by the Reformation; the Anglo-Saxon mind had been free all along. By serving as "Anglo-Saxons in the woods again," the Virginians not only demonstrated their oneness with their primitive ancestors, but they performed again their ancestors' function: to carry the whole germ of a system which, though maturing in a later century, was essentially complete in their own time.[19]

One can see this idea clearly in Bancroft's emphasis on the same relationship in New England towns. In a more "scientific" tone than Bancroft's, Herbert Baxter Adams complained in 1882 that "the older New England historians" had neglected "the Germanic origin of New England towns" and the function of New England's village democracies as the germ of America's democratic system. Bancroft, it is true, did not study the question thoroughly in his narrative history; but one does not need a microscope to see in his second volume the germ of the later theory. At least forty-five years before Adams published his three essays on Germanic origins, Bancroft not only asserted the "Teutonic tradition" of liberty but called the New England town system "the natural reproduction of the system, which the instinct of humanity had imperfectly revealed to our Anglo-Saxon ancestors."[20]

By recognizing this bond Bancroft gave an added meaning to the "naturalness" of the American people. Both groups of pioneers relied frequently on "the instinct of humanity," and the second system was a *natural* reproduction of the first. It seemed especially fitting, moreover, that on the virgin continent destined for the fulfillment of all races' hopes by *representatives* of all races—that here descendants of the first democratic tribes should be the first tenants of "the woods." The connection reemphasized Bancroft's idea that America was the scene of a new beginning for humanity.

Language, too, was a patriotic property. Along with the freest agents of "the Teutonic race" went the English language, which, after the vast English conquests of the eighteenth century, "was now to spread more widely than any that had ever given expression to human thought." Cataloguing "all that was best" in a New England community, Bancroft combined character, race, and language: "A moral, well-educated, industrious people; . . . all of unmixed lineage, speaking the language of the English bible." The English Bible proclaimed the highest religious truths; the mission of the English language as of the Anglo-Saxon people was to proclaim through the world the highest political truth. Although the search for "an American epic" had failed before Bancroft began writing his history, he was still able to find his Ossian. In the same year in which Prescott compared *The Cid* to the poems of Homer, Bancroft announced that America's heroic poetry had been written in a new form:

There is an analogy between early American politics and the earliest heroic poems. Both were spontaneous, and both had the vitality of truth. Long as natural affection endures, the poems of Homer will be read with delight; long as freedom lives on earth, the early models of popular legislation and action in America will be admired.[21]

During the twelve-year interlude between the appearance of his third and fourth volumes, Bancroft himself served as an agent of progress. As Polk's Secretary of the Navy and Acting Secretary of War, he helped his party work out America's Manifest Destiny at the start of the Mexican War. Minister to England during the revolutions of 1848, he was able to visit Paris during that hopeful summer; for a while he had great hopes for French democracy, and he boasted that at the same time "we are working along toward the [Far] East with the democratic principle." He published his fourth volume, on England's conquest of North America, at the very peak of America's expansionist movement. The comparison between the conquests of 1763 and those of 1848 was too tempting to resist, and in one of the most extravagant effusions in his *History* he reemphasized the mission of the language:

Go forth, then, language of Milton and Hampden, language of my country, take possession of the North American continent! Gladden the waste places with every tone that has been rightly struck on the English lyre, with every English word that has been spoken well for liberty and for man! . . . Utter boldly and spread widely through the world the thoughts of the coming apostles of liberty, till the sound that cheers the desert shall thrill through the heart of humanity, and the lips of the messengers of the people's power . . . shall proclaim the renovating tidings of equal freedom for the race![22]

In the tenth volume of his *History*, which was published in 1874, Bancroft wrote two long chapters on the relations between Germany and the American colonies: the first, entirely on bonds of race and principle; the second, on Germany's moral and diplomatic support during the Revolution. He had been noticing both kinds of relationship in his *History* since 1837; and in stressing Luther's importance as the founder of Protestantism, he had promised to show more direct German contributions to the United States when the proper time came. Surely, however, his interest in contemporary world politics and his seven years' experience as Minister to Berlin encouraged him to write these chapters, repeating some of the ideas that he had already expressed. New German sources, moreover, had been opened to him the year before he went to Berlin. Very helpful in sending him new documents was General von Moltke, later to defeat the army of Napoleon III and to be described by Bancroft in the rhetoric reserved for representative military heroes.[23]

Partly, I believe, because he wanted his readers to feel more closely related to the new Germany, Bancroft began this digression by tracing the German people "to their origin, not recounting the annals of the German nation, but searching for the universal interests which the eternal Providence confided to their keeping." After establishing through England the immortality of their customs, the Germanic tribes had unfortunately "lost the tradition that they were brothers." But "the creative energy of the house of Saxony," by establishing a long-lived empire, saw to it that the idea of German unity "worked its way indissolubly into the blood and marrow of all the people."[24]

The spirit of the race lived on in Germany. Although the Anglo-Saxons had laid the foundation of empire in America, Bancroft argued, the continental Teutons had also made substantial contributions. Mind ruled the world: in the doctrines of Luther, "Germany, which appropriated no territory in America, gave to the colonies of New Netherland and New England their laws of being." Inspired by the same principle of Protestant reformation and belonging to one race, the people of New England and of Germany worked under "an unwritten alliance or harmony, not written in the archives of states, showing itself only in moments of crisis." The crises were the Thirty Years' War, the Seven Years' War, and the American Revolution. Bancroft symbolized the alliance by noting coincidental actions in the Thirty Years' War for Protestant freedom. The New Englanders' function was to open a second front:

The day on which Winthrop sailed into Boston harbor, Gustavus Adolphus was landing fifteen thousand men in Pomerania. The thoughts of Germany and of the new people in America ran together: one and the same element of life animated them all. The congregations of Massachusetts, too feeble to send succor to their European brethren, poured out their souls for them in prayer.

The alignment of "races" in this war showed again that the Teutonic peoples naturally loved liberty. Ninety per cent of "the Germans," if let alone, would have "peacefully embraced" Protestantism. "It was by hordes of other races and tongues that the battle of Jesuit reaction was fought."

Not only Germany, but "its kindred in the Netherlands and Switzerland," led commercial and intellectual progress while France was being "rent in pieces by bloody and relentless feuds."[25]

As Parkman, too, pointed out, Germany made a more tangible contribution to American destiny during the Seven Years' War, when the nations of the Teutonic race were finally allied for the first time in centuries. In that crisis England and Germany stood alone in Europe against the combined forces of Catholicism. The English people, Bancroft believed, recognized their affinity with Germany, and when George II and Newcastle tried to subsidize a Russian attack on Frederick the Great,

> . . . England shot so wildly from its sphere that Newcastle was forced to bend to William Pitt; and then England, Prussia, and the embryon United States,—Pitt, Frederic, and Washington,—worked together for human freedom. . . . "We conquered America in Germany," said the elder Pitt, ascribing to Frederic a share in the extension of the Germanic race in the other hemisphere.

Defender of Protestant freedom against seemingly overwhelming odds, and the man who inspired the German people to become once again "the hardiest nation in Europe," Frederick seemed to Bancroft the counterpart of Washington, with the best traits of the representative man. When he had to decide "with which branch of the Teutonic family" to sympathize during the Revolution, Frederick naturally chose the branch that was fighting for freedom. Bancroft rejoiced at finding original evidence that Frederick encouraged France to enter the war on the American side.[26]

The German people also supported the Americans. In the eighteenth century as in the seventeenth, the "thoughts" of the two peoples "ran together." While Providence guided America's revolt against materialism and despotism in government, it was also guiding in Germany the great philosophical revolution against "the despotism of the senses." The greatest minds in Germany were perpetuating the Teutonic traditions of liberty. Bancroft, himself influenced by "the sublime lessons of Kant," called those lessons the Reformation in philosophy and gave Kant "a place among the wise beside Plato and Aristotle." He declared, moreover, that Kant was "one of the first, perhaps the very first, of the German nation to defend, even at the risk of his friendships, the cause of the United States"; and he demonstrated that Lessing, Herder, Klopstock, Goethe, and Schiller had also spoken for freedom and wished the Americans well.[27]

The highest unifying force in history was eternal principle. "The movement for intellectual freedom" was the force, Bancroft said, that "brought all influences harmoniously together" and prompted France to support the colonies in 1777. This announcement led him to "the largest generalization thus far in the history of America": that Luther and Descartes had discovered two sides of the truth most important to human freedom, the idea of spiritual and intellectual self-reliance. As he worked out this theory in the following pages, Bancroft had to return to the penultimate unifying force, that of race and nation. The Protestant countries, those which achieved freedom for the individual mind by following Luther's influence, "went forward in their natural development, and suffered their institutions to grow and to shape themselves according to the increasing public intelligence. The nations that learned their lessons of liberty from Descartes were led to question everything, and by creative power renew society through the destruction of the past." Jonathan Edwards, Thomas Reid, Kant, and Rousseau were the four great representative heirs of "Calvinistic Protestantism" in "four great nationalities" in the eighteenth century. But while the representatives of Germanic Protestant countries "were expositors of the active powers of man," Rousseau "spoiled his doctrine by dreamy indolence."[28]

For all one's faith in the unity of the human race, it seemed obvious that the Germanic "races" were at once more energetic and more naturally moderate than the Celtic. Having noted in his early twenties that the Germans' "fondness for abstract studies has given their national character firmness and energy, has lent new vigour to their poets and new force to their historians," Bancroft was bound to be waiting for political evidence of that vigor and the Germans' love of "truth." The revolutions of 1848 persuaded him that monarchy was dead in France and Germany and extremely feeble in England, where he was United States Minister. A week after telling Prescott that "Germany is . . . the great imitator just now of the model republic," he wrote a letter to President Polk, congratulating him on the defeat of Mexico and predicting that the United States was elected to bring democracy to the Far East. In Paris when France had no government but the people, he wrote happily that "the moderation of the people is marvelous, and will be rewarded." But when he returned to Paris several months later, he had to admit that "All parties are in the wrong: everybody is in the wrong. Common sense has disappeared: impatience triumphs over reason."[29]

By the time Bancroft was sent to Berlin as Andrew Johnson's Minister, the theory seemed to be even more emphatically supported by contemporary evidence. Prussia was moving forward under Bismarck, who not only worked for German unity but also recognized the relationship between the German and American people. A man of "clear vigorous vehement will," Bismarck explained his theory of "male" and "female" races to Bancroft at their first meeting. At Bancroft's house on the day of President Grant's inauguration, Bismark spoke of the "cordial understanding" begun by Washington and Frederick, and Bancroft replied "in the same spirit." Bismarck seemed to be working for the unity of the human race. Later on he asked the Republican Motley to dissuade the new administration from recalling Bancroft. Against this man and the German people stood Louis Napoleon, representing both "the scarlet woman of Babylon" and the old monarchy of "Louis Quatorze." It was "the old contest between evil and good; and the victory as at Marathon, and on the plains of Abraham [was] on the side of civilization and freedom." Although he had hopes for the revival of the French republic, Bancroft believed that the country was still "given to extremes: when the Protestants were driven out, France was maimed, and left to the struggle of extremes."[30]

The unification of Germany, Bancroft wrote to the State Department, was "completely in harmony with natural laws" and was "thoroughly the concurrent act of government and people." The system of petty states, under which tyrants like the landgrave of Hesse-Cassel had exploited their people, had to fall before the natural forces of popular will and racial unity. When the Franco-Prussian War was imminent, Bancroft advised Secretary Seward that Napoleon III was pursuing "a policy hostile to any further improvement of the unity of the German people." France, not Germany, was "belligerent." The United States, he said, should try to restrain France for the mutual benefit of Germany and America.[31]

3

At the same time that Bancroft was deploring "French ignorance,"[32] Motley was demonstrating that he, too, had brought down to the present the combined theory of racial superiority and inevitable progress. "I don't believe much in Latinized Celtic Republics," he wrote to Bancroft on December 1, 1870, "and Great Germany the mother of us all, is sure to become a free and magnificent Commonwealth—under whatever political name it is first to be baptized." In Austria during the Austro-Prussian crisis of 1864–66, he had at first condemned both sides, proclaiming himself uninterested in the outcome because the struggle involved no worthwhile principle. But he changed his mind. He began to notice that

the peoples are getting stronger. Somehow or other there is a dim consciousness in the Teutonic mind all over the country, from Schleswig to the Carpathians,

that this miraculous success of Prussia is not needle-guns, nor her admirable
organisation, nor the genius of Bismarck, nor the blunders of the Bund in all
its dotage, but the democratic principle.

And in 1872, after visiting the Bismarcks and attending their twenty-fifth
wedding anniversary party, he praised Bismarck's accomplishments in
racial terms:

the substitution of the solid, healthful, Teutonic influence for the Latinized
Celtic, the control of Central Europe by a united nation of deepthinkers and
straightforward, honest strikers for liberty and Fatherland. . . . .

These are not dynastic victories, military combinations, cabinet triumphs.
They are national, natural achievements, accomplished almost as if by magic
by the tremendous concentrated will of one political giant, aided by a perfect
military science.[33]

Bismarck was not only "the greatest living man," but the representative
man. His genius, Motley said, "consists in the instinctive power of governing by conforming to the spirit of the age." That spirit was "consolida-
tion." Motley felt so strongly about this principle that when he waved the
bloody shirt in a campaign speech for Grant, he appealed to "those holy
words—Nation and Union."[34]

By 1868, then, Motley was able to focus on a contemporary problem
the basic values and theories that I have discussed so far: naturalness, inevitable progress, the principle of nationality, America's mission, the theory
of Teutonic superiority, and representativeness. "Time will show," he said
that year in his speech on "Historic Progress and American Democracy,"
"that progress and liberty are identical. It is impossible that the success
of Prussia is to end in the establishment of one military empire the more.
The example and the retroaction of America; the success here of freedom
and progress—forbid that result."[35]

The only new element here was Motley's faith that Prussia's "military
despotism" would do "more for liberty than all the Garibaldis, Kossuths,
and Mazzinis of half a century." The other ideas had appeared in his histories since the beginning. As the fair heroine in his novel *Morton's Hope*
had been "a perfect incarnation of Germany,—the blonde, blue-eyed, fair-
haired Germany"[36]—so the Dutch people who rebelled against Philip II
were the natural heirs to Teutonic libertarianism. The Introduction to
The Rise of the Dutch Republic goes conventionally to the origins of the
nation and of liberty. But Motley combines naturalism, Teutonism, Protestantism, and libertarianism so tightly that atavism becomes a major theme
of his history.

The Introduction begins with a brief description of the natural features of the country, after a reminder in the first two paragraphs that Caesar and Tacitus praised the "heroic" Teutonic "savages" of the Netherlands. Here Motley first sounds the theme of the people's long conflict with Nature, and then he moves to the subject of race. Throughout this discussion of Dutch origins he iterates the superiority of Teutons over Celts. Noting that Caesar called the Belgae the bravest of the Celts, he attributes their superiority partly to "the presence of several Germanic tribes, who, at this period had already forced their way across the Rhine, mingled their qualities with the Belgic material, and lent an additional mettle to the Celtic blood." The Batavians, main stock from which grew the Dutch traditions of liberty and the willingness to defend it, had been forced out of "the Hercynian forest" and had settled in the Netherlands. They and the "free Frisians," with whom they later combined to form the Teutonic group in the Netherlands, were part of a "homogeneous nation of pure German origin." Against this racial group Motley ranged the Celtic or "Gallic" tribes, the other "race" of the Netherlands. Anticipating the male-female racial theory that Bismarck later outlined for Bancroft, he regretted that the two races had not merged to form the most powerful race in Western Europe. But if Providence had really prevented "a fusion of the two races," the decree had done Motley a literary favor.[37] Made up of Celts and Teutons, the Netherlands was the perfect literary testing ground for the merits of the two races. And the differences between the early Teutons and the Celts formed a perfect primitive background for Motley's interpretation of the rise of the republic.

Behind the sixteenth-century choice of Catholicism over Protestantism, of obedience over rebellion, of artificiality over naturalness, lay "racial" traits formed centuries earlier. In his Introduction Motley was careful to lay the groundwork for every major contrast in the main body of his history. The Gauls wore flamboyant clothes; the Germans were "simple" and unostentatious. The Gaul was "irascible, furious in his wrath, but less formidable in a sustained conflict with a powerful foe." Because the Gaul was "inflammable, but too fickle," his confederacy dissolved before Caesar's attack; but "the Nervii, true to the German blood in their veins," swore to die rather than surrender, and they kept their oath. The Gauls, though republican, were an aristocracy, with two high orders, the nobility and the priesthood; the Germans gave sovereignty to the whole people. The Gauls were agricultural; the Germans, rugged marauders who lived on "carnage." The Gaul was "priest-ridden," and with his "smoke-and-blood-stained priests" sacrificed thousands "to the savage gods whom they served"; the German, "in his simplicity," surpassed "the sensuous Roman and the super-stitious Gaul" by rising to faith in one supreme God. The Gaul was "singu-larly unchaste"; the German, monogamous. The former gave his bride "bracelets and gold necklaces"; the latter, "oxen and a bridled horse, a sword, a shield, and a spear." Even the German burial was less material-istic.[38]

The parallel to Motley's view of the sixteenth century was not coinci-dental. He observed that the religious contrast was the most extreme con-trast, and that it was the Celts who later "contaminated" the purer Ger-manic religion, before both "faded away.in the pure light of Christianity." The religious question was the central question, of which political freedom was only a part, in the sixteenth-century war between the Netherlands and Spain. It was well to show that the Celts had always been less natural in both. To forewarn the reader of the Celts' later fate, Motley announced that "time has rather hardened than effaced" their racial traits.[39]

After discussing the two races' contrasting responses to Caesar's inva-sion, Motley turned—as Schiller had done before him—to the heroic deeds of Batavia's representative man, Claudius Civilis. He emphasized Civilis' eloquence and love of liberty, his sublime constancy and endurance in pathetic isolation. The battle of Civilis with Rome was "a remarkable foreshadowing of the future conflict with Spain." When he compared Civilis and William of Orange, "two heroes of ancient German stock," Motley brought together individual and racial atavism. For in both the first and the sixteenth centuries, he declared, the "petulant" southern peoples had been the first to "defy the imperial power. . . . In both wars the south-ern Celts fell away from the league, their courageous but corrupt chieftains having been purchased with imperial gold."[40]

Having established the relationship between the old Germans and the Dutch, the old Celts and the obedient provinces, Rome and Spain, Motley contrives to set his history in a still larger framework. For the "free Frisians," into whose group the old Batavians have "melted," are "the near-est blood-relations of the Anglo-Saxon race," and they "now occupy . . . the whole future European territory of the Dutch republic." Blood is so important to at least one Frisian chief, Radbod, that, like some of Cooper's and Parkman's Indians, he refuses to be baptized and go to Heaven when he learns that his ancestors are all in Hell. Only when "their brethren from Britain" come as missionaries do the Frisians accept Christianity.[41]

This noble choice, however misguided, prepared the way for the largest generalization thus far. In the whole race the love of freedom and "manly resistance to despotism" were paramount, "whether among Frisian swamps, Dutch dykes, the gentle hills and dales of England, or the pathless forests of America." The Dutch patriots were related to the Americans not only by principles, but also by blood. It was not only naturalness but something in the Teuton's blood that gave the race the most important quality for natural achievement: vigor. Whatever the excesses of the wild Frisian tribes, "at any rate there was life. Those violent little commonwealths had blood in their veins. They were compact of proud, self-helping, muscular vigor." It was here that Motley first pronounced their bloodiest riots "better than the order and silence born of the midnight darkness of despotism." Even the women, Motley said later, were "distinguished by beauty of form and vigor of constitution."[42]

The entire Introduction, including the passages on the Catholic excesses that provoked the Reformation, was intended to review sixteen centuries of Dutch adherence to "one master passion—the love of liberty, the instinct of self-government." The source of this passion was racial, the compound of "the bravest Teutonic elements, Batavian and Frisian." It was in the person of these brave Teutons that "Humanity, bleeding but not killed," still stood at bay and defied "the hunters." It was against this inspiring background that Motley, with a fine dramatic sense, placed the theatrical scene of Charles V's abdication; against this history of racial enthusiasm that he brought onstage Philip II, "a prince foreign to their blood, their tongue, their religion, their whole habits of life and thought." It was against this proud lineage that he emphasized and reemphasized Philip's Spanishness; that he found in William "a worthy embodiment of the Christian, national resistance of the German race to a foreign tyranny."[43]

I have concentrated on this Introduction not only because it contains the basic theory, but also because it suggests virtually every application of the theory in almost all the romantic histories. Motley's cross-references go backward as well as forward. Sixteenth-century Dutchmen fight on the sites of primitive Teutonic battles for liberty; Englishmen rely in crises on their Anglo-Saxon blood, "ever mounting against oppression"; representing "the best energies of the English people," Drake and Frobisher, Hawkins and Essex, Cavendish and Grenfell—all Anglo-Saxons or Anglo-Normans—emulate their primitive kindred as they go out to capture "the old world and the new" from Spain; Dutchmen are resolute after William's assassination, and Frenchmen fall to pieces after the murder of Henry IV; Sir Philip Sidney appears as "an Anglo-Norman representative of ancient race," and Maurice of Nassau represents a lineage older in nobility than that of Philip II; Flemings ignore their blood relation to the patriots and murder them in the name of a foreign tyrant and a decadent religion; Anglo-Saxons and Hollanders, though bleeding in their fight against "sacerdotal despotism," can "spare enough [from their] superfluous energies to confront the dangers of polar oceans, and to bring back treasures of science to enrich the world"; "English frankness" confronts "Spanish legerdemain"; "stout-hearted" Anglo-Saxon sailors long for "open war with the Jesuits" when their queen wants peace. The Netherlanders offer the most "spotless examples of patriotism to be emulated in all succeeding ages"; they fight "for the liberty of all" and save "the proud history of England, France, and Germany" from being "written in far different terms." Their refusal to allow "peaceful dismemberment" teaches their American kindred the importance of fighting through the Civil War.[44]

4

Parkman alluded to these racial origins far less frequently than Bancroft or Motley. The main reason seems to be not that he dissented from the common faith in Germanic superiority, but that he saw no need to go back formally to the origins of liberty. Except for a few allusions to "our barbarous ancestors" he stayed out of the Hercynian forest and concentrated on the American forest—a sufficiently primitive laboratory for the testing of American character. When he contrasted the Frenchman and the Englishman, he was usually content to show each as nationally representative and to focus on the two principles, Absolutism and Liberty, behind which lay the racial distinction. A large part of his history, moreover, described the brave deeds of vigorous Frenchmen from Champlain to Montcalm. Except for his strictures on corrupt French nobles and colonial officials—and for some traits in the heroic Montcalm—it was on the behavior of the *peoples* of the two colonies that Parkman regularly concentrated his demonstration of racial difference. The difference appears most emphatically in the repeated presentation of energy against passiveness.

But Parkman certainly accepted the conventional theories. His Frenchman was "fiery"; his Saxon, of "stubborn mettle." His Breton clung to old superstitions with "Celtic obstinacy"; in his English woodsman he saw "renewed, with all its ancient energy, that wild and daring spirit, that force and hardihood of mind, which marked our barbarous ancestors of Germany and Norway." The air of liberty was "malaria" for his colonial Frenchman, because only the Englishman had "learned to breathe it." Parkman, too, called England "the great mother of nations" and the American people her "gigantic progeny" who, despite their independence, "joined with her in a triple kinship of laws, language, and blood."[45] And he praised Frederick as the father of modern Germany.

One should notice, too, that Parkman did write the conventional essay on the natives of the country that provided the scenes for his history. It is in his comments on the Indians that he refers most constantly to race. But before considering the Indians and their literary "kindred," one should examine the unnatural, non-libertarian, non-Teutonic subject of priestcraft, which had a central place in most of the romantic histories.

CHAPTER V

Priestcraft and Catholicism

---

*Holy Mother Church, linked in sordid wedlock to govern-
ments and thrones, numbered among her servants a host of the
worldly and the proud, whose service of God was but the service
of themselves,—and many, too, who in the sophistry of the
human heart, thought themselves true soldiers of Heaven, while
earthly pride, interest, and passions were the life-springs of their
zeal. This mighty Church of Rome, in her imposing march
along the high road of history, heralded as infallible and divine,
astounds the gazing world with prodigies of contradiction: now
the protector of the oppressed, now the right arm of tyrants;
now breathing charity and love, now dark with the passions of
Hell; now beaming with celestial truth, now masked in hypocrisy and lies; now a virgin, now a harlot; an imperial queen,
and a tinselled actress. Clearly, she is of earth, not of heaven;
and her transcendently dramatic life is a type of the good and ill,
the baseness and nobleness, the foulness and purity, the love and
hate, the pride, passion, truth, falsehood, fierceness, and tenderness, that battle in the restless heart of man.*

PARKMAN, *The Jesuits in North America
in the Seventeenth Century*

All the romantic historians regarded Spain and New France as grim
historical exhibits of the Roman Church's influence on government and
society. Both countries, one should remember, were ruins, almost unique
as antiprogressive phenomena; and both had tried to remain exclusively
Catholic, giving large policy-making powers to religious orders and leaders of the Church. To the progressive nineteenth-century historian the
lesson seemed plain: "Whoever wishes to be made well acquainted with
the morbid anatomy of governments," Macaulay said, "whoever wishes
to know how great states may be made feeble and wretched, should study
the history of Spain."[1] One cannot understand the treatment of Catholi-

cism in the romantic histories—and it is a central force in almost all of them—without looking at it from this point of view. Although the epithets may seem in the end to have the same meaning, one should notice that the historians were anti-authoritarian and anticlerical before they were anti-Catholic. What enervated Spain and New France was what Parkman called Absolutism, a term that applied to political and social action. In post-Reformation history the Catholic Church seemed to have been consistently reactionary, except in some of its conflicts with Islam and barbaric polytheism. All the historians believed that the Church's religious teachings were responsible for this bias, but the central target of their criticism was authoritarianism, "Absolutism," "regal and sacerdotal despotism"—not so much religious doctrine as temporal policy, including Church government.

The historians' religious and political heritage made it difficult for them to understand a total commitment to piety, a total religious conviction. Not only as admirers of the natural but as Unitarians, they had almost no use for theology, and they leaned toward what Joseph Haroutunian has called "moralism" rather than toward "piety." Perhaps the best example of this religious attitude is the story of Prescott's reexamination of Christian doctrine after his four-year-old daughter's death in 1829. In his first entry describing this project, Prescott resolved "to prosecute this examination with perfect impartiality" and to avoid being "influenced by the present state of my feelings" except as they led him "to give the subject a more serious attention." To insure his "sober impartiality," he called in his father, because he was confident that an experienced judge would be severely critical in evaluating Biblical testimony.[2] This faith that a civil judge was the best man to determine the validity of divine testimony exemplifies the reversal of emphasis that had occurred in New England between the seventeenth and nineteenth centuries. The burden of proof had been placed on the Bible.

Prescott reopened the question almost a decade later, after the first part of Andrews Norton's *Evidences of the Genuineness of the Gospels* had been published. Although he wrote in his journal that Norton had done more to authenticate "the gospels as a whole than any other modern writer except Lardner or Paley," the arguments of other writers forced him to doubt the historicity of miracles. Both Prescott's language and his conclusions emphasize the vast difference between the religious Unitarian's habits of mind and those of the orthodox Protestant or Catholic. "The cautious inquirer," he said, "has a right to demand far stronger testimony for the truth of a miraculous story, than for any other." It was at once hard to believe and "harder to disbelieve" the stories of the miracles. Prescott wished that "the vouchers for the narrative" had been "of an intelligence most unlikely to be deluded, a probity incapable of even a pious fraud"; and he regretted that "the good, the learned, & wise of their own age" had not been convinced. Turning to contemporary arguments, he had to admit that the conflicting hypotheses of some Unitarians showed "a credulity and superstition . . . not much less unfavorable to the cause, than the blind faith required by Orthodox interpreters." At the same time he feared that some liberal interpretations showed "such an allegorical latitude of expression, as will shake the solidity of every doctrine and declaration in the Scriptures—according to the same principles of interpretation." Still unconvinced, after a month of thorough study, by Norton's arguments against the Trinity, but convinced that the Trinitarians' doctrine was "monstrous," he could only conclude that "the study of polemics, or biblical critics," would never "settle principles, or clear up doubts. They [sic] rather tend to confuse the former, and multiply the latter."[3]

Reliance on works, or morality, seemed to be the only answer: "To do well, act justly, to fear and to love God—and our neighbor as ourselves—in these are the essence of religion. . . . For what we can believe we are not responsible (supposing we examine candidly and patiently). For what we do, we shall indeed be held accountable." One must concentrate on following "the code of morals" preached by Jesus and for all else " 'Wait the great teacher Death, and God adore.' " In the same year (1837) Prescott announced these conclusions to the world in his introductory chapter on Castile. Even before the Castilian people had been duped into supporting the persecution of the Moors, the corrupt morals of the clergy and some nobles had "confused" the people's "moral perceptions." From these superiors the people learned, Prescott said, "to attach an exclusive value to external rites, to the forms rather than the spirit of Christianity; estimating the piety of men by their speculative opinions, rather than their practical conduct."[4]

Most of the language quoted here refers to Protestants, even to Unitarians. The "orthodox" who demand "blind faith" and who are characterized by "credulity and superstition" are orthodox Calvinists, not Catholics. And the last two epithets apply equally to Unitarians who demand more faith than the "cautious inquirer" can give. Bancroft, referring to the orthodox Unitarians' position on miracles, even condemned Unitarian "bigotry."[5] It is important to notice the wide range of beliefs over which this kind of language was applied, for its frequent application in the histories to Catholic ideas, and the historians' repeated allegiance to the Protestant side in Catholic-Protestant conflicts, might easily lead one to believe that they were offended only by Catholic "superstition" and intolerance. The historians were not always fair to Catholicism, but one must see their objections to it in the proper context.

In his study of the Jeffersonians' attitude toward metaphysics, Daniel J. Boorstin has said that they were able to "view the disputes of metaphysicians and theologians with detached amusement or indifference, because it is easy to tolerate anarchy in a realm where one has never really entered and which one is glad to see discredited." In the same way, it was easy for Motley to announce his impartiality in the Preface to his two volumes on the Arminian-Calvinist battle for control of the Netherlands. If "practical conduct" was the criterion of piety, and if theology was, as Motley said, "a maze whence there was no issue," then one's religious convictions were relatively unimportant. Motley recognized that the controversy over Barneveld was still alive, but he was apparently unaware that his own allegiance to Unitarian principles made him a partisan. His bias against Calvinist doctrines (a bias that appears plainly in his history) is not so important here as is its basis. He was almost wholly incapable of understanding the force of strong doctrinal loyalty, and, like some economic determinists of a later generation, he suspected the evidence of those loyalties and sought other motives.[6]

Throughout his *Life of Barneveld* Motley deprecates theological interest as a waste of time or an expression of ridiculous vanity. He dismisses James I as a pedant who wanted "to turn a throne into a pulpit, and amaze mankind with his learning." Even in his account of the Arminian controversy at Leyden, Motley skims over the theological details; he merely says that a schism resulted from the Calvinists' claim that they were the true church, and he announces that the debates accomplished "the usual result of confirming both parties in the conviction that to each alone belonged exclusively the truth." The issue of "absolute predestination" is a "theological quibble"; Motley says a great deal about "theological hatred," but in discussing the issues themselves he concentrates on the relationship between church and state, relegating the "five points" of the Remonstrants and the seven of the Contra-Remonstrants to a footnote. After a brief, extremely simplified statement of these issues, he promises that "there shall be no more setting forth of these subtle and finely wrought abstractions in our pages. We aspire not to the lofty heights of theological and supernatural contemplation, where the atmosphere becomes too rarefied for ordinary constitutions." Although he breaks his promise a few pages later, he is obviously uneasy with the subject. He finally confesses the difficulty he has in believing

that out of this arid field of controversy so plentiful a harvest of hatred and civil convulsion could have ripened. More practical than the insoluble problems, whether repentance could effect salvation, and whether dead infants were hopelessly damned, was the question who should rule both Church and State.

For one who does not believe in damnation the question of how to avoid it is naturally impractical. Motley's moral is not that either side was right but that this was no time for "the great Protestant party in the Netherlands to tear itself to pieces for a theological subtlety, about which good Christians might differ without taking each other by the throat."[7]

All the romantic historians believed that the mission of Protestantism was to encourage intellectual and political liberty. Motley said that "liberty of thought" was "the only [lesson] worth learning of the reformation." Parkman criticized the early Puritans for being "unfaithful to the principle of freedom," for appealing to Liberty and then closing "the door against her," for grafting "on a stock of freedom . . . a scion of despotism." "All Protestantism," he said, "is an appeal from priestly authority to the right of private judgment."[8]

Of the four historians, only the transcendentalist Bancroft expressed a personal view of piety which emphasizes the sovereignty of God. In a letter to George Ripley during the Revival of 1857 he condemned superstitious people who, by praying for special favors, "demand of God to break his own laws, which his providence necessarily upholds." The true believer, he said, tries to "bring his own will into harmony with the divine will. Piety studies the law, obeys the law, loves the law, and through perfect obedience becomes perfectly free. For liberty is the daughter of necessity." This attitude bore some fruit in Bancroft's interpretation of Jonathan Edwards; ignoring Edwards' harsher doctrines, he insisted that Edwards had given Calvinism its "political euthanasia" by proclaiming universal love as the highest virtue. But the law with which Bancroft's believer had to harmonize his will was natural law, which every man could perceive and obey. And "justification by faith alone" meant to Bancroft intellectual freedom.[9] He was no more willing than were the other three historians to endorse an "artificial" religion or submission to the doctrines of theologians.

Motley's, Parkman's, and Prescott's view of Puritanism, then, resembled Hawthorne's view and sometimes that of Cooper and Scott. Both Parkman and Motley portray the Calvinist yeoman as a comic figure, a caricature, with more redeeming traits than Cooper's Jason Newcome, but with the same frailties of ridiculous pretension and long-winded disputatiousness that appear in Newcome and in Scott's Douce Davie Deans. Both historians bring forth their best comic rhetoric when describing the Calvinist yeomanry. In two of the best chapters in *A Half-Century of Conflict*, Parkman presents the siege of Louisbourg in 1744 as "broad farce," and the New Englanders' pretentiousness is an important ingredient in the comedy. Parkman begins with a sardonic chapter on the ridiculous preparations for the expedition, and then moves to the siege itself. Impossible to discipline, the "raw" Yankee soldiers in the camp race, wrestle, pitch quoits, and fish while the battle goes on at the front.

Yet through all these gambols ran an undertow of enthusiasm, born in brains, still fevered from the "Great Awakening." The New England soldier, a growth of sectarian hotbeds, fancied that he was doing the work of God. The army was Israel, and the French were Canaanitish idolaters. Red-hot Calvinism, acting through generations, had modified the transplanted Englishman; and the descendant of the Puritans was never so well pleased as when teaching their duty to other people, whether by pen, voice, or bombshells. The ragged artillerymen, battering the walls of papistical Louisbourg, flattered themselves with the notion that they were champions of gospel truth.

Although this passage clearly reveals the stereotyped view of the Puritan, it tries to describe the Yankee's attitude accurately, and at the same time to judge it. The ultimate effect of Parkman's humor, however, is to increase the Yankee's stature, for his tone changes as the heroic energy and endurance of these pretentious yokels and the timidity and folly of the French give the Yankees an incredible victory.[10]

As supporting figures in this portrayal of the New England character, Parkman is fortunate to have General Pepperell's son-in-law—"a thrifty merchant, with a constant eye to business," and aptly named Nathaniel Sparhawk—and the zealous Parson Moody. Parkman makes the most of both opportunities for caricature. He introduces Sparhawk's persistent requests for booty when Pepperell is most worried about restraining his victorious troops. Moody, a notoriously long-winded "village pope," moves into action at the dinner celebrating the victory. The officers wait fearfully for his endless invocation, but he surprises them with a brief, two-sentence grace. To achieve his caricature, Parkman must then draw on "tradition":

Moody, it seems, "had been seen in the French church hewing at the altar and images with the axe that he had brought for this purpose; and perhaps this iconoclastic performance had eased the high pressure of his zeal."[11]

The Protestant who claimed to belong to the true church, who demanded state endorsement of a theological system, who denied religious liberty to dissenters from his creed, who gave authority to the clergy—this man betrayed the promise of the Reformation. The right of private judgment was guaranteed by natural law, the separation of church and state was a natural law, and theology was artificial. If the historians condemned these faults in Protestantism less vigorously than they condemned the same faults in Catholicism, the reason was not that the principles were less reprehensible. It was here that the relativism of progressive law was applied most frequently. Motley was lenient in his judgment of Protestant persecution of Catholics because some Catholics had provoked it, because Queen Elizabeth's very life had been threatened by Jesuit conspiracy, because the "rough and unlovely husk of Puritanism" contained the germ of a new freedom. Parkman praised the fruitful energy and manliness of the intolerant Puritans; and Bancroft defended early Puritan intolerance as a necessity to ensure moderation in Protestant progress. That movement had succeeded, Bancroft said, in the Seven Years' War. With characteristic directness in abstracting basic principles from a worldly conflict, he arranged the issues of this war in ascending order: the American question was whether "English Protestantism and popular liberty" or Catholicism and France's "tottering legitimacy" would control the continent; the European question was whether "a Protestant revolutionary kingdom, like Prussia," could survive. But "considered in its unity, as interesting mankind, the question was, Shall the Reformation, developéd to the fulness of Free Inquiry, succeed in its protest against the Middle Age?"[12]

This interpretation, exactly the same as Parkman's, named the worst fault in Catholicism: it was the Church of the Past. Parkman specified the trouble when he said that the Church was clearly of earth, not of heaven. For if it was not divine and yet it refused to change, it could only fight against the natural law of progress. In this struggle, which had lasted for centuries and seemed to be renewed occasionally even in the nineteenth century, the Church had broken other natural laws. It had enlisted political support whenever it could, forming unholy alliances with the state to prevent religious and intellectual freedom; it had entered into "conspiracies" against the people of various countries; it had even incited ferocious savages to attack Protestant women and children. The Church is extremely important in these histories not only because the historians interpreted so many of the conflicts as crises in the development of Protestantism, but also because of its continuity. Political absolutism, the principle of monarchy, had different agents during the centuries about which the historians wrote. But despite the fact that in the Netherlands, England, and colonial America religious absolutism was defended sometimes by Anglicans and sometimes by Calvinists, there was one identity, one institution, that consistently represented this principle. The Catholic Church almost becomes a character in the histories; until the end of the Seven Years' War it almost always acts as a reactionary force.

The function of Catholicism in these histories can be examined most clearly under two broad headings: the institution and representative characters.

2

The most telling charge against the institution was that it had permitted external forms to corrupt or consume the religious essence. This objection was first stated in the journals that the historians wrote as young men on the grand tour; later they transferred it—usually with more restraint, but sometimes with less—to the histories themselves. In Rome on Christmas Eve, 1821, Bancroft watched "the display of pretended devotion" and grew "heartily sick of the mockery of religion, & the tireless profusion of ceremonies, which are intended to inspire the Roman with piety." At twenty, Prescott had found it interesting, as the citizen "of a free country, flourishing under the influences of a benign religion, to contemplate the degradation to which human nature may be reduced when oppressed by arbitrary power and papal superstition." Parkman, at the same age, watched "the scum of humanity" pour out of one of the rear gates of Messina; most of the crowd were "literally hung with rags, half hid in dirt, hideous with every imaginable species of deformity," and covered with lice. "The next numerous class" were the priests, "fat and good-looking men" who drew "life and sustenance from these dregs of humanity—just as tall pigweed flourishes on a dunghill."[13]

These faults which appeared in the nineteenth century seemed to be merely the logical result of what had been clear in the sixteenth. Like monarchy and Calvinism, Catholicism had had an important progressive mission, to spread Christianity through Europe. But it had achieved this mission before Luther nailed his theses to the door, and its last glorious progressive act was to inspire Christians to victory at Lepanto. Shocked into action by the Reformation, but "unable to advance," the Church had

tried to return, by establishing the Jesuit order, to the Middle Ages.[14]
As monarchy had become "kingcraft," priesthood had become "priestcraft."
The same change had occurred in Massachusetts during the reign of the
Mather dynasty, but there the vigor of the people and of other principles
within the creed of Calvinism had made the struggle very brief. Catholi-
cism had a great system, imposing forms, and an alliance with monarchy.

There were many ways of showing in the histories themselves that
Catholicism was a religion which raised forms above essence, but underneath all of them lay the assumption that any sensible man could see the
faults plainly. In the presentation of both institution and characters the
technique was simplification. As natural moral laws were simple, so were
natural institutions and characters. Picking from the records of history the
clearest contrasts of principle and practice, the historian was able to show
plainly the "real" character of reactionary Catholicism.

Motley's Philip II took great care to protect the body of a "saint who
had been buried for centuries, while dogs [gnawed] the carcasses of the
freshly slain men" of the saint's city and "troopers" drove into "perpetual
exile its desolate and mutilated women." Here Motley merely presents an
ironic arrangement of documented facts, but when he describes the siege
of Harlem, during which the patriots used religious statues to mend
breaches in the city's walls, he attacks the Catholics' sincerity. The Dutch
had merely sought "a more practical advantage from those sculptured saints
than they could have gained by only imploring their interposition"; but
the Spaniards, who had been "daily butchering their fellow-beings, and
hanging their prisoners in cold blood, affected to shudder at the enormity
of [this crime] against graven images." Philip II, ill when a messenger
brought in the report that Harlem had capitulated and that two thousand
people had been treacherously killed, was cured by the news.[15]

Bancroft's and Parkman's De Soto brings iron fetters, bloodhounds,
monks, and priests to bind, hunt, and convert the Indians. Their Menéndez slaughters Huguenots and then orders that mass be said; he builds a
church "on ground still smoking with the blood of a peaceful colony." In
Bancroft's Ponce de Leon and De Soto "avarice" and religious zeal are
united, and their typical Spanish credulity leads them to folly, crime, and
death; superstition and credulity fight against Nature, and Nature wins.
Prescott's wretched Jews, expelled from Spain and attacked by rapacious
Moors in Africa, return in such numbers that the Spanish priest must baptize them with a "mop"; and the priest is proud of the remarkable Providence which had delivered the Jews from "'their ancient heresies.'"[16]

There were many variations of this kind of contrast, but almost all of them placed a simple moral alternative against a corrupt religious action. Motley ended a long paragraph on the sale of absolutions with a rhetorical question that had only one "natural" answer: "Was it unnatural that plain people, who loved the ancient Church, should rather desire to see her purged of such blasphemous abuses, than to hear of St. Peter's dome rising a little nearer to the clouds on these proceeds of commuted crime?" Again, when describing the Protestant siege of Paris, he quoted an anti-League source that charged Parisian priests with having condoned the eating of babies as an act preferable to surrendering the city to heretics. At the time, he reported that this charge was mere hearsay; but two hundred pages later, when trying to explain the premature capitulation of Gertruydenberg during a Protestant siege, he used the charge again as a rhetorical weapon:

It was known that even if the public ceremonies of the Catholic Church were likely to be suspended for a time after the surrender, at least the rights of individual conscience and private worship within individual households would be tolerated, and there was no papal legate with fiery eloquence persuading a city full of heroic dupes that it was more virtuous for men and women to eat their own children than to forego one high mass, or to wink at a single conventicle.

Here Motley implied that restriction to "private worship" is no more inconvenient to the Catholic than to the Protestant; and that the alternative to eating one's children was not surrendering the true faith and the city to heretics, but forgoing one high mass.[17]

Such distortions demonstrate that on the subject of Catholicism Motley was often the extreme rather than the representative of the four historians. Within the bounds of honesty, however, all four used the same technique of simplified contrasts. Motley, too, tried to state fairly the issue of toleration, and he made it very clear that he opposed persecution of Catholics as well as of Protestants. He was simply unable, it seems, to understand or respect the Catholic's or "the red-hot Calvinist's" view of the alternatives. Convinced that the age of cathedrals had given way to the age of good works, he could not "dare censure in very severe language" the "havoc" wrought "among stocks and stones" by Dutch iconoclasts who had hurt no living people. For this desecration had occurred "in a land where so many living men and women, of more value than many statues, had been slaughtered by the inquisition."[18]

The most striking of the simplified contrasts revealed the artificiality of Catholic ideas by presenting them in conflict with the mind of the simple man. Variations of this device had been used in other contrasts, as in

Bancroft's chapter on "The King of Spain Baffled by the Backwoodsmen of Virginia." The device was inevitable in the works of "naturalists." Cooper used it repeatedly in his fiction—with Natty Bumppo outwitting Hiram Doolittle and defeating the "learned" Obed Battius in religious and ethical discussions; with Duncan Middleton, hero of *The Prairie*, using his plain "common-sense" to confute the unscrupulous priest who tried to convert him.[19] In the histories the most common form of the contrast—along with rhetorical devices such as Motley's—was the juxtaposition of Catholic and savage.

In this dramatic meeting of formalist and barbarian, both savage and missionary (as well as the latter's religion) show up badly. But whether the reflection on the savage is good or bad, the result almost always reflects unfavorably on the missionary or his religion. The Indian cannot understand Catholic Christianity; his artless questions, by their very naïveté, expose the fallacies in Catholicism. If the savage does not ask the right question, the historian may even supply it for him. Prescott's Montezuma, highpriest of a cannibalistic religion, "may have, perhaps, thought it was not more monstrous to feed on the flesh of a fellow creature, than on that of the Creator himself." The hypothesis shows the "barbarian's" inability to comprehend "abstruse" doctrines, and it characterizes the doctrine itself.[20]

Parkman's *Jesuits in North America* turns the same doctrine against the missionaries, but as a part of a much more elaborately ironic scheme. The Jesuit mission to the Hurons is having difficulties. Even in the distress of a smallpox epidemic, converts who really comprehend the religion are very hard to find. "Nature [triumphs] over Grace" when a Huron woman chooses to go to Hell, "if my children are there, as you say."

No admirer of the Indian's mental capacity, Parkman also points out that in other Indians this same refusal comes from the inherent worldliness of the race's imagination, which leads the savage to argue: No hunting; no heaven. Some Indians, however, have nobler motives for rejecting Paradise, and one retort quoted by Parkman hits almost providentially on a major fault that the historians believed that Catholicism encourages: the blight of indolence. "I will not go," an Indian declares. "It is not good to be lazy."[21]

The theme of these episodes is more than the Jesuits' repeated failure, "cheaply as they offered salvation, . . . to find a purchaser." Parkman emphasizes not only the Indian's intractability but the cheapness of the offer. The succession of amusing, sometimes pathetic misunderstandings shows the irony of the entire Catholic effort to Christianize the Indian, the weakness of Catholicism as well as that of the Indian mind. Offering salvation "cheaply" to any Indian who will confess his faith and show some understanding of Catholic doctrine—offering it also to dying children who cannot even believe—the Jesuits find that their zeal in baptizing the dying naturally convinces many Indians that baptism *causes* death.[22]

In later chapters, especially one called "Persecution," the number of such ironies accumulates impressively for Parkman's doubly didactic purpose. One "half-instructed neophyte," misunderstanding the idea of the Eucharist, spreads the story that the priests have hidden a corpse in their houses, and that this is what has "infected the country." The pictures that the Jesuits have brought to facilitate conversion have the opposite effect when a painting of the Last Judgment becomes "an object of the utmost terror" to the Indians. Parkman then writes a telling summary to show how the priests' best objects of wonder (a clock, for example) and the highest truths they have brought with them are turned against them. The final irony is the Indians' charge that the Jesuits' "sorceries" have caused a smallpox epidemic. For the Jesuits, of course, have bravely complained of Indian sorcery, and they attribute their persecution to "the fury of the Devil."[23]

Whether or not one is offended by this method of displaying a religious doctrine, one cannot deny that in these passages Parkman has achieved excellent dramatic irony. He writes frankly as a "heretic" and, like Prescott and Motley, for a predominantly heretical audience. His characters do not know the meaning that their actions will convey to the audience; by a skillful presentation of their speeches, Parkman makes that meaning very clear. His method differs from Motley's juxtaposition of brutality to human beings and solicitude for "stocks and stones." In Parkman's book the results are ironic even within the framework of the Jesuits' conscious purpose, and he does not attack the Jesuits' sincerity. Sometimes, though rarely, he points explicitly to the larger irony that he expects non-Catholics to see so clearly. After arguing that the Indians' primary motive for interest in Christianity was a desire for good "medicine," he remarks that the Jesuits "themselves, indeed, firmly believed that saints and angels were always at hand with temporal succors for the faithful."[24]

In the face of the Indians' hostility to their own welfare, even the best Jesuits resorted to the "duplicity" that the historians considered characteristic of the order. They baptized dying infants surreptitiously and lied to suspicious parents who asked questions. Although he admired the "self-sacrificing zeal" demonstrated by this risky behavior, Parkman deplored the method; the "nimble-fingered" baptisms seemed like the work of pick-pockets.[25]

This deceptive behavior in the service of a noble motive was only the prelude to later duplicity in an ignoble cause. The later missionaries were not heroic men, nor was their dominant purpose to save Indian souls; to contrast them with Indian simplicity, Parkman focused not on the Indian's naïve questions or suspicions, but on their own deliberate distortion of Catholic doctrine. In *Count Frontenac and New France* he recorded and condemned the acts of many Acadian missionaries who had "hounded" their Indian converts "on the track of innocent blood." Relying on Cotton Mather and Jeremiah Dummer as sources, he recorded the more lurid perversions of doctrine by which some politically motivated priests had imposed on the savages' ignorance: Jesus was a Frenchman; Mary, a French lady. The English had murdered Jesus, and the best way to gain his favor was to revenge his death on the English. From this example of blasphemy Parkman turned back to the antithesis of forms and essence. Throughout Canada, he said, missionaries had taught all other Christian virtues but those of peace: "temperance, conjugal fidelity, . . . the rites of their religion, and submission to the priest; but they left the savage a savage still." They kept him separate from the French and neglected to teach him the French language. The Indian convert, in short, "wore a crucifix, hung wampum on the shrine of the Virgin, told his beads, prayed three times a day, knelt for hours before the Host, invoked the saints, confessed to the priests; but, with rare exceptions, he murdered, scalped, and tortured like his heathen countrymen."[26]

From the bloodhounds, fetters, and monks of De Soto, through the heroic but ironically fruitless missions of the Jesuits, to the half-century of conflict in the eighteenth century, Catholic missionaries had meant to bring Christianity to the Indians. A major purpose of Parkman's contrasts of "priest and pagan" was to show that the result was always failure, often positive harm. He summed up the moral in one sentence in *Count Frontenac and New France*. Noting that some French officers had invited their Indian allies to burn and eat their Iroquois prisoners, Parkman described the burning and then wrote: " 'It was the mission of Canada,' says a Canadian writer, 'to propagate Christianity and civilization.' "[27]

Bancroft used the Indian-Catholic contrast to emphasize the virtues of the simple mind. Despite the Indians' paganism, Bancroft said, "belief was free; there was no monopoly of science, no close priesthood." He compared the Indians who had resisted De Soto to the Athenians "in the days of Themistocles"; and he often put quotation marks around the words "the Christians" when referring to the Spaniards. By stressing the quiet resolution of those Indians who had deliberately led the credulous "Christians" into "morasses," and the plight of those who had been terrorized into fabricating descriptions of golden countries, he used the Indians to expose the hollowness of the Spaniards' "superstition."[28]

Motley had no Indians at his historical disposal, but he had "Philip the tyrant's" heir: "Philip the simpleton." The ignorant dupe of his own political favorite, Philip III was a man whose entire "stock of erudition" consisted of a few phrases in French, Italian, and Flemish, and the Catholic catechism. But "he was as devout as a monk of the middle ages," and he liked to shoot rabbits while the Duke of Lerma governed the empire and grew rich by peculation. With commendable sensitivity, Motley confessed that it would be cruel to unearth a "simpleton's" character merely for ridicule; but it was instructive, he insisted, to see what kind of character could be given absolute power under a despotic system. Nor could he resist combining all of these characteristics (including the rabbit-shooting) with an allusion to the Catholic "superstition" of his own time, in order to show the ridiculousness of Catholic doctrine. "In one respect," he confessed, Philip III "was in advance of his own age. In his devotion to the Madonna he claimed the same miraculous origin [sic] for her mother as for herself. . . . He had frequent interviews with doctors of divinity on the subject, and instructed many bishops to urge upon the pope the necessity of proclaiming the virginity of the Virgin's mother."[29]

The image of Catholicism as a religion appears in these histories in extremely distorted form. The distinguishing features of the religion—as they appeared to the historians—stand out much more prominently than do the tenets common to Catholicism and Protestantism. Aside from any intentional or unintentional bias, one major reason for this distortion is that the peculiarities of the religion against which the historians objected were naturally those that appeared as distinctly Catholic in ideological conflicts. The peculiar features of anti-Protestant and antidemocratic reaction were the doctrines or "myths" most useful and, it must have seemed, most relevant to these histories. Thus ultramontanism, the Inquisition, the privileges and claims of priests, the intercession of saints, the Immaculate Conception, transubstantiation, faith in the value of relics, the confessional, rituals, the need to baptize dying infants—these are the Catholic ideas that receive the most attention. All of these, moreover, appear most frequently in connection with reactionary political action. They all belong in the category of "superstitions"—a word by which all four historians, at one time or another, characterized Catholic belief.[30]

3

The power of this distortion is magnified by the literary devices that the historians employed, by their emphasis on moral conduct, and above all by the large number of evil or contemptible people who had acted, at one time or another, in the name of the religion. Consider Motley's portrayal of Henry of Valois, the cowardly, effeminate king. An important ingredient in the portrait is his use of relics and his punctilious observance of religious forms:

Now sauntering, full-dressed, in the public promenades, with ghastly little death's heads strung upon his sumptuous garments, and fragments of human bones dangling among his orders of knighthood—playing at cup and ball as he walked, and followed by a few select courtiers who gravely pursued the same exciting occupation—now presiding like a queen of beauty at a tournament to assign the prize of valour, and now, by the advice of his mother, going about the streets in robes of penitence, telling his beads as he went, that the populace might be edified by his piety, and solemnly offering up prayers in the churches that the blessing of an heir might be vouchsafed to him,—Henry of Valois seemed straining every nerve in order to bring himself and his great office into contempt.

The reactionary Catholic was vulnerable to this kind of treatment because of the *objects* of his prayer. Motley rarely neglected the opportunity to use a prayer for some ridiculous blessing—such as an heir for Henry III or Philip II, which any manly man could come by without special prayer; or a victory over heretics, which no man less energetic than they could possibly win.[31]

The first unsuccessful attempt to assassinate William of Orange gave Motley a perfect opportunity of this kind, and he used the evidence (supplied by Dutch Protestants, but apparently not contradicted elsewhere) to create two powerful symbols of the warring religions. By observing chronological order and withholding the assassin's name, he was able to describe the man's possessions before revealing the name, which had been discovered only after an examination of his papers. The description of the papers enabled Motley to cram into one paragraph nearly every kind of "superstition" which was used to describe Catholic villains in the histories. Immediately after noticing the pistol and poniard which lay on the floor beside the dead man, Motley turned to his other possessions:

In his pockets were an *Agnus Dei,* a taper of green wax, two bits of hareskin, two dried toads—which were supposed to be sorcerers' charms—a Jesuit catechism, a prayer-book, a pocketbook containing two Spanish bills of exchange—one for two thousand, and one for eight hundred and seventy-seven crowns—and a set of writing tablets. These last were covered with vows and pious invocations, in reference to the murderous affair which the writer had in hand. He had addressed fervent prayers to the Virgin Mary, to the Angel Gabriel, to the Saviour, and *to the Saviour's Son*—"as if," says the Antwerp chronicler, with simplicity, "the Lord Jesus had a son"—that they might all use their intercession with the Almighty towards the certain and safe accomplishment of the contemplated deed. Should he come off successful and unharmed, he solemnly vowed to fast a week on bread and water. Furthermore, he promised to Christ a "new coat of costly pattern"; to the Mother of God, at Guadalupe, a new gown; to Our Lady of Montserrat, a crown, a gown, and a lamp; and so on through a long list of similar presents thus contemplated for various shrines. The poor fanatical fool had been taught by deeper villains than himself that his pistol was to rid the world of a tyrant, and to open his own pathway to Heaven, if his career should be cut short on earth. To prevent so undesirable a catastrophe to himself, however, his most natural conception had been to bribe the whole heavenly host, from the Virgin Mary downwards, for he had been taught that absolution for murder was to be bought and sold like other merchandise. He had also been persuaded that, after accomplishing the deed, *he would become invisible*.[32]

The forcefulness of the gruesome caricature does not depend on this symbol alone. In Juan Jauregy and his intended victim one sees the symbols of reaction and Reformation, forms and essence. Beside this product of Catholic "superstition" and corruption, who has been taught to buy absolution with bribes for the heavenly host, stands the Christ-like image of William himself. Although shot point-blank by a pistol ball that went into his neck and out through the roof of his mouth, carrying two teeth with it; although his beard and hair were on fire; William, before falling, had shouted: 'Do not kill him—I forgive him my death!'[33]

The most damning fault in Catholicism was that, in its career of opposition to freedom, its agents were so often "deep villains"—kings, politicians, priests. The Church's most consistently damaging agent was the priest; the encouragement of priestcraft was its most unnatural act, from which grew such others as the crimes of the Inquisition. But before considering the priest, one should remember that the historians were consistent in their anticlerical emphasis. Gauls, Aztecs, Moors, Calvinists—all were duped at times by the self-interested authoritarianism of priests. In his volumes on Barneveld, Motley, who had made the Gauls' submission to priestcraft one of their determining traits, referred to Dutch Calvinists as the "sacerdotal element," and as the "priesthood." Prescott, who criticized the same faults in Aztecs and Peruvians, praised Bancroft for "showing up the good old times of witchcraft and priestcraft" in Massachusetts; Bancroft's chapter on witchcraft, he said, "carried me back to the Inquisition." Again, however, Catholicism provided the most powerful and long-lived tradition of priesthood.[34]

Parkman was very careful to place his discussion of priestcraft explicitly in this framework. He was led to a generalization about priests by the reflection that the "social atmosphere" of Quebec under the seventeenth-century Jesuits was "more suffocating" than that of Puritan New England itself. In a paragraph reminiscent of Hawthorne, he insisted that "no degree of personal virtue is a guaranty against the evils which attach to the temporal rule of ecclesiastics." He admitted that the "fervent and conscientious priest" burns "with love and devotion to Christ and his immaculate Mother," and that this piety leads him to work strenuously for the salvation of "every rash wanderer." But the crucial issue, as in politics, was authority, and here Parkman made the mistake of all four historians, and of many Protestants before and since:

And while he, the priest, yields reverence and obedience to the Superior, in whom he sees the representative of the Deity, it behooves him, in his degree, to require obedience from those whom he imagines that God has confided to his guidance. His conscience, then, acts in perfect accord with the love of power innate in the human heart. These allied forces mingle with a perplexing subtlety; pride, disguised even from itself, walks in the likeness of love and duty; and a thousand times on the pages of history we find Hell beguiling the virtues of Heaven to do its work. The instinct of domination is a weed that grows rank in the shadow of the temple, climbs over it, possesses it, covers its ruin, and feeds on its decay. The unchecked sway of priests has always been the most mischievous of tyrannies; and even were they all well-meaning and sincere, it would be so still.[35]

This frank statement is as earnest an attempt at impartiality as any that appears in the romantic histories. Despite the exaggeration of the priest's idea of his legitimate authority, it would be hard to question Parkman's good faith; and one should notice that history gave Parkman many examples of priests who had demanded complete temporal and spiritual obedience of their wards. But just as important as the emphasis on authority in this paragraph is the emphasis on psychology. Parkman, it seems, found it hard to describe an entirely devoted Catholic without making some psychological comment on the devotee's mixed motives—some comment that questioned the whole basis of Catholic piety. The best of his priests and nuns had been misled not by their love of authority, but by other earthly needs of the human heart; the worst had been motivated by greed, bigotry, and "the instinct of domination."

Consider the Jesuit martyr Brébeuf, "that masculine apostle of the Faith—the Ajax of the mission," and his associate Charles Garnier. In describing them Parkman set the pattern for his psychological interpretation of Catholic martyrs; at the same time, he suggested a judgment of religious orders which typifies all the historians' interpretation of priestcraft:

Nature had given [Brébeuf] all the passions of a vigorous manhood, and religion had crushed them, curbed them, or tamed them to do her work,—like a damned-up torrent, sluiced and guided to grind and saw and weave for the good of man.

Although Brébeuf appears as a hero, the lofty position of naturalness and vigorous manhood in Parkman's hierarchy of virtues suggests an adverse judgment of an order and a Church that require a man to make such a sacrifice. Beside Brébeuf in this scene, standing "in strange contrast," was the frail, beardless Garnier, extremely sensitive, saintly from boyhood. "The affections of his sensitive nature," Parkman said, "severed from earthly objects, found relief in ardent adoration of the Virgin Mary." Although he said that only psychologists could account for the Jesuit "visions" and their quest for martyrdom, Parkman repeatedly explained Catholic piety in these terms. "A subtle element of romance" pervaded Marquette's devotion to the Virgin, toward whom he turned "the longings of a sensitive heart, divorced from earth"; and the female "enthusiast" was also capable of sublimation, exemplified in the love of Marie de l'Incarnation for Christ.[36]

Despite the "enormous spiritual pride" of Sister Marie, these characters stand among the finest examples of Catholic piety in all the romantic histories. Yet even these descriptions of heroic piety lead, in Parkman's *Jesuits*, to a pathetic example of the "stifling" of Nature. The widowed Marie de l'Incarnation, wanting to be married to Christ, resisted the desire for a long time because of her love for her young son; "but at last, fortified by her confessor, she left him to his fate, took the vows, and immured herself with the Ursulines of Tours." Her son, "frenzied by his desertion," came to the convent "screaming to the horrified nuns to give him back his mother." The moral of abandoning one's natural duty for an illusory spiritual one becomes clear when Parkman reports that the boy fell "into bad company" and ran away from his guardian; it is the moral taught by the Quaker mother's behavior in Hawthorne's story "The Gentle Boy."

But Parkman directs his final criticism against the artificial power of the confessor. When she heard that her son had run away, "the wretched mother, torn with anguish, hastened for consolation to her confessor." This unnatural man, the same one who had encouraged her to leave her son for the convent, "met her with stern upbraidings."[37] Marie de l'Incarnation herself does not receive Parkman's approval until she is "no longer lost in the vagaries of an insane mysticism," until she has busied herself with the duties of Christian charity and the responsibilities of an arduous post."[38]

As a contrast to this story, the supremacy of the natural, even in piety, becomes perfectly clear some twenty pages later in Parkman's description of Marguerite de Bourgeoys. Considering the quality of her piety and the way in which Parkman wanted to use it, he was very fortunate that her portrait had survived into the nineteenth century; for, by indulging in conventional abstraction, he was able to observe that "her face is a mirror of frankness, loyalty, and womanly tenderness." This comment introduces his description of her character. Such features as these cannot introduce a zealot, and her essential traits naturally follow: "good sense, conscientiousness, and a warm heart." With this sound basis her piety has to be natural:

She had known no miracles, ecstasies or trances; and though afterwards, when her religious susceptibilities had reached a fuller development, a few such are recorded of her, yet even the Abbé Faillon, with the best intentions, can credit her with but a meagre allowance of these celestial favors. Though in the midst of visionaries, she distrusted the supernatural, and avowed her belief that, in His government of the world, God does not often set aside its ordinary laws. Her religion was of the affections, and was manifested in an absorbing devotion to duty. She had felt no vocation to the cloister, but had taken the vow of chastity, and was attached, as an *externe,* to the Sisters of the Congregation of Troyes, who were fevered with eagerness to go to Canada. Marguerite, however, was content to wait until there was a prospect that she could do good by going; and it was not till the year 1653, that, renouncing an inheritance, and giving all she had to the poor, she embarked for the savage scene of her labors.

This was the one fair heroine associated with a religious sisterhood in Parkman's history, and he used her to demonstrate the virtues of natural piety. She was the one pious member of a religious order who could distinguish between "visionary" religion and a "religion of the affections"; she displayed her piety through good works; she was prudent, she remained outside the cloister, she gave all she had to the poor, and her virtue was "unobtrusive."[39]

The admirable and "lamentable" examples of superhuman Catholic devotion—here and in Prescott and Motley—point clearly to the same objection that Schiller had made to a change in control of the Inquisition.

Innocent III, Schiller said, had replaced the bishops and the secular clergy, who, because they still had some contact with "civil life," were "still too much attached to humanity for his purpose"; the office was turned over to the monks, "*a half-denaturalized race of beings who had abjured the sacred feelings of nature,* and were the servile tools of the Roman See."[40] The priest, by his vow of celibacy; the monk, by his withdrawal from the world; the Jesuit, by his vows of obedience—all struggled to repress the feelings of nature. Good and bad, all appear in the histories as partly, if not half-, denaturalized.

4

This stifling of the feelings of nature is the key to one of the most ubiquitous stock characters in the histories: the monk. The word priest is often used without any pejorative intent; the word monk, almost never.[41] In a system of "natural" values, an unnatural or artificial religion was bad enough; an unnatural man was detestable. The monk who appears repeatedly in these histories originated not so much in historical fact as in literature. His actions and his name may have individualized him, and his actual portrait may have conformed to the literary portrait painted by the historian; but this resemblance, when it occurred, was a fortunate coincidence. Even when no physical characteristics are given, the rhetoric reserved for monks (and, sometimes, for priests) alludes to a picture that the reader already has in mind. The traits are those of Mrs. Radcliffe's Schedoni, of Lewis's *Monk,* of the Elizabethan stage Jesuit.

Prescott repeated several times the anti-natural explanation of monkish behavior. The chronicler Mariana was "incompetent" because he was a monk—cut off, as his colleagues were, "from sympathy with any portion of the species save their own order." Torquemada, a Dominican friar, was "one of that class . . . who compensate for their abstinence from sensual indulgence, by giving scope to those deadlier vices of the heart, pride, bigotry, and intolerance, which are no less opposed to virtue, and far more extensively mischievous to society." And "in every part of the odious scheme of the Inquisition" it was "easy" to see "the contrivance of the monks, a class of men, cut off by their profession from the usual sympathies of social life, and who, accustomed to the tyranny of the confessional, aimed at establishing the same jurisdiction over thoughts, which secular tribunals have wisely confined to actions."[42]

That the monk was frankly recognized as a literary type can be seen in Prescott's final essay on Cardinal Ximenes. It was his custom to begin every obituary essay of any length with a portrait or sketch. But he began his obituary of Ximenes with praise for the Cardinal's virtues—simplicity, endurance, resolution, courage, directness. Only when he came to Ximenes' versatility and his military talents did he prepare to introduce the portrait: "In every situation, however, he exhibited the stamp of his peculiar calling; and the stern lineaments of the monk were never wholly concealed under the mask of the statesman, or the visor of the warrior." The portrait itself, which would have been out of place beside his greatest virtues, appears with a reference to his unnatural "austerities":

His complexion was sallow; his countenance sharp and emaciated, his nose aquiline; his upper lip projected far over the lower. His eyes were small, deep set in his head, dark, vivid, and penetrating. His forehead ample [sic], and what was remarkable, without a wrinkle, though the expression of his features was somewhat severe. His voice was clear, but not agreeable; his enunciation measured and precise. His demeanor was grave, his carriage firm and erect; he was tall in stature, and his whole presence commanding. His constitution, naturally robust, was impaired by his severe austerities and severer cares; and, in the later years of his life, was so delicate as to be extremely sensible to the vicissitudes and inclemency of the weather.[43]

The stereotype was so generally accepted that Motley, when describing a villainous Franciscan who did not have the proper physiognomy, was able to make a point of the exception. He compensated for the friar's "visage of more than Flemish frankness" by using serpentine imagery again and again, by calling him "the smooth friar," "the monk," "the Franciscan," "the very smooth Flemish friar." In his novel *Morton's Hope* a French priest in Canada "was none of your ordinary, well-fed, greasy priests. There was genius in his crafty eye and in his scornful mouth. But it was an evil genius." In his *United Netherlands,* "rabid" Parisian monks "foamed with rage." Spain, he said, would have been better off if she had expelled half a million mendicant monks instead of half a million Moors. "Evil black eyes," a "dark, restless eye"; "a dark, martial face and dangerous eyes"; a "mean visage," a "meagre" form—these are the features of different villains.[44]

The romantic histories support Mario Praz's contention that romantic literature "reproduces to the point of frenzy some of the characteristics of the Elizabethan age." Motley's affection for Elizabethan characters and Elizabethan prose, the racial overtones in Motley's and Prescott's strictures on "southern" diplomacy, Prescott's comments on proverbial Neapolitan dishonesty—all this evidence supports the conclusions of recent scholars about the sixteenth- and seventeenth-century influence on Melville, Thoreau, Cooper, Scott, and other contemporaries. Most interesting in this context are the historians' explicit references, in their portrayal of "jesuitical" villains, to the language and character of Shakespeare's Iago.[45]

Parkman headed a chapter on Vinal, the villain of *Vassal Morton,* with a quotation from Iago, and then described Vinal's traits, which included "the courage of the intriguer—a quality quite distinct from the courage of the soldier." Prescott's Alvaro de Luna resembles Iago in his courage and ability, his "insinuating address," his presumptuous insolence, his amazing control of his master (King John of Castile), and the mute impassiveness with which he faces his horrible execution; but Prescott compared him only to Cardinal Wolsey. Motley, on the other hand, liked *Othello* so much that he not only used its language occasionally in his own prose, but also cast two different historical villains in the role of Iago.[46]

Motley's first Iago was Cardinal Granvelle, who "dealt mainly by insinuation," and who "was apt to conclude his statements with disclaimers upon his own part, and with hopes of improvement in the conduct of the seignors." The letter that Motley used to begin his comparison justifies it completely, and his skillful paraphrase echoes Iago's speeches in the third act of *Othello.* Motley was aware, moreover, that the intended victim of the intrigue, Count Egmont, reinforced the comparison; for Egmont was a loyal, forthright, and not too prudent soldier whom Philip II eventually executed on the basis of unjustified suspicion. The letter, Motley said, showed the Cardinal's "masterly style of innuendo . . . , by which he was often able to convince his master of the truth of certain statements while affecting to discredit them." It was "characteristic" of Granvelle to "add that, after all, he considered [Egmont] one of the most honest of all, if *appearances did not deceive.*" It is characteristic of Motley that even after this he should make the *Othello* comparison still more emphatic:

It may be supposed, however, that all these details of a plot which was quite imaginary, were likely to produce more effect upon a mind so narrow and so suspicious as that of Philip, than could the vague assertions of the Cardinal, that in spite of all, *he would dare be sworn that he thought the Count honest, and that men should be what they seemed.*[47]

Motley not only continued to use the *Othello* comparison in later descriptions of Granvelle, but made it the theme of his treatment of Maurice of Nassau in the *Life of Barneveld.* Maurice was the all-conquering general "who found himself at the conclusion of the truce with his great occupation gone." The very next sentence is a long comment on the "potent principle" of jealousy; the next, a one-sentence paragraph: "And there were not to

be wanting acute and dangerous schemers who saw their profit in augment-
ing its intensity." The loyal, honest Barneveld, object of the Prince's jealousy, is robbed of his good name and eventually executed. Even the language in which Motley described calumny is reminiscent of *Othello*. Again
and again calumny was a thing dirty and slimy, calling forth images of
reptiles and monsters; at the height of the slanders against Barneveld, "it
was as if a whole tribe of noxious and obscene reptiles were swarming out
of the earth which had suddenly swallowed him." The implied comparison
of Maurice with Othello was especially useful to Motley because it might
prepare the literate reader to accept Motley's hypothesis about Maurice's
motives—a hypothesis supported largely by hearsay evidence and conjec-
ture.[48]

The Iago of this drama is Francis Aertsens. He is not, as Granvelle was,
a priest, but in him, too, Iago and the monk coalesce. With his "shrewd"
face, his "restless eye," and his "close-fitting skull cap," he has "something
the look of a monk, but with the thoroughbred and facile demeanour of
one familiar with the world; [he was] stealthy, smooth, and cruel, a man
coldly intellectual, who feared no one, loved but few, and never forgot or
forgave." It is by this man's "almost devilish acts" that "the imperious,
rugged, and suspicious nature" of Maurice has "been steadily wrought
upon."[49]

The use of these stock characters does not, of course, mean that every
monk, every member of a religious order in the histories, is a villain. But
when the monk appears as monk, he usually works for political or social
reaction, and his cloth is the garb of a villain. Whatever his virtues, moreover, all the historians make it clear that his social situation, his religious
vows, and his political duty are artificial forces resistant to natural virtue.
These forces act on all priests, and especially on the Jesuits.

If any proof were needed of the similarity of Motley's Catholic clergy
to the Elizabethan Jesuit, one paragraph from the *United Netherlands*
would suffice. Describing the last attempt to revive in the Netherlands the
"blood-dripping edicts against heresy," Motley blamed "the Jesuits" as
instigators of the movement. The paragraph introduces the "last religious
murder" committed in the sixteenth-century Netherlands, the burial alive
of a Protestant girl. Preparing to contrast the heroic girl's constancy with
the easy apostasy of Henry IV, Motley wrote a ringing paragraph on "the
Jesuits"—for it was they who "denounced this maid-servant to the civil
authority"—as another contrast to her simple character. He followed a
simple rhetorical technique: to play on the sound of "the Jesuits" while

recording their insidious behavior. The edicts, he wrote, had been dead for twenty years;

but the devilish spirit which had inspired them still lived in the persons of the Jesuits, and there were now more Jesuits in the obedient provinces than there had been for years. We have seen that Champagny's remedy for the ills the country was enduring was "more Jesuits." And this, too, was Albert's recipe. Always more Jesuits. And now the time had come when the Jesuits thought that they might step openly with their works into the daylight again. Of late years they had shrouded themselves in comparative mystery, but from their seminaries and colleges had gone forth a plentiful company of assassins against Elizabeth and Henry, Nassau, Barneveld, and others who, whether avowedly or involuntarily, were prominent in the party of human progress. Some important murders had already been accomplished, and the prospect was fair that still others might follow, if the Jesuits persevered. Meantime those ecclesiastics thought that a wholesome example might be set to humbler heretics by the spectacle of a public execution.

Throughout his account of this execution, Motley referred to "the Jesuits" as actors and conspirators, specifying only once—when the martyr walked "between two Jesuits" to the place of execution—the number of Jesuits engaged in any action.[50]

The prevailing moral trait in the Jesuit, and in almost every priest who worked for reaction, is duplicity. Even in the best of Parkman's Jesuits it begins, as I have said, with the relatively harmless artifice of surreptitious baptism. But Parkman wanted his reader to see in these heroic martyrs the same principle of corruption that in others had produced the worst treachery. He pointed out that their

equivocal morality, . . . built on the doctrine that all means are permissible for saving souls from perdition, and that sin itself is no sin when its object is "the greater glory of God,"—found far less scope in the rude wilderness of the Hurons than among the interests, ambitions, and passions of civilized life. Nor were these men, chosen from the purest of their Order, personally well fitted to illustrate the capabilities of their elastic system.

This was the basic crime of the Jesuit order, the basic fault in Catholic morality, the principle behind the stereotype. "The end justifies the means," "No faith with heretics"—the historians waved these slogans like a bloody shirt. Detail after detail was thrown onto the scales of historical justice to show nineteenth-century readers their results. Despite all the criticisms of "incessant supernaturalism," superstition, and ceremonialism, the main battleground was that of morality.[51]

One should remember the importance of truthfulness in the historians' list of virtues. The Jesuits are "adepts in dissimulation," and other politically active priests have similar skills. A confessor advises a virgin, whose father will disinherit her if she does not marry, to execute a sham marriage in order to assure her inheritance, and then to take her religious vows; Jesuits advise Acadians to break their oaths of loyalty to the British crown; Jesuits incite Indians to attack English settlers "in time of peace," and some even lead them to battle; "the devilish arts of the Jesuits" change a Prince's moral character; assassins are encouraged by Jesuits; friars try to bribe republican patriots. Popes release kings from "solemn promises"; "the most Catholic king" renounces all his mercantile contracts and takes "God to witness" that it is "to serve his Divine will"; "casuists" approve the breaking of an officer's word of honor; a "zealous missionary" pays Indians a bounty for English scalps and is rewarded for "good service to religion and the state." A Dominican "friar" encourages Pizarro to murder: "'Set on, at once; I absolve you.'" Missionaries are encouraged to "hound" their Indian and Acadian "flocks" against the English but are advised to avoid being "found out," so that the Governor, "by means of falsehood," can have the attackers "punished as felons." The fact that one Acadian priest keeps his oath to the English crown is so exceptional that his name must be given.[52]

All these examples are used to show that the political habitat of the priest is the region of intrigue. Nor are they manufactured examples of horror; all but one[53] are well documented in the histories. Indeed, a major technique of all four historians was to let a Philip II, a Menéndez, a Granvelle, a Father Piquet, damn himself before posterity with the words from his own private letters. Parkman, moreover, was able to quote Catholic contemporaries who had shared his opinion. One Frenchman had declared that "'nobody . . . was more fit than [Father Le Loutre] to carry discord and desolation into a country.'" And other French officers had written more succinctly: "'What is not a wicked priest capable of doing?'"[54]

Second in reprehensibility only to his duplicity is the priest's belief that he should engage in politics at all. Beside the imagery of diabolical and sinuous winding with which Parkman and Motley describe duplicity stands the rhetoric of "rabid" foaming, of "goading" and "hounding." The key to this language, and to the priests' political activity, is the word "fanaticism." Although this word was also applied to Protestant intolerance, Protestant priestcraft had only a very small part in these histories, it was not internationally organized, and it did not seem to be so essential to Protestantism as Catholic priestcraft was to Catholicism. "Superstition"

describes "blind faith," in Protestants and Catholics alike; Catholic belief in
visions, miracles, and the intercession of saints; and submission to a "sacerdotal" hierarchy. "Fanaticism" describes religious exclusiveness and political action to establish it. Intriguing priests are subtle, stealthy, smooth, and
serpentine; soldier-priests, inquisitors, and priestly demagogues are rabid,
frantic, furious. Their passion is somehow a cold passion, like the fanaticism
of Scott's Protestant Balfour and the revenge of Hawthorne's Chillingworth.

Prescott reveals the fanatic type in Torquemada. Some wealthy Jews
have tried to prevent the expulsion of their "race" from Spain by offering
the crown "thirty thousand ducats" toward paying the debts incurred in
the Moorish war. Torquemada bursts into the room where Ferdinand and
Isabella are talking to the Jewish deputy, and,

drawing forth a crucifix from beneath his mantle, [holds] it up, exclaiming,
"Judas Iscariot sold his master for thirty pieces of silver. Your Highnesses would
sell him anew for thirty thousand; here he is, take him, and barter him away."
So saying, the frantic priest threw the crucifix on the table, and left the apart-
ment. The sovereigns, instead of chastising this presumption, or despising it
as a mere freak of insanity, were overawed by it.[55]

The same "fanatical temper," described in even more violent language, appears in Motley's demagogic Parisian monks and Parkman's demagogic
eighteenth-century missionaries.

Fanaticism, Prescott argued, was even worse than atheism, for while
atheism (like superstition) does not require evil social action or blindness
to "just moral perceptions," fanaticism "enjoins the commission of the most
revolting crimes as a sacred duty." In the denaturalization of the priest, as
Schiller's remark and Prescott's language show, the historians considered
no trait more telling than his insensitivity to human suffering. If he was
not an active villain, this quality could be revealed through his willingness
to regard catechizing children as more important than economic survival.
Even Parkman's heroic seventeenth-century Jesuits seemed above Nature
in their "unquenchable" desire "to suffer and to die."[56] And when they were
confronted by the Huron torture of Iroquois captives, they did not "come
up to the requirements of modern sensibility." Though "offended" by such
atrocities, these Jesuits "were wholly given to the saving of souls," and they
had only "scorn" for the corrupt body, which deserved "the worst inflictions
that could be put upon it. What were a few hours of suffering to an eternity
of bliss or woe?"

This passage expresses the best priest's attitude. When his fancied duty
called him to villainous action, the priest could stage an *auto da fé,* or con-

nive at the massacre of Huguenots, or conspire for political purposes against the welfare and safety of his own Acadian parishioners, or calmly offer to confess a wounded Dutch officer in whose execution he concurred. In this last instance the confessor is a Jesuit, and, although the soldier Farnese opposes the hanging, an archbishop has asked him to carry it out "as a personal favor to himself."[57]

Naturally, then, the unnatural qualities in priests and monks enabled the historians to use them regularly as Gothic characters. Even Parkman's image of rank weeds growing in the shadow of the temple suggests the pattern. In scenes of secret execution or deep intrigue; in scenes set in the grim, quiet Escorial from which Philip II tried to govern the world; in wild, dark forest settings where enraged Indians jumped about in shadows cast by their fires; the "frantic priest" or cool "ghostly counsellor" demonstrated his Gothic lineage. His "monastic weeds" or black priestly clothes, his dark complexion, and his "elastic" morality added to the effect. And when the historian could paint devil and priest together, as Parkman did to describe a raid on the Senecas by a party of Frenchmen and Iroquois converts, the Gothic convention could have immense value:

On their left were the Iroquois converts from the missions of Saut St. Louis and the Mountain of Montreal, fighting under the influence of their ghostly prompters against their own countrymen. On the right were the pagan Indians from the west. The woods were full of these painted spectres, grotesquely horrible in horns and tail; and among them flitted the black robe of Father Engleran, the Jesuit of Michillimackinac.[58]

5

Besides contrasting the priest with simpler men and with natural feelings and morality, the historians also exploited his relationship with other Catholic characters. Many of Parkman's heroic French explorers, from La Salle onward, vehemently oppose the Jesuits, and the Jesuits fight them with intrigue. In all the histories, moreover, reactionary or corrupt kings are frequently not only "superstitious" but "priest-ridden" or "priest-led." Louis XI, Ferdinand of Aragon, Louis XIV, Louis XV, and James I ("Catholic at heart," Motley says) follow disastrous policies in close cooperation with priestcraft.[59] Prescott's representative villain is Torquemada. Parkman's appears first as Louis XIV and then as Louis XV. The father, Parkman said, had a clear, free choice between a policy of toleration and progress, and a policy of bigotry and ruin. He chose the latter, crippled the empire, and helped to cause the French Revolution. The "manifold ills" of eighteenth-century France were summed up in his son. Fearing damnation, the superstitious Louis XV tried to "propitiate Heaven by a new crusade" against the Protestant powers.[60]

Of all the representative evil men in the histories, however, the one who most closely unites Catholicism and evil is Philip II of Spain. In this amazing character the historian's duty as judge and teacher, the theories of representativeness and of racial inferiority, and the unnatural evils of priestcraft and kingcraft are harmoniously combined. Prescott called him "the most perfect type of the Spanish national character," and Motley showed even more clearly how much this statement meant. In his final arraignment of Philip before "the Judgment-seat of history" he made it very clear, first of all, that despite Philip's accomplishment of more evil than almost any man in history the "fate" of nations "is and ought to be in their own hands." From the very beginning of *The Rise of the Dutch Republic,* he had emphasized Philip's Spanishness; and although in this last pronouncement on Philip he called the Spanish people "brave and quick-witted," he insisted that "it was certainly the ignorance and superstition of the people on which the Philippian policy was founded"; that both "liberal" and "despotic" institutions grow out of "the national biography and the national character." With monotonous regularity, moreover, Motley had iterated through six volumes his belief that the only good reason for studying the crimes of king, priest, and noble was their instructive value; before sentencing Philip II, he restated this conviction.[61]

Although Motley said that Philip would not be his "head devil" again in the *United Netherlands,* the key to his final verdict, as to his entire presentation of Philip, is the Devil. In action, Philip has been described as "the great father of lies," as "more dangerous than the Turk," as a false angel of light who "murdered Christians in the name of Christ," as "the common enemy of Christendom," and as a man whose "malignity and duplicity" were almost "superhuman." Throughout the six volumes Philip has acted as an invisible, silent, mysterious manipulator who controls the fate of others from a distant, secluded writing desk. "The only plausible explanation . . . of his infamous career [was] that the man really believed himself not a king but a god."[62] Obviously in the manner of the Devil, and with a system of bribery almost as extensive as the Devil's,[63] he has bought the souls of patriots. He has not "a single virtue"; only the human being's inability to "attain perfection even in evil" has prevented him from having every possible vice. "Falsehood" is the great basis of his character, and in direct contrast to William of Orange—who was "overreached only by those to whom he gave his heart"—he is "false, most of all, to those to whom he gave what he called his heart." Having learned from Machiavelli, "the great schoolmaster of iniquity," he has even duped the Pope, robbed Catholics, betrayed his own generals.[64]

As Philip is diabolical, so is his Church. Motley never lets his reader forget Philip's title of "Most Catholic King" or his exemplary observance of forms. In the final arraignment it is extremely important both that the most powerful churchmen were "dependants" of this devil, and that the Inquisition—which worked mysteriously and punished by burning—was the instrument of his diabolical will:

He never doubted that the extraordinary theological system which he spent his life in enforcing with fire and sword was right, for it was *a part of himself*. The Holy Inquisition, thoroughly established as it was in his ancestral Spain, was a portion of the working machinery by which his absolute kingship and his superhuman will expressed themselves. A tribunal which performed its functions with a celerity, a certainty, and invisibility resembling the attributes of Omnipotence; which, like the pestilence, entered palace and hovel at will, and which smote the wretch guilty or suspected of heresy with a precision against which no human ingenuity or sympathy could guard—such an institution could not but be dear to his heart.[65]

The contrast between Motley's diabolical emphasis and Prescott's portrayal of Philip II indicates clearly just how far the romantic historians varied from each other as they worked within the same fundamental system. Prescott and Parkman were willing, and Motley reluctant, to concede that the sixteenth-century Spaniard's desire to convert American Indians had not been hypocritical.[66] But, along with Bancroft, all three treated the Spaniard's self-interest and evangelism ironically. The historians differed not on the function of Catholic morality, piety, and characters, but in the severity with which they judged individual actions and characters. As Prescott's remarks on Philip demonstrate, these differences resulted not from fundamental disagreement but from different conceptions of the techniques of judgment and narrative, different points of view required by different subjects, and differences in prose style and temperament.

After he had published the first two volumes of his unfinished *History of the Reign of Philip the Second,* Prescott wrote to his friend Pascual Gayangos about the criticisms of his treatment of Philip. Defending himself against conflicting charges of partiality to Philip and unfairness to both Philip and the Duke of Alva, he insisted that no one who had read carefully his "remarks on the Inquisition and the mischief it has caused to unhappy Spain" could call his condemnation of Philip's persecutions luke-

warm. He reminded Gayangos that it was not the persecution of Protestants, but persecution itself which "excites my indignation," and he suggested that "those who criticize my lukewarmness" might not "have felt
equally indignant if the persecution had fallen on the Catholics." Then he
generalized on the historian's duty:

I will only add that in exhibiting a character like that of P. or Alva I think the
historian gains nothing by throwing about hard names and calling the miscreant
a demon like Southey and others of that plain spoken school. I think it is better
to give a plain narrative of the events, which truly told will best convey its own
moral. I don't believe that any one ever rose from the perusal of my pages with
a love of P. or Alva either.[67]

This statement, written in the year Motley's *Rise of the Dutch Republic*
was published, is reasonably accurate. Often, of course, the epithets in
Prescott's narrative expressed as plain if not so severe a judgment as Motley's. He not only cast suspicion on "monkish bookmen," but also showed
surprise that any priest had seen the merit in Columbus' ideas. Yet he did
try to present clearly the Catholic's position—usually reserving his formal
judgment for paragraphs that followed his "plain narrative," and for his
final review of the subject's character in the conventional obituary essay.
He did not call Philip II a demon; he criticized Motley for the unrelieved
blackness of his portrayal; and he praised Bancroft for letting the reader
"judge for himself" how much "knavery" and how much "fanaticism"
motivated the actors in the Salem witchcraft episode.[68]

Of the other, less theoretical reasons for the difference, the most important is point of view. My discussion of Prescott's Isabella has already shown
that (as Theodore Parker saw immediately) Prescott was no model of
impartiality when defending the fair name of his heroine. Even more
pertinent to the *History of Philip the Second* is his attitude toward Charles
Brockden Brown. After he had written his complimentary essay on Brown
for Sparks's *Library of American Biography,* he confessed in his journal that
he did not like Brown well enough to finish reading "one of his novels,
unless as a job." But in spite of his own judgment, Prescott said, the biographer had to present as "favorable a view" of his subject as the evidence allowed. He hoped that his "halting or overleaping praise" would betray his
adverse judgment of Brown "quite as much as my censure [might have
done]."[69] Therefore, although he did criticize with varying severity the
faults of Isabella, Ferdinand, Cortés, Pizarro, and Philip II, one must remember that Prescott wrote Spanish history, that he narrated much of the
action from the Spanish point of view, and that he felt obliged to emphasize

the virtues and progressive achievements of Spanish characters. In his frank letter criticizing Motley's severity to Philip, he took "comfort" from "the reflection that you are looking thro a pair of Dutch spectacles after all."[70]

In Motley's histories Spain and Catholic leaders are the enemy. Motley does not mention Philip II in connection with the victory at Lepanto; Prescott describes it as a progressive victory. Motley says little of Spanish literature during Philip's reign; Prescott describes it favorably. Motley uses the Escorial only as a symbol of Philip's egotism and the scene of his mysterious manipulations; Prescott describes it as a monument to his piety, however "gloomy," misguided, and disastrous that piety was. Motley says that Philip had not "a single virtue"; Prescott, who considers Philip pious, treats his independence of the Pope, and some of his administrative changes, as political accomplishments. Motley scorns Philip's "contemptible intellect," his miserable handwriting, his "sluggishness"; for him, Philip's habit of poring over "interminable dispatches" illustrates a pedestrian mind's concern with trivia. Prescott commends Philip's interest in art and architecture, the architectural achievements of his administration; for him, the dispatch-reading and -writing illustrate administrative industry. Motley blames Philip directly for Spanish atrocities at St. Quentin; Prescott says that Philip, "touched" to the "heart," instantly ordered an end to personal violence, although it was impossible to prevent the customary pillage. The "chief amusement" of Motley's Philip is to be "grossly licentious . . . in the common haunts of vice"; his William, on the other hand, is so thoroughly virtuous that the sudden appearance of his "natural son" in the *United Netherlands* (without comment from Motley) comes as a complete surprise. Prescott's Philip is not licentious; but his William, who has followed Machiavellian rules in arranging his second marriage, is "addicted to gallantries, which continued long enough, it is said, to suggest an apology for the disorderly conduct of his wife."[71]

The final distinction is stylistic and temperamental. Prescott did not command so explosive a rhetoric as Motley's. Even when both men condemn the same crimes or institutions (the Inquisition and the secret execution of Montigny), Prescott's judgment seems much less severe; their language on these subjects differs more than their opinions. The stronger force of Motley's images and epithets, his vigorous use of alliteration, his long periodic sentences; his use of incremental repetition, of cumulative details, of Elizabethan prose rhythms, and of Saxon monosyllables—these seem to express a much sharper judgment than do Prescott's more stately sentences.

Motley, moreover, seems to have been much more eager to "pitch into" an evil character. He enjoyed writing a racy, forceful paragraph on a royal villain. His histories contain a whole gallery of royal rogues, from Charles V to James I. Before he had even begun to study about Philip II, he was able to write a paragraph which, while it anticipates his own judgment of Philip, has no rhetorical parallel in all the works of Prescott. The passage condemns Peter the Great for the "judicial murder" of his son (a crime similar to Philip's alleged execution of Don Carlos):

Up to this time Peter seems a man—a hard-hearted, despotic man, perhaps—but he is still human. He now seems only a machine, a huge engine of unparalleled power, placed upon the earth to effect a certain task, working its mighty arms night and day with ceaseless and untiring energy, crashing through all obstacles, and annihilating everything in its path with the unfeeling precision of gigantic mechanism.[72]

Prescott never used this kind of image. He did not write of "blood-dripping edicts," he never called a Pope a "querulous dotard," and he wrote no letters about "pitch[ing] into the Duke of Alva and Philip the Second."[73] Motley's political speeches, his Civil War letters, and the tone of his histories reveal an intensity of emotional participation—and sometimes a vindictiveness—that one cannot find in the writings of Prescott, whose letters and histories consistently show a temperament more tolerant, more urbane.

6

I have not included Bancroft in my discussion of the villainous priest, because there is no place in his *History* for the character. His objections to Catholicism as a religion of forms, and to its reactionary role in the history of progress and the early history of America, are perfectly clear in his *History*. He was able to bring out the rhetoric of the Reformation for his description of the principles involved in the Seven Years' War; among the medieval sights of which "all Europe had grown weary" were "idlers and beggars, sheltering themselves in sanctuaries," and "the countless monks and priests, whose vows of celibacy tempted to licentiousness." But he had said in his second volume that "priestcraft had no motive to emigrate," and the priestcraft in his *History* is European priestcraft. The individual priests who do appear in his volumes are the early Jesuit martyrs, whom he praises for their purity and heroic devotion. Some of his corrupted European villains, however, bear the conventional stamp. General William Howe, described immediately after George Washington, has the proper markings: "Six feet tall, of an uncommonly dark complexion, a coarse frame, and a sluggish mould, he was unresistingly ruled by his sensual nature."[74]

In a letter from Berlin, moreover, Bancroft wrote perhaps the best summary of the romantic historians' treatment of Catholicism. It is an angry letter, one of several he wrote from Berlin during five years when it seemed to him that an ultramontane conspiracy was trying once again to sustain tyranny against natural laws—laws which, in this battle, were defended by Bismarck and Germany.[75] The letter repeats in one paragraph nearly all the kinds of objection raised against Catholicism in the romantic histories:

Many, very many, all too many ways lead to Rome. Idleness leads there; for Rome saves the trouble of independent thought. Dissoluteness leads there, for it impairs mental vigor. Conservatism, foolish conservatism, leads there, in the hope that the conservatism of the oldest abuse will be a shield for all abuses. Sensualism leads there, for it delights in parade and magnificent forms. Materialism leads there, for the superstitious can adore an image and think to become purified by bodily torments, hair-shirts, and fastings, turning all religion into acts of the physical organs.[76]

Bancroft's objection to "bodily torments" is especially interesting, because Parkman criticized the same peculiarity not as materialism but as unnatural unworldliness, a loathing of the flesh. Yet Parkman, too, criticized the excessive materialism in the Catholic missionary's presentation of Christian truth; this appeal to the senses, indeed, was what made the greatest impression on the Indians.[77] Catholicism was at the same time too unworldly and too materialistic.

Bancroft's letter is representative not in its vehemence but in its reliance on a belief in intellectual liberty and its assumption that "Rome" opposes this liberty. One must notice, too, that Bancroft was at times more tolerant of Catholic piety; for the most vehement criticisms of Catholicism in the romantic histories were provoked by "unnatural" political policies, by some form of active tyranny, and by historical lapses from simple morality. It was possible, but difficult, to be an "obedient" Catholic and a progressive "Christian." Evidence of the Church's political influence abounded in Spain and New France, two supremely Catholic countries. The one was "the bulwark of the Church, against whose adamantine wall the waves of innovation beat in vain"; the symbols of colonization in the other were "a musket, a rosary, and a pack of beaver skins."[78] The one expelled its most industrious population because they were infidels; the other never let them in, because they were heretics. The stifling of free thought, free trade, free immigration—these seemed to be the natural results of a religion that misdirected piety to "images," taught that the end justifies the means, and required its priests to stifle the affections of Nature.

CHAPTER VI

The Infidel: Vanishing Races

*The picture of the unequal contest inspires a compassion
which is honorable to humanity. The weak demand sympathy.
If a melancholy interest attaches to the fall of a hero, who is overpowered by superior force, shall we not drop a tear at the fate
of nations, whose defeat foreboded exile, if it did not indeed
shadow forth the decline and ultimate extinction of a race?*

BANCROFT, *History*

*And thus forever with reverted look
The mystic volume of the world they read,
Spelling it backward, like a Hebrew book,
Till life became a Legend of the Dead.*

LONGFELLOW, "The Jewish Cemetery
at Newport"

Besides the Teutonic nations and the "southern" Catholics, Bancroft,
Prescott, and Parkman portrayed, among them, three other "races." Indian, Moor, and Jew round out the cast of antiprogressive characters in the
romantic histories, and in portraying them all three historians again followed literary convention. The Indians posed some perplexing moral problems for Bancroft and Prescott, but the literary conventions allowed the
historians to use these "races," too, as valuable illustrations of progressive
law, and to fulfill the sentimental requirements of contemporary fiction.
In their relationship to progress, their sentimental and moral function, and
some of their "racial traits," Indian, Moor, and Jew were literary kindred.

I

In Bancroft's system the Indian was an anomaly. Like the Connecticut
colonists, he was "near to nature"; like Daniel Boone, "ever fond of tracking the deer on foot"; like George Washington, "a pupil of the wilderness."
Almost wholly dependent on Nature and his own instincts for instruction
and livelihood, he lived in the most extreme simplicity. Yet his nearness

to Nature was embarrassing. He might seem a valuable property when one wanted to prove that language was the gift of Providence rather than the product of civilization; Bancroft, following Emerson's *Nature*, argued that even the Indian dialects were vocal symbols of Nature. But lacking the corrupt motives of George III and Parliament for opposing American progress, the Indian stood squarely in the path of the English colonies, which were growing according to natural law. He was an incorrigible pagan. Nearer to Nature than the simple Greeks had been, he had almost nothing to show for his opportunity: no Homer, no "gentle philosophers," no simple architects and sculptors. He was deficient in the faculty of abstraction, and his "knowledge of architecture [was] surpassed both in strength and durability by the skill of the beaver."[1]

The answer to this problem lay in a distinction between simplicity and barbarism. The Indian was little more than a part of physical Nature; "not yet disenthralled from Nature," he was "still in that earliest stage of intellectual culture where reflection has not yet begun." Nature, then, held him to what Bancroft considered the most damnable conclusion of Voltaire's philosophy, "the despotism of the senses":

As the languages of the American tribes were limited by the material world, so, in private life, the senses held dominion. The passion of the savage was liberty; he demanded license to gratify his animal instincts. To act out himself, to follow the propensities of his nature, seemed his system of morals. The supremacy of conscience, the rights of reason, were not subjects of reflection for those who had no name for continence. . . . their love never became a frenzy or a devotion; for indulgence destroyed its energy and its purity.

It was a virtue for the natural man to "follow the propensities of his nature," but the Indian was not natural; he was savage.[2]

To clarify this distinction, Bancroft used a device that Parkman also used again and again. He placed the Indian in "harmony" with the wildest of forest settings, emphasizing the sublime, Gothic characteristics of Nature in the New York of 1609. This was a scene in which "sombre forests shed a melancholy grandeur over the useless magnificence of nature," a scene made grotesque by "the fantastic forms of withered limbs," a scene where "reptiles sported in the stagnant pools." "Vegetable life and death were mingled hideously together. The horrors of corruption frowned on the fruitless fertility of uncultivated nature." The Indian, of course,

was wild as the savage scene, in harmony with the rude nature by which he was surrounded; a vagrant over the continent, in constant warfare with his fellow man; . . . his religion the adoration of nature; his morals the promptings of undisciplined instinct; disputing with wolves and bears the lordship of the soil.

Against this scene Bancroft placed the Arcadian order in which the natural man of the nineteenth century lived a useful, virtuous life. There, man was "still in harmony with nature, which he has subdued, cultivated, and adorned. . . . The passions of society are chastened into purity; manners are made benevolent by civilization; and the virtue of the country is the guardian of its peace."[3]

Had the Indian's condition before the European invasion been the only problem, this distinction might have sufficed, with slight changes in emphasis and rhetoric, for Bancroft found some evidence on which to base hope for improvement. In conflicts between the corrupted European and the Indian, he was able to show that the corruptions of the thralls of tyranny were often worse than those of Nature's bondmen. Bancroft's Indian never submitted to the persecutions of priestcraft; he had at least the instinct of religion, and he never succumbed, as did the eighteenth-century materialist, to a "worship of humanity." Although he was a "faithless treaty-breaker," he did not "exalt falsehood into the dignity of a political science." He had no fear of death, he believed in immortality, his political organizations were democratic, and he respected the marriage vows. In conflict with a De Soto or even a Frontenac, such Indians could be described as "wild republicans."[4]

What made the distinction unsatisfactory was the problem of progress. One had to defend the Indian not only to prove that some of his customs and instincts were superior to corrupt "civilized" practices, but also to show "that the moral affections are planted everywhere," that the human race is one. As the Jeffersonian had done, Bancroft argued that "the fellowship which we should cherish with the race, receives the Comanche warrior and the Caffre within the pale of equality. Their functions may not have been exercised, but they exist." There was an "exact correspondence" between the powers of Caucasian and Indian, but a "comparison" of the powers in different races showed "the existence of degrees." The Indian was "inferior in reason and the moral qualities," and this inferiority was not "simply attached to the individual; it is connected with organization, and is the characteristic of the race." The Indian, it is true, had made some progress by learning to use modern weapons and farming tools, and the Cherokees had even increased in population. But Bancroft added this hopeful information only after a long argument leading to gloomy conclusions respecting the Indians' moral "inflexibility."[5]

How could Nature be relieved of responsibility for the Indian's failings? If the Indian had the instinct to worship a supreme Deity, why had he not been quick to embrace the truths of Christianity? Marie de l'Incarnation had said that the Indian showed "even a greater tendency to devotion" than the Frenchman; but Bancroft had to report that the total efforts of the Jesuits, Roger Williams, John Eliot, Jonathan Edwards, David Brainerd, and the Quakers and Moravians had failed to instruct or elevate the Indian. Even enrollment at Harvard College "could not close the gulf between the Indian character and the Anglo-American." Human progress was a natural law, but the Indian, one with Nature, clung to the Past as tightly as the corrupt prelacy of France:

The copper-colored men are characterized by a moral inflexibility, a rigidity of attachment to their hereditary customs and manners. The birds and brooks, as they chime forth their unwearied canticles, chime them ever to the same ancient melodies; and the Indian child, as it grows up, displays a propensity to the habits of its ancestors.[6]

This view of the Indian foretold his doom in all his conflicts with natural men in Bancroft's *History*. Bancroft's treatment of the Indian follows a fairly consistent pattern. When the Indian stands alone against the corrupted European, he represents natural virtue; when he clashes with the natural man, he is an opponent of progress, often a merciless butcher of defenseless mothers, maidens, and babes.

The point of view can even shift within the account of a given episode. Bancroft's account of South Carolina's Indian relations during the Seven Years' War shows how the method worked when an antiprogressive governor and natural colonists were involved at different stages of the conflict. Lyttleton, the royal governor, had been trying to reestablish his authority over the colonists, and his love of power and lack of natural understanding brought on a war with the Cherokees: "He could not discern in the red man's morals the eternal principles which inspire all justice; and as he brought the maxims of civilized society into conflict with the unwritten law of the Cherokees, the European rule proved the most treacherous and cruel." In 1758 "the backwoodsmen of Virginia" had killed and scalped several of their Cherokee allies—as punishment for a series of thefts. The Cherokees, following their eye-for-an-eye code, had killed the same number of colonists, and had then sued for peace. The South Carolina legislature had consented—for the natural man understood "eternal principles"—but Lyttleton, representing royal authority, "could not hear the voice of humanity as it spoke from the glades." Insisting on war, he executed twenty-seven Indians who had come to sue for peace. In turn, although they had captured 200 Englishmen, the Cherokees executed four officers and twenty-three privates. "The Cherokees were very exact in that number, as being the amount of hostages Lyttleton had killed to start the war." They still wanted peace, but Lyttleton would not treat with them.[7]

In narrating this episode Bancroft sympathized entirely with the Indians. He stated their grievances carefully and pointed out their integrity and their loyalty to the colonists against the French. A logical conclusion would have been to take the Cherokees' point of view in describing the war. Bancroft, however, used the same method that William Gilmore Simms had used in *The Yemassee*; after he had presented a good case for the Indian, he shifted his sympathies as soon as the colonists became involved against them. In this battle the change came when the Indians ambushed "the provincials": "the Highlanders and provincials drove the enemy from their lurking-places; and returning to their yells three huzzas and three waves of their bonnets and hats, they chased them from height and hollow."[8]

Here the Indian, though "inferior" in moral capacity, represents eternal principles of justice and "the voice of humanity" until the colonists' entry into the war consigns him to a "lurking-place." Had the corrupted European alone collided with the Indian, Bancroft might have been able to praise consistently the Indian's resistance to unjustified encroachment on his rights. Had the Indian been capable of adapting himself quickly to civilization and Christianity, he would have fitted neatly into the progressive pattern. But contact with civilized man began his degradation, and when he became dependent on civilization, he was at the mercy of both corrupt and virtuous European.

Natural law was another problem. When the Indian tried to retain possession of his own land, he was certainly in harmony with a natural law. Bancroft had no great problem so long as he was describing the record of New Englanders, who "had never, except in the territory of the Pequods, taken possession of a foot of land without first obtaining land title from the Indians." Unlike Washington Irving, he did not pass moral judgment on the prices paid or on what the colonists' purchase did to Indian ability to make a livelihood.[9]

There was only one real solution to this problem, and that solution violated Bancroft's contention that no natural law can contradict another. By invoking the natural law that guaranteed him his native lands, the Indian obstructed progress, represented by the American who sought new dominions for the common man. Guided by a favoring Providence, the colonists were an irresistible force. "Nothing," Bancroft said, "could restrain the Americans from peopling the wilderness." The final appeal, then, was to what Theodore Parker called the international principle of eminent domain, what John L. O'Sullivan called Manifest Destiny, what Prescott and Bancroft called, simply, destiny. Bancroft's Indian chief knew as well as Simms's Sanutee, Cooper's Chingachgook, and Prescott's Montezuma which was the higher law. After the colonists had pushed back the Chero-kee frontier more than seventy miles, Attakulla-kulla went to Charleston to ask for peace. " 'As to what has happened,' he added, 'I believe it has been ordered by our Great Father above.' " The Indians, Bancroft said, "knew that they had come into the presence of a race more powerful than their own; and the course of their destiny was irrevocably changed."[10]

This was not, for the transcendentalist, a perfect answer, because of the conflict of natural laws. But it was at least the better choice in a plain di-lemma. Arguing that the Indian had never had a right to his lands would have denied him the rights of Nature, denied that "the gifts of mind and heart" were universally diffused, and denied the unity of the race. At the same time, the destinarian method gave the historian the same sentimental advantages enjoyed by dramatists and historical romancers. He could now sympathize with both sides. The Indian could be the heroic child of Nature destined to death or exile in the cause of human freedom; serving history by touching the reader's heart and—in the best manner of the fiction of sensibility—calling forth his more benevolent instincts. Bancroft made it quite clear that the "compassion" inspired by contemplation of the In-dian's sad destiny is "honorable to humanity." Under this dispensation it was even possible to explain the Indian's method of fighting without doing him too much dishonor. Although his attacks on innocent civilians still left him open to pejorative language, the Indian's awareness of his fate explained his general ferocity:

The individual, growing giddy by danger, rushes, as it were, towards his fate; so did the Indians of New England. Frenzy prompted their rising. It was but the storm in which the ancient inhabitants of the land were to vanish away. They rose without hope, and therefore they fought without mercy. For them as a nation, there was no tomorrow.[11]

The problem of the colonists' land title also disappeared. The New Englanders and the first Kentuckians had paid for their land, but the gen-eral movement beyond the Alleghanies did not depend on a conveyance of title from the Indians: "Every where an intrepid, hardy and industrious population was moving westward through all the gates of the Alleghanies; . . . accepting from Nature their title deeds to the unoccupied wilderness."[12]

2

The Indian's complex role as child of Nature, slave to his "animal instincts," and sentimental victim of destiny must be kept constantly in mind by anyone who compares Bancroft's and Parkman's histories. It is well known that Parkman, relying on his own experience of western Indians, set out to prove that the Indian was no fit subject for the romances in which some nineteenth-century fiction and poetry had cast him. But the difference between Parkman's attitude and that of other writers has been exaggerated.[13] Even Bancroft's most laudatory language shows agreement with Parkman's contention that the Indian race was inferior. And Bancroft also used extremely uncomplimentary rhetoric when he described the Indian as an ally of reaction. The British government's most unnatural crime during the Revolution had been the hiring of German mercenaries and the encouragement of slaves and Indians to fight against the colonists. The French, Bancroft said, had had more reason than the English for using Indian allies, for they had adopted the policy "from despair at their own relative inferiority in numbers," and they had not been fighting against "their own colonies and kindred." What made the use of the Indian worse was his barbarous method of fighting:

. . . he was a deadly foe only as he skulked in ambush; or prowled on the frontier; or burned the defenceless farmhouse; or struck the laborer in the field; or smote the mother at her household task; or crashed the infant's head against the rock or a tree; or tortured the prisoner on whose flesh he was to gorge.[14]

Here the tone, revealed largely through Bancroft's monosyllabic verbs, is very close to Parkman's.

Although Parkman measured the moral actions of many countries and individuals against the natural standard, he was not so intent as Bancroft on proving a "natural" thesis. His subject, too, helps to account for differences between his emphasis and Bancroft's. In Parkman's "forest drama" individual exploits and small skirmishes were much more important than in Bancroft's history of English colonization and the Revolution. Parkman was unencumbered by the details of English colonial problems, of English mercantile policies, of the settlement and growth of English colonial towns, and of the Revolutionary battles. Indian diplomacy and Indian methods of fighting had a prominent place in his history. Before considering Parkman's Indians, one should also notice Parkman's own delineation of the issue in two frank letters that he wrote to Bancroft in 1882. The indefatigable Bancroft, at eighty-two, was revising his *History*, and he had asked Parkman to send him a list of errors in the ten volumes. Parkman could not "recall a single point where the statement of fact seems to me to call for correction." He suggested, however, that Bancroft's "interpretation of the facts" (a question, he confessed, "of opinion") had not always agreed with his own. When Bancroft, persisting, asked for details, Parkman discussed only two major questions: Bancroft's partiality to the colonial legislatures, including the Quaker-dominated Assembly in Pennsylvania, in his account of their struggle with royal governors over funds for defending the West; and Bancroft's partiality to the Acadians whom the English had expelled. He did not criticize Bancroft's Indian.[15]

The difference between Parkman's and Bancroft's treatment of the Indian is a difference of degree, based largely on different reactions to three "traits" that the Indian revealed during the colonial period: his use of deceit in diplomacy, his method of fighting, and his cruelty. With a much more elaborate role in Parkman's history than in Bancroft's, the Indian displays these unattractive "characteristics" more consistently there than in Bancroft's work.

Even in his long "philosophical" discussion of Indian habits and traits, Parkman used much more consistently critical language than Bancroft's, -although both described the same "faults." Instead of vacillating between a kind and a critical judgment, as Bancroft's language seems to do, Parkman's prose is that of a man who, convinced that the race is inferior, has organized his essay clearly around his conviction. Thus, while Bancroft had said that the Indian was deficient in the faculty of abstraction, Parkman concluded his discussion of religion with a blunt announcement: "The primitive Indian, yielding his untutored homage to One All-pervading and Omnipotent Spirit, is a dream of poets, rhetoricians, and sentimentalists." Although these differences in emphasis produce a different over-all effect, the Indian's function in the scheme of progress is the same in both histories, and in both he has the same limitations. He is baffled by abstractions, dominated by his senses, limited to materialism, difficult to improve, addicted to treachery, loose in morals, irresolute in formal combat.[16]

In Parkman's "forest drama" the Indian's role was more often that of Bancroft's "skulker" than that of his "wild republican." Parkman said that the savage lived in a stage of culture that had not yet developed the concept of honor. Echoing Scott's statement that all children are habitual liars, he confessed that even "the barbarous ancestors of our own frank and manly race" had been "prone to treachery and deceit." But within eight pages he was again alluding to "the deep dissimulation which seems native to [Indian] blood." Two later examples of Indian honor were only "a ray of light out of Egyptian darkness" to show that "the principle of honor was not extinct in these wild hearts."[17] However persuasive the "childhood" theory might have been, it was apt to be forgotten in a fast-moving dramatic narrative in which the historian's sympathies and moral preferences were engaged. The key to Parkman's portrayal of the Indians is in their place in his drama.

From the very beginning Parkman's hostile Indians form an integral part of the wild forest scene. By using the Indians' own imagery, he portrays them as forest beasts. The widespread group of tribes which Frontenac tried to keep together as allies was, for example, "like a vast menagerie of wild animals; and the lynx bristled at the wolf, and the panther grinned fury at the bear, in spite of all [Frontenac's] efforts." The connotation, however, more often displays the European's than the Indian's attitude toward the animal, and "panther" and "wolf" are Parkman's favorite epithets for fighting Indians. The forest, too, is consistently characterized in this imagery. In *The Conspiracy of Pontiac*, the "surrounding forests" of the West are "peopled by a race dark and subtle as their own sunless mazes." In *Montcalm and Wolfe*, the marauding Indians, "a pack of human wolves," are "sudden as the leaping panther"; they would not have been so terrifying, Parkman says, had they lived on the open plains,

but the forest was everywhere, rolled over hill and valley in billows of interminable green,—a leafy maze, a mystery of shade, a universal hiding-place, where murder might lurk unseen at its victim's side, and Nature seemed formed to nurse the mind with wild imaginings.[18]

This is not only the Gothic Nature that Bancroft used and that Prescott praised Brockden Brown for describing; it is the Nature of Herman Melville—wild, "subtle," deceptive; overpowering the individual settler with an appalling loneliness and a hidden terror. By the time he wrote *A Half-Century of Conflict*, Parkman was incorporating Darwinism into this kind of picture, but the fundamental relationship of Indian and forest remained the same. Describing the "savage waste of vegetation" in the ancient forest of Maine, he wrote a brief essay on the constant, brutal war of the plants and trees—"the same struggle for existence and mutual havoc that mark all organized beings, from men to mushrooms." Using the same device of contrasting points of view that Melville had used in *Pierre*, Parkman again emphasized the deceptive appearance of the forest: "Seen from above, their mingled tops spread in a sea of verdure basking in light; seen from below, all is shadow, through which spots of timid sunshine steal down among the legions of lank, mossy trunks, toadstools and rank ferns, protruding bushes, and rotting carcasses of fallen trees."[19]

One cannot make a Melville out of Parkman; this passage is part of an ill-executed analogy which compares the suffocation of young saplings in the forest and the leveling that "is said" to go on in a "democratic society." One must recognize, however, that the passage depicts a deceptively vicious tangle of which the Indians form a harmonious part. Parkman moves from "this grim solitude" to "the life and light" in its "countless streams and lakes," then to "its beasts of prey"—including "savage, cowardly, and mean" wolves—and finally to "the human denizens of this wilderness." Quickly, then, he recounts another example of these denizens' duplicity.[20]

The Iroquois, especially, are a consistently destructive force of Nature. From Champlain to Montcalm, they are "the destroyers," "the scourge of Canada." It would have been factually accurate for Parkman, especially in his first four volumes, to devote only a single chapter to the Iroquois' destructive effect on French evangelism and colonization. He chose instead to bring them onto his stage periodically, trying to approximate the terror of their constant presence in the wings and the suddenness of their attacks. By this method and by his manipulation of point of view, he conveys the impression that the Iroquois were a really determining force in the ruin of French plans. There were, of course, many reasons why the Jesuit missions failed, but always present, always the same while other conditions changed, was the Iroquois terror. Whenever diplomatic or religious victory seemed achieved, there were the Iroquois to destroy the priests' gains. The imagery, often trite, is consistently natural: a "portentous cloud of war," a storm "gathering in the east," "the crash of a thunderbolt." In less hackneyed imagery, Parkman associates the Iroquois with other natural blights: "Famine, destitution, disease, and the Iroquois were making Canada their prey." And he makes their regularity seem as certain as Nature's: "Spring came at length, and brought with it the swallows, the bluebirds, and the Iroquois."[21]

Natural imagery, however, did not suffice. Parkman's fighting Indian was not only man and wolf; he was "man, wolf, and devil, all in one." With a consistency and thoroughness rivaled only by Cotton Mather's

Decennium Luctuosum, Parkman emphasized supernatural as well as natural analogies to Indian behavior. Indian duplicity was, of course, one of the qualities in this portrayal, for the Indians were "forest Machiavels." Parkman also used his own experience of the western Indians' facial characteristics to add force to the caricature. In a passage in *La Salle*, frankly based on his own experience, he described what La Salle's aide Tonty must have seen when the Iroquois attacked the Illinois: "the contorted forms, bounding, crouching, twisting, to deal or dodge the shot; the small keen eyes that shone like an angry snake's; the parted lips pealing their fiendish yells; the painted features writhing with fear and fury, and every passion of an Indian fight."[22]

The diabolical imagery gains its power not only from this emphasis on "fiendish" appearance, but also (as in Mather's *Decennium Luctuosum*) from the Indian's invisibility, his ubiquity, and the difficulty of catching him. And all of these qualities grow more mysterious in the ghastly forest. "The Iroquois were everywhere, and nowhere." The Iroquois "seemed invulnerable as ghosts." "To hunt Indians with an endless forest behind them was like chasing shadows." The Indians were "a wily enemy, silent and secret as fate, choosing their own time and place of attack." Retreating Indians "glided away through the gloom with the silence of shadows." The Indian attacked stealthily, fled mysteriously into the forest which was as much "his element" as the sea was a sailor's, and disliked "civilized" warfare in the open. Pontiac, the most gifted Indian leader, was "the Satan of this forest paradise."[23]

One explanation for all this rhetoric is, of course, Parkman's desire to bring history alive on his pages, to re-create the actual experience. The ghost imagery, and even the simile invoking the snake's eyes, can be justified in this way, especially in Parkman's account of what a character such as Tonty, or a settler returning to his clearing after an Indian attack on his family, must have felt. The devil comparison, moreover, had been made by some of the Jesuits themselves before Cotton Mather wrote his *Decennium Luctuosum*. But Parkman does not always maintain this integrity in point of view. The rhetoric often reveals Parkman's own judgment of Indian appearance, Indian tactics, Indian character, and he himself seems to become a partisan. Montcalm, for example, has advised the defeated English officers to stave in their rum barrels before letting the French and Indian force take over, and the English have followed his advice;

but the Indians were drunk already with homicidal rage, and the glitter of their vicious eyes told of the devil within. They roamed among the tents, intrusive, insolent, their visages besmirched with war-paint; grinning like fiends as they handled, in anticipation of the knife, the long hair of cowering women, of whom, as well as of children, there were many in the camp, all crazed with fright.

Parkman might use the survival of the fittest to explain the development of Iroquois cruelty, but his picture of the fighting Indians and their forest had evolved from the seventeenth century.[24]

One can defend the battle cries of Parkman's Indians on the same ground of accuracy. But they also reinforce the diabolical impression, and Parkman uses them to distinguish Indian racial traits from "white" traits, savage from civilized man. At the crisis of a battle between Indians and "whites," the romantic historian is apt to distinguish between "the deliberate courage" of civilized man and the "impulse of savage passion." The words are Bancroft's, but Parkman underscores the same distinction. Reminiscent of Prescott's juxtaposition of French "impetuosity" and Spanish "coolness," this idea is often reserved for battles in which the Indian is not necessarily cruel or vicious. Like Bancroft's "huzzas," Parkman's "shouts and cheers" suggest harmoniously the "whites' " "steadiness and coolness in using their guns"; the Indians' "whoops," wolf-like "howls," and "enraged yells" accompany their "greater agility and skill in hiding and sheltering themselves." Like the contrast between French and Spanish character, this contrast displays the "rock-like strength of the Anglo-Saxon," against which "all the combined tribes of the forest might have chafed in vain rage."[25]

One feature of Parkman's portrayal of the unattractive in Indian culture has no counterpart in Bancroft or Prescott; it is the sense of grotesque, repulsive dirt that overpowered a civilized gentleman who visited an Indian village. Into the Indian village scenes scattered throughout his history Parkman regularly paints the "shrivelled hags" of the village. Their condition not only invalidates the ideal picture of Indian love that had been painted by "poets and sentimentalists," but it also stands as a severe indictment of Indian culture. In his long essay on the Indians Parkman has already remarked that "the Huron woman" was a "wanton" before marriage and "a drudge" afterward, and he has used this information to explain the number of hags who snarl in every village. Later, in the scene dramatizing the Jesuits' first baptism of a Huron adult, he contrasts the splendor of the priests' ceremonial equipment with the Indians' squalor:

It was a strange scene. Indians were there in throngs, and the house was closely packed: warriors, old and young, glistening in grease and sunflower-oil, with uncouth locks, a trifle less coarse than a horse's mane, and faces perhaps smeared with paint in honor of the occasion; wenches in gay attire; hags muffled in a filthy discarded deerskin, their leathery visages corrugated with age and malice, and their hard, glittering eyes riveted on the spectacle before them.[26]

Whether the Indian was a "child" with "the passions of a devil," a "wily" enemy, or merely a childlike savage "unstable as water," all the characteristics that I have described support the fundamental justification for the Anglo-Saxon's conquest of the continent. For Parkman as well as Bancroft, that justification was progressive destiny. Pausing to survey the forest before beginning his account of Pontiac's War, Parkman, too, emphasized the vast area of "waste fertility," where only a few Indian squaws "turned the black mould" in an occasional meadow. Despite the sadness with which he viewed the passing of the forest and of the Indian's highest virtues, he considered it inevitable and proper that an energetic race colonizing according to natural law would cover the continent and use it more efficiently.[27]

But this aggressively unsentimental picture of the Indian race did not prevent Parkman from exploiting the sentimental value of Indian destiny. Even his worst tribes have a positive progressive role, a clear instructive value, and when their destiny becomes most clear he withholds his severest rhetoric and uses their sad fate to illustrate the cost of progress.

The Indian's chief virtue, like that of Parkman's good Jesuit missionaries, is courage and endurance. Although he can rarely attain the "whites'" courage in open battle, or their concept of honesty, the Indian can endure extreme torture without effeminate complaint, and he has a characteristic respect for the European's martial courage. Bloodthirsty and treacherous though they often are, the Iroquois are morally superior to the Hurons and to the Illinois, and this superiority determines the fate of both. Indeed, Parkman's Iroquois even teach a moral lesson to corrupt European officials. They are the agents of retribution against the venal La Barre, the contemptible governor of New France whom Parkman characterizes as a lawyer rather than a soldier. The eloquence of their leader Big Mouth reproves La Barre's dishonesty, declares the Iroquois' independence of both French and English, and demonstrates the justified contempt that La Barre's "rhodomontade" and cowardice have inspired in the brave Indians.[28]

The spirit of nationality was so important to these historians that Parkman used the Iroquois' exemplary political union as a moral example for the Anglo-Saxon himself. In his essay on Indian culture, Parkman said that no nation since Sparta had "fused" individual and national life so completely as did the Iroquois; and in *Montcalm and Wolfe* he used the courage, eloquence, and nationalism of an Iroquois chief to emphasize the worst political fault of the English colonies. Sneering at English cowardice after the English had retreated from Crown Point, an Onondaga chief lectured an American delegation on courage and preparedness: " 'You desire us to speak from the bottom of our hearts, and we shall do it. Look at the French: they are men; they are fortifying everywhere. But you are all like women, bare and open, without fortification.' " The scene was the Albany Congress of 1754; before introducing Franklin's plan of union, Parkman mentioned a contemporary writer who also "held up the Five Nations for emulation." Neither the Crown nor the colonies were as wise as the Iroquois orator, and both rejected Franklin's plan.[29]

Like many antiprogressive Europeans, Parkman's antiprogressive Iroquois were, from the very beginning of his history, involuntary agents of progress. As "destroyers," they were the "obvious" cause of the failure of the Jesuit missions; although the will of Providence must have seemed "dark and inexplicable" to the Jesuits, Parkman said, it was "clear as the sun at noon" to anyone looking from the viewpoint of "Liberty." As Liberty could thank "the fatuity of Louis XV and his Pompadour," she owed thanks to "the Iroquois, that, by their insensate fury, the plans of her adversary were brought to nought, and a peril and a woe averted from her future." In the seventeenth century they destroyed the western allies of the French; a hundred years later they forgot what their "cooler judgment" must have told them, that French and Indian interests were one, and they foolishly helped to destroy New France.[30]

While engaged in savage battle, Parkman's Indian is contemptible or loathsome, but when confronted by his destiny he is pathetic. In the long "march of humanity" the Iroquois represents an inevitable casualty. He appears at his noblest when he recognizes his doom in the actions of the two European powers between whom his tribes have been squeezed. An Onondaga chief tells Sir William Johnson, the Indians' best friend among colonial officials, that

"we don't know what you Christians, English and French, intend. . . . We are so hemmed in by you both that we have hardly a hunting-place left. In a little while, if we find a bear in a tree, there will immediately appear an owner of the land to claim the property and hinder us from killing it, by which we live. We are so perplexed between you that we hardly know what to say or think."

This is the lament of Natty Bumppo, and the only humane response is Bancroft's "tear of compassion." There are no tears in Parkman, but the

leaders of a race doomed to vanish stand up and speak eloquently of the
cruelty of civilized progress, the pretentiousness of European royalty. Before reporting the speech of the Onondaga chief who laughs at the English as "women" without fortifications, Parkman quotes his blunt reproof
of both England and France: " 'The Governor of Virginia and the Governor of Canada are quarreling about lands which belong to us, and their
quarrel may end in our destruction.' "[31]

   The most pathetic victims of destiny in Parkman's history are the
Hurons ("A Doomed Nation"), the Acadians, and those Canadians who
are trapped between the conflicting threats of their own governor and
General Wolfe. As in Bancroft, the behavior of Parkman's Indians "when
the knell of their common ruin had already sounded" hastens their
ruin. "It was a strange and miserable spectacle" to see the Indians, "in this
crisis of their destiny, . . . tearing each other's throats in a wolfish fury,
joined to an intelligence that served little purpose but mutual destruction."
This not very sympathetic analysis prepares for the Huron-Iroquois war.
In the following chapters the stories of Jesuit martyrdom are mixed in with
the destruction of the Huron nation, of which Brébeuf's death is the symbol. And when the Hurons are actually ready to die as a nation, they have
no more "wolfish fury" left in them; they are merely pathetic. "All was
over with the Hurons. The death-knell of their nation had struck. Without a leader, without organization, without union, crazed with fright and
paralyzed with misery, they yielded to their doom without a blow. Their
only thought was flight." Stumbling wretchedly through the wilderness,
and then reaching Isle St. Joseph, they make a pathetic picture: "groups
of famished wretches, with dark, haggard visages and uncombed hair, in
every posture of despondency and woe." Here, during the winter, they
die "by scores daily" as the priests try to comfort and cure them. Some
dig up the bodies of their own relatives to avoid starvation. Most of them
have become Christians, since misery has "softened their hearts." Half of
the 6,000 to 8,000 refugees perish.

   An important ingredient in such sentimental pictures is the enforced
migration. Parkman follows the survivors of the war through more terror and misery until he comes to "the last of the Hurons." "It is a matter
of some interest," he says, "to trace the fortunes of the shattered fragments
of a nation once prosperous, and, in its own eyes and those of its neighbors,
powerful and great. None were left alive within their ancient domain."
Some join other Indian tribes, including the Iroquois, but the Iroquois,

meanwhile, pursue the last surviving group, the Tobacco Nation, even into the islands of Lake Michigan. Some reach the Sioux country, but the Sioux drive them out. A much smaller remnant move at last to Quebec, even there to be moved about several times, until they finally settle on

a wild spot, covered with the primitive forest, and seamed by a deep and tortuous ravine, where the St. Charles foams, white as a snow-drift, over the black ledges, and where the spotted sunlight struggles through matted boughs of the pine and fir, to bask for brief moments on the mossy rocks or flash on the hurrying waters.

There one can still find "the remnant of a lost people, harmless weavers of baskets and sewers of moccasins, the Huron blood fast bleaching out of them, as, with every generation, they mingle and fade away in the French population around."[32]

The fall of this doomed race was also the end of the Jesuit mission, symbolizing the failure of Catholicism and the Indian's inability to progress. The pathetic description of the vanishing, or expelled, or doomed "race" is a common picture in the romantic histories—inspiring honorable compassion, showing the force of destiny, suggesting one's proper attitude toward the Indian. Although Parkman argued persuasively that the Acadians immortalized by Longfellow had brought on their own expulsion by obeying the treacherous advice of their missionaries, when he came to the actual scenes of expulsion, he treated them in much the same way.[33]

3

Prescott's infidels include not only Indians, but Moors and Jews. From the very first Prescott regarded the subject of the Moors as "a rich study for the poet and the novelist," and Irving's decision to write *The Conquest of Granada* troubled him, he said, because "this would have formed the most interesting part of my narrative." As "Orientals" and as victims of progressive destiny, the Moors were just as "poetic" a subject as Montezuma. They had contributed to Spanish progress by "fertilizing" the European intellect at the moment when "the long night of darkness, which divides the modern from the ancient world," had descended on Europe. By the end of the fifteenth century, of course, their progressive value had been exhausted, and they stood in the way of the natural law which guaranteed Peninsular unity. The climate of Spain and their contact with Christian Europeans had prolonged their moment of cultivation, but by the nineteenth century they had inevitably lapsed into their original barbarism. Like any ruin, the decline of their empire deserved a few moments of melancholy contemplation, and Prescott introduced his account of the conquest of Granada by pointing the moral in a melancholy picture worthy of Irving:

The empire, which once embraced more than half of the ancient world, has now shrunk within its original limits; and the Bedouin wanders over his native desert as free, and almost as uncivilized, as before the coming of his apostle. . . . Darkness has again settled over those regions of Africa, which were illumined by the light of learning. The elegant dialect of the Koran is studied as a dead language, even in the birth-place of the prophet. Not a printing press at this day is to be found throughout the whole Arabian Peninsula. Even in Spain, in Christian Spain, alas! the contrast is scarcely less degrading. A death-like torpor has succeeded to her former intellectual activity. . . . Her most interesting monuments are those constructed by the Arabs; and the traveller, as he wanders amid their desolate, but beautiful ruins, ponders on the destinies of a people, whose very existence seems now to have been almost as fanciful as the magical creations in one of their own fairy tales.[34]

The Moorish infidel has the characteristics of both decadent civilized man and savage. As an Oriental who loves splendor, he has been weakened by "effeminate indulgence" and by his "sensual religion." For all the Moors' accomplishments and all their industry, Prescott said,

they had long since reached their utmost limit of advancement as a people. The light shed over their history shines from distant ages; for, during the later period of their existence, they appear to have reposed in a state of torpid, luxurious indulgence, which would seem to argue, that, when causes of external excitement were withdrawn, the inherent vices of their social institutions had incapacitated them for the further production of excellence.

This corruption justifies the "wise" Providential decree under which the Spaniards appropriated the Moors' lands, for the Spaniards' religion and government, "however frequently misunderstood or perverted, qualified them for advancing still higher the interests of humanity."[35]

The Moor's savage characteristics appear most plainly in the battle scenes. Like Parkman's Indian, he is "impetuous," easily discouraged, and thus no match for Spanish firmness. Ali Atar's impulsive charge cannot succeed against "Ferdinand's coolness." Like Parkman's Indians, the Moors "wantonly" fight a war among themselves at the very time when they should stand united against the Spaniards. Later on, having lured the Spaniards into wild, mountainous country, they show that they are "trained to the wild tactics of mountain warfare," but they cannot fight so well in "an open reach of valley." In a dark Gothic scene they appear on the mountain tops at night, and their own fires show them "flitting to and fro like so many spectres"; to harass the retreating Spanish army, they use not only guns and crossbows but wild Nature itself as a weapon—rolling masses of rock down onto the compact groups of Spaniards. To this weird scene their "shrill war-cries," which seem to come from every quarter, add more terror and confusion. When the Spaniards decide to climb the sierra and at least die fighting, the Moors, fighting from the higher ground, keep retreating, avoiding frontal attack, and they seem to have "the powers of ubiquity."[36] The defeat of the Spaniards is comparable in kind and degree to that of Braddock by the French and Indians.

The final result, however, is inevitable. Spanish resolution and ingenuity go to work, and "the moorish garrisons, perched on their mountain fastnesses, which, like the eyry of some bird of prey, seemed almost inaccessible to man," watch "with astonishment the heavy trains of artillery emerging from the passes, where the foot of the hunter had scarcely been known to venture." Inspired by some timely eloquence from their commander, the Spaniards win.[37]

Even Moorish imagery resembles that of the Indians. Prescott relieves his accounts of these battles with tales of individual generosity to show the "romantic" character of the war and the chivalry of an occasional Moor. The Moors fight fiercely, as do Bancroft's Indians, out of "despair," but in this war they do not butcher children. One Moorish noble tells some displaced Spanish children to go back to their mothers, and when his comrades ask him why he let the children escape so easily, he answers: " 'Because I saw no beard upon their chins.' " Later the deposed king Abdallah heaves his famous last sigh as he takes his last look at Granada from "a rocky eminence." His "more masculine mother" tells him that he does well " 'to weep like a woman, for what you could not defend like a man!' "[38]

In the two deposed kings, Abdallah and El Zagal, Prescott has perfect "poetic" subjects, and he exploits both opportunities for pathos, increasing the effect by his emphasis on destiny. Like the great but unsuccessful Indian chiefs, Prescott's Abdallah recognizes the divine hand in his fate, and he tells Ferdinand to honor his Providential good fortune by following a policy of "clemency and moderation." On hearing his mother's rebuke as they move off into the Alpuxarras, he exclaims, " 'when were woes ever equal to mine!' " Prescott not only compares his fate to that of his uncle, El Zagal, but uses the same expression—"pined away"—to describe the reaction of both to life without a kingdom. The one, he says, went to Africa, where he was "plundered" and "condemned to starve out the remainder of his days in miserable indigence"; the other was killed in Africa while serving under a royal relative. The account of Abdallah ends with a sentence on the sealed gate of Granada, "a memorial to the sad destiny" of her kings.[39]

In the war for Granada the Moors were the victims of progress, but when they rebelled against Philip II in the next century, they were the victims of tyranny. The long story of this rebellion begins as a tale of retribution. Here little of the chivalry that marked the earlier war appears in Prescott's pages. Philip II, at the advice of a junta including the Duke of Alva, has decided to destroy the Moriscoes' past by forbidding them to observe their customs, and, eventually, to read their literature or speak their language. This edict was the more unnatural, Prescott observes, because Philip II destroyed their past and then denied them any future. The war is ferocious on both sides from the start. The Moriscoes who begin the rebellion in the Alpuxarras are "barbarians." Like Pontiac's followers, they have successfully masked their deep-seated hatred of the Spaniards. The Christians, who have not anticipated the uprising, flee to the churches, to the protection of the priests, who have had charge of Morisco and Spaniard alike. "But the wild animal of the forest, now that he had regained his freedom, gave little heed to the call of his former keeper,—unless it were to turn and rend him." In his description of the ensuing battles, Prescott again takes advantage of wild scenery which is not only sublime but "gloomy." Again he consistently describes the fighting Moriscoes as savages; again he emphasizes, in almost identical language, their skill "in the mountain wilds in which they had been nurtured from infancy," their astonishment at Spanish resourcefulness, the grotesqueness of their mountain "watchfires" and their "shrill war-cries," their "wily tactics" (which depend on "ambushes and surprises"), their loss of heart if these tactics failed—a discouragement like that of "the lion, who, if balked in the first spring upon his prey, is said rarely to attempt another"—and their ferocious cruelty even to women and children. This "diabolical cruelty," Prescott says, is as extreme "as anything recorded of our North-American savages."[40]

The behavior of the Spaniards as conquerors is, of course, no better, but in dramatizing the battles themselves Prescott always writes from the Spanish point of view. It is before the battles and after the victories, when the Moriscoes can appear as a doomed people, that he condemns Spanish bigotry and cruelty. Again the accounts of battles precede a scene of pathetic exile, but this time (as in Parkman) the exile of an entire people:

It was a sad and solemn spectacle, that of this company of exiles, as they moved with slow and uncertain step, bound together by cords, and escorted, or rather driven along like a gang of convicts, by the fierce soldiery. There they were, the old and the young, the rich and the poor, now, alas! brought to the same level, the forms of most of them bowed down, less by the weight of years than of sorrow, their hands meekly folded on their breasts, their cheeks wet with tears, as they gazed for the last time on their beautiful city, the sweet home of their infancy, the proud seat of ancient empire, endeared to them by so many tender and glorious recollections.

As they leave the city, the morning light breaks "on the red towers of the Alhambra," and they turn "their faces toward new homes,—homes which many of them were destined never to behold." Prescott summarizes the wretched demise of many of the ill-provisioned exiles and then turns to the decay of their "light and airy edifices," their "exotic" gardens, the "sparkling fountains" in their courtyards and public squares.[41]

This scene precedes the assassination of the Moriscoes' heroic leader, Aben-Aboo. As Parkman's Pontiac, who showed some of "the high emotion of the patriot hero," was still "a thorough savage" who represented, "in strongest light and shadow, the native faults and virtues of the Indian race"; so Aben-Aboo, though "remarkably free from some of the greatest defects in the Moorish character," though "temperate in his appetites," though "cool and circumspect in his judgments," showed clearly in his faults and virtues that "the blood of the Moor flowed in his veins." He stood firm under inhuman tortures, and he remained so loyal to his race and his creed that he preferred living and dying " 'as a Mussulman' " to " 'all the favors which the king of Spain could heap on him.' " Yet he was, Prescott reminds the reader, "a despot, and a despot of the Oriental type." Here Prescott's emphasis differs from Parkman's, for he argues that Aben-Aboo's faults were those of his "race" and its institutions; but whatever the reasons, Aben-Aboo is a member of that large literary family of admirable, pitiable heroes whose greatness is restricted by their racial traits.[42]

Despite Ferdinand's "shrewd" device of exorbitant ransom, the original conquest of Granada had been justified by its good moral results as well as by progressive necessity. The religious war against the infidel, Prescott said, had planted the sentiment of nationality firmly in the Spanish consciousness. The Moriscoes' rebellion, however, taught an opposite moral. Religious "enthusiasm" had become "the blindest fanaticism," which provoked the rebellion, motivated the Spaniards' atrocities, and prompted the foolish expulsion of the Moriscoes from Granada. After he had described the pathetic scene of exile and the subsequent ruin of Granada, Prescott drove home the moral of retribution: the hatred and cruelty encouraged by these acts led inevitably to the Moriscoes' expulsion from the Peninsula by "the imbecile Philip the Third"—to one of the "principal causes" of the ruin of Spain.[43]

Although Prescott did not describe the Jews in language reserved for savages, they, too, vanished from Spain during the reign of Ferdinand and Isabella, and they bear a marked literary relationship to his Moors. Not only their pathetic destiny but their "racial" traits mark them as literary kindred of Moor and Indian alike. Prescott's experience of Jews was largely literary, and he went to tradition and literature, including Sir Walter Scott, for their traits. There is nothing unique in this. Motley, for example, set off against the "Teutonic" blonde heroine of his *Morton's Hope* a Jewess whose

> features, although very Jewish, were very handsome. Her eyes were long and black as death; her nose was of the handsomest Hebrew cut, slightly aquiline, but thin and expressive. . . . Her figure was certainly superb, and the rounded luxuriance of the outlines, and the majestic fullness of the whole development, accorded well with her Eastern origin.[44]

Here the "Oriental" qualities in the conventional dark heroine are quite explicit, as indeed they are in Scott's Rebecca and Hawthorne's Hester Prynne, Zenobia, and Miriam Schaeffer (a Jewess); as they are in Zahara, the Moorish beauty whose "voluptuous" dancing and "bewitching" singing and lute-playing lead one of Prescott's Moriscoes to his death. Motley, moreover, gave his Jewess a "large greasy looking" corrupt banker for a father, and in his history itself he manipulated the evidence to show that the Jewish doctor who agreed to poison Queen Elizabeth for Philip II had "stipulated for a handsome provision in marriage" for his daughters.[45]

Prescott, too, regarded the Jews as Oriental, and he used this common origin to explain their affinity with the Moors. Like the Moors and the American Indians, the Jews had an unshakable attachment to the customs of their ancestors. No other "nation" except the Spanish, Prescott said, revealed so intense a feeling of nationality. They had "preserved their unity of character unbroken, amid the thousand fragments" into which they had been scattered. Choosing the Spanish Jews as the typical subjects through whom to explain the techniques of the Inquisition, he relied repeatedly on this conception of "racial" character, both in criticizing and in defending the Jews. Under the benevolent tolerance of the Moors, they had "accumulated wealth with their usual diligence"; despite their lack of originality in "speculative philosophy" (which might have been the result of their excessive attachment to ancestral traditions), their "natural aptitude" for financial work and their skill in "practical and experimental science" won them national respect and royal patronage. Even this high favor, however, could not protect them after they had done so well as "to excite popular envy, augmented, as it was, by that profuse ostentation of equipage and apparel, for which this singular people, notwithstanding their avarice, have usually shown a predilection." Here Prescott referred the reader to *Ivanhoe,* in which Scott had portrayed these "opposite traits" in Rebecca and Isaac as a means of contrasting "the lights and shades of the Jewish character." Scott's picture was not at all analogous to the Jews' financial, social, or intellectual condition in Spain, Prescott admitted, but it represented accurately the "race's" character.[46]

All this is but a prelude to wholly unjustified persecution. Although the traits of Prescott's Jews include "their usual crafty policy," and although he might have considered "profuse ostentation" a source of understandable malice, he always sympathizes with the Jews rather than the Spaniards. The sense of destiny here comes from the Bible rather than "Nature," for Spanish Jewry was already a "fragment"; the "race" had already been scattered. Prescott begins by reminding the reader of the Jews' Biblical destiny, introducing them as "the unfortunate race of Israel, on whom the sins of their fathers have been so unsparingly visited by every nation in Christendom, among whom they have sojourned, almost to the present century." From this hint of what is to come, he moves to their prosperity and respectability, and then to the nonreligious motives various Spaniards had had for persecuting them. After he has ridiculed the various slanders against them, he describes their downfall, noticing not only the number destroyed in *autos da fé* but also the illogicality in governmental decrees that completely trapped them. He points out, for example, that giving a child a Hebrew name was evidence of relapse, although a previous law had forbidden Jews to use Christian names.[47]

Prescott also made the inevitability of Jewish destiny more poignant by underscoring the greed and envy of their persecutors. Even their ability brought this people into trouble. The "wealthy," Prescott said, were "the least pardonable offenders during times of proscription." Moreover, the "thrift and dexterity peculiar to their race" made the common people as well as the wealthy relatively prosperous, and the whole people thus became "personally more sensitive to physical annoyance, and less fitted to encounter the perils and privations of their dreary pilgrimage." Before they were expelled, the Jews of Aragon were cheated out of their property on the pretext, Prescott said, that their debts exceeded their assets. It was "strange indeed, that the balance should be found against a people, who have been everywhere conspicuous for their commercial sagacity and resources!"[48]

The expulsion began another series of dilemmas that narrowed further and further the possible alternatives of the marked "race." In his conventional paragraph on the pathetic condition of an exiled nation, Prescott stressed the unique stigma attached to these exiles:

They were to go forth as exiles from the land of their birth; the land where all, whom they ever loved, had lived or died; the land, not so much of their adoption, as of inheritance; which had been the home of their ancestors for centuries, and with whose prosperity and glory they were of course as intimately associated, as was any ancient Spaniard. They were to be cast out helpless and defenceless, with a brand of infamy set on them, among nations who had always held them in derision and hatred.

Following the different groups of Jews along Spanish roads that were "swarming with emigrants," Prescott exploited thoroughly the effect of the traditional stigma. Not only had Torquemada forbidden Spaniards all gestures of sympathy or "succour" to the exiles, but those who went to Africa were attacked by "roving tribes," who "ripped open" dead bodies in their search for concealed gold. The survivors were later charged a heavy ransom by the Algerian Moors who, defeated by Ximenes, had to agree to surrender all their Christian captives. Here the Jews' position was that of Parkman's Canadians, Iroquois, and Acadians, for "it was of little moment to the wretched Israelite which party won the day, Christian or Mussulman; he was sure to be stripped in either case." Those Jews who went to Italy carried with them a deadly symbol of their infamous brand, "an infectious disorder" that killed 20,000 people in Naples during the first year and spread "over the whole Italian peninsula." The law allowed them to stay in Genoa only three days, long enough to deposit the germs of their plague, before they were forced to move on again.[49]

Like the tale of the Moriscoes, this story serves the triple purpose of inspiring compassion, characterizing the exiles, and showing the evils of bigotry. As the Inquisition was the major cause of Spain's decline, so the expulsion of the Jews was the moral turning point in Spanish history. Prescott not only stressed the tremendous cost which the loss of both "industrious races" forced the country to pay; he gave added moral force to the expulsion of the Jews by showing that it came at the high point of Spanish achievement. He placed his chapter on expulsion just after his description of Columbus' departure for America, which had followed immediately after his last chapter on the conquest of Granada. The "most disastrous edict" against the Jews had been published before either of these achievements,[50] but Prescott placed it where it would have its most emphatic moral significance. By signing the edict, "as it were, with the same pen which drew up the glorious capitulation of Granada and the treaty with Columbus," Ferdinand and Isabella revealed Spain's fatal flaw. At the moment when they most clearly represented natural law, they accepted the advice of inquisitors and violated an essential natural law. Prescott made the moral more impressive by arguing that, whatever the greed of the Pope and the inquisitors and whatever the envy of some of the people, the motives of Ferdinand and Isabella were religious. Although, in defense of Ferdinand and Isabella, he pointed out that similarly atrocious acts were decreed in England, France, and Portugal "a few years later," these countries had no permanent Inquisition, and they had other industrious subjects. The faults of the age might entitle Ferdinand and Isabella to clemency, but the punishment of Spain was inevitable.[51]

4

This sentimental, Oriental, and moral context is the proper one in which to read Prescott's portrayal, in his volumes on Mexico and Peru, of American Indians. It is obvious that besides the amazing endurance and unparalleled "romantic" achievements of two resolute adventurers, these subjects gave Prescott the advantage of describing the destruction of two empires. The reader of both histories is intended to have from the beginning a sense of doom. The grand subject combines progressive enterprise, however unscrupulous its agents and their methods, and the symptoms of national death. The founding of Vera Cruz, for example, leads Prescott to a melancholy observation that he echoes frequently in both histories. The "simple natives" were pleased, but

alas! they could not read the future, or they would have found no cause to rejoice. . . . Their fetters, indeed, would be broken; and their wrongs be amply avenged on the proud head of the Aztec. But it was to be by that strong arm, which should bow down equally the oppressor and the oppressed. The light of civilization would be poured on their land. But it would be the light of a consuming fire, before which their barbaric glory, their institutions, their very existence and name as a nation, would wither and become extinct! Their doom was sealed, when the white man had set his foot on their soil.[52]

These natives are the Totonacs, who have been forced to pay tribute to the Aztecs. The doom of the Aztecs and the Peruvians is just as clear as theirs, but those powerful nations are not to be liberated, except from their emperors. It is in this distinction that the Oriental theme is important. Both Aztecs and Peruvians are at once civilized, in an Oriental fashion, and savage. The Oriental comparison is not confined to speculation about the origins of the two empires. When Prescott told Bancroft that the Aztec "civilization smacks strongly of the Oriental," he named an essential ingredient of his literary and moral recipe for the Indian.[53]

The analogy pervades the histories from the beginning of *The Conquest of Mexico*. Prescott's Cholula resembles his Granada. His first picture of the Valley of Tenochtitlan makes "the fair city of Mexico, with her white towers and pyramidal temples," look like "some Indian empress with her coronal of pearls." Both Aztec and Peruvian love splendor and display their taste richly. The lavish use of jewels, gold, and silver in the temples corresponds to the first picture of Tenochtitlan, and a later allusion to Mecca and Jerusalem adds to the exotic effect.

Obviously this kind of emphasis provides "color," and it shows that in these episodes romance and history are one, that the Spanish knight-errant had, in a way, really found the Indies. But the Oriental analogy applies also to the character of the two nations. Their very institutions are Oriental. Both governments are despotisms that require a slavish obedience—"an Oriental adulation"—of their subjects. The "truly Oriental" pomp of the emperors and subordinate kings, who travel in splendid litters; the institution of polygamy; the vacillating weakness of both Montezuma and the Inca Atahuallpa—in these qualities Prescott shows a languor produced by the same kind of "effeminate indulgence" that ruined the kings of Granada. The religion of Mexico, moreover, is even more grossly "sensual" than that of the Moors. Like fifteenth-century Spanish Moors, Prescott's Aztecs have corrupted an older civilization, and their religion is the main source of corruption. Human sacrifice, though horrible, is not, Prescott says, wholly degrading; but cannibalism, though in Mexico a religious rite, makes any great "moral or intellectual" progress "impossible." Like the fifteenth-century Moors and the Jews, the Aztecs do show some "proficiency" in "that material culture . . . which ministers to the gratification of the senses," but they can make no "purely intellectual progress."[54]

The Peruvian is no cannibal, his despotism is benevolent, and his religion is relatively pure; but he, too, is a materialist, and "the great law of progress was not for him." The suffocating benevolence of the Incas' welfare state supplies his material needs but destroys his moral identity by denying him "free agency" and by deliberately keeping him in ignorance. As Prescott compares the Incas' method of proselyting to the Mohammedans', so the character of the Peruvian people has its Oriental analogy: "patient and tranquil," they more nearly resemble "the Oriental nations, as the Hindoos and Chinese, than . . . the members of the great Anglo-Saxon family, whose hardy temper has driven them to seek their fortunes on the stormy ocean." The Peruvian has not corrupted his inherited religion, but "the defects" of his government are "those of over-refinement in legislation,—the last defects to have been looked for . . . in the American aborigines." This overrefinement, Prescott says, caused a passivity that enervates patriotism and bows too quickly to the invaders.[55]

This is not to say that Prescott minimized the attainments of either the Aztecs or the Peruvians. He had high praise for different accomplishments of both civilizations. The comparisons of Indian and Oriental character, government, and religion had an important function, however, in Prescott's application of progressive law. He was frankly troubled by the problem of the "right of conquest," and his doubts produced some confusion, if not downright self-contradiction. The problem was made more perplexing by several plain facts about both conquerors and conquered. These Indians, unlike Parkman's, had not roved over vast areas of "waste fertility"; they had been industrious farmers and artisans. Nor had the conquerors been religious exiles or the industrious overflow of an expanding society; they had been greedy, occasionally or consistently perfidious, and consistently cruel. In his own time, moreover, Prescott opposed the annexation of Texas and the Mexican War, and in both *The Conquest of Mexico* and *The Conquest of Peru* he criticized his contemporaries' belief that they had a "mission" of conquest.[56]

In "Reflections" prompted by Cortés' massacre of the Cholulans, Prescott questioned both Spanish and "Protestant" arguments for the right of conquest, referring the reader finally to Diedrich Knickerbocker's ridicule of European pretentiousness. Here his explicit solution was twofold: to compare sixteenth-century Spanish atrocities to even more horrible French and British atrocities in the more recent Peninsular War; and to *assume* the right of conquest in order to judge the men of the sixteenth century by the standards of their own time. He did not, he said, mean to "vindicate the cruel deeds of the Conquerors," which should properly "lie heavy on their heads." But he insisted that judging the *men* fairly required the historian to use the standards of their own time in order to give them "the same justice which we shall have occasion to ask from Posterity, when, by the light of a higher civilization, it surveys the dark or doubtful passages in our own history, which hardly arrest the eye of the contemporary."[57]

Although one might say that using sixteenth-century Spanish standards would "vindicate" the "cruel deeds," Prescott moved on in his next paragraph from morality to "policy." Whatever the massacre's "moral" worth, he said, "as a stroke of policy, it was unquestionable." This statement might surprise the reader who has noticed the regularity with which Prescott insisted that "principle and policy go together"—an axiom that he had used in this very moral discussion when praising Cortés for a humane action! The contradiction, however, reveals a moral pattern. The wisdom in Cortés' policy lay in his exploitation of Aztec superstition. The massacre proved that the Spaniards were "white gods," and the natives "trembled." "None trembled more," Prescott said, than Montezuma, whose superstitious fatalism "read in these events the dark characters traced by the finger of Destiny." Frightened by the defection of some of his subject tribes, he again asked the advice of "his impotent deities; but, although the altars smoked with fresh hecatombs of human victims, he obtained no cheering response."[58]

As Prescott has picked up the thread of his narrative after a pause for reflective moral doubts, he has also recovered his moral control of the narrative. Properly impressed by the smoking hecatombs, one reads of Cortés' desire to convert the Cholulans as quickly as possible; when his enthusiasm is tempered by the "wise" restraint of his chaplain, he at least has "the satisfaction" of liberating the Cholulans' intended sacrificial victims and of building a "gigantic" Cross on the great Cholulan temple. On this spot, Prescott observes, "where his ancestors celebrated the sanguinary rites of the mystic Quetzalcoatl," an Indian "descendant of the Cholulans [now] performs the peaceful services of the Roman Catholic communion."[59]

Despite Prescott's "reflective" doubts about the right of conquest, he has supplied the answer in his narrative technique. The way has been prepared not only for one's judgment of Montezuma within the narrative, but for one's long-range judgment of the conquest itself. Immediately after this passage Prescott turns to the behavior of Montezuma, which he finds so "pusillanimous" that he cannot contemplate it "without mingled feelings of pity and contempt." Not until he has completed the narrative of Montezuma's life does he ask one to judge "superstitious fatalism" from Montezuma's point of view. Montezuma's perception of his destiny, unlike that of Bancroft's and Parkman's chiefs, is not the recognition of natural law. Based on superstition, it produces conduct as effeminate as that of the Moor Abdallah. He is not a brave man standing against the forces of destiny, but a decadent despot whose "lofty and naturally courageous spirit" has been "subdued by the influence of superstition." Courage is an absolute virtue, the highest virtue of the Indian; when Montezuma is measured against this standard, one can see that his Oriental institutions have subverted the strength of his Indian character. On the same page Prescott measures Cortés against the same standard. Montezuma's effort to bribe Cortés is ridiculous; "the man, whom the hostile array of armies could not daunt, was not to be turned from his purpose by a woman's prayers."[60]

Similar weaknesses also taint the nobler Inca Atahuallpa, who reads his doom in the appearance of a strange comet, and who, although he later dies resolutely, is at first "unmanned" by the news of his sentence by Pizarro's drumhead court. Throughout this Inca's melancholy story, moreover, Prescott emphasizes his misdeeds as well as Pizarro's treachery. The Inca's execution of his brother was striking proof that polygamy weakened the natural "bonds of brotherhood"; "the arm of the despot" was quick to sweep away "any obstacle that lay in his path."[61]

The moral function of this Orientalism, then, was to help account for the "beneficent" decree of Providence that destined both empires to ruin. "The debasing institutions of the Aztecs" were "the best apology for their conquest." Although the Spaniards brought the Inquisition with them, the purer truths of Christianity, destined to outlive "fanaticism," destroyed "those dark forms of horror which had so long brooded over" Mexico. Despite the relative purity of the Peruvians' religion, their institutions were both "artificial" and "repugnant to the essential principles of our nature." The justification for Anglo-Saxon conquests has been reversed. No roving savage, but a farmer and a builder of cities, Prescott's Indian is *too* civilized; to denote the fault, Prescott chose the word "semi-civilized."[62]

In Prescott's "reflective" passages the question of the right of conquest is never settled. When he considers Pizarro's character for the last time, he contrasts "the ferocious cupidity of the conquerors with the mild and inoffensive manners of the conquered"; in such a contrast, he says, "our sympathies, the sympathies even of the Spaniard, are necessarily thrown into the scale of the Indian." Although he insists that Cortés' primarily religious motive entitles him, rather than the Aztecs, to our "sympathies," these differing judgments do not alter Prescott's faith in the wisdom of Providential decrees. Despite Pizarro's greed and cruelty, the Peruvian is as clearly the cause of his own downfall as was the Aztec. *The Conquest of Peru* ends with a symbolic return from the "artificiality" of Incan institutions and the vicious corruption of the conquerors to the method of

Nature. The conquerors are defeated by "a humble missionary" whose greatest powers are his virtue, his "common sense," and his mastery of moral persuasion. His methods and the permanence of his achievements resemble "the slow, insensible manner in which Nature works out her great changes in the material world, that are to endure when the ravages of the hurricane are passed away and forgotten."[63]

While the Oriental comparison helped to explain the ruin of "semi-civilized" nations, Prescott's Indian, both in his faults and his virtues, is also a savage. His greatest virtues are courage and endurance, a strong spirit of independence (confined largely to leaders, many of whom behave less passively than "Hindoos"), and an intense tribal or racial loyalty.

The proper course for the hero of a doomed or vanishing race is resistance to the end. Prescott is not content to make the point only in his pitying and contemptuous judgment of Montezuma. As if to emphasize the distinction between Oriental and savage, he presents several Indian leaders whose resistance to the conquerors is "manly" and uncompromising. In both Mexico and Peru he contrasts these chiefs with their more effeminate predecessors, and he calls their constancy an Indian virtue. The "spirit" of Guatemozin, Montezuma's successor, is admirable in spite of the "vicious system" that he has inherited. And Xicotencatl, defeated chief of the Tlascalans, stands forth in the posture of the Byronic hero; the impartial reader, Prescott says, "may find much to admire in that high, unconquerable spirit, like some proud column, standing alone in its majesty amidst the fragments and ruins around it." The Inca Manco, eventual successor to Atahuallpa, also dies fighting, having reverted to the heroic type of his ancient predecessors. "With the ancient institutions of his ancestors lying a wreck around him, he yet struggled bravely, like Guatemozin, the last of the Aztecs, to uphold her tottering fortunes, or to bury his oppressors under her ruins." This resolution forces him to retreat to the "mountain fastnesses," where he maintains his "savage independence" instead of living as "a slave in the land" once ruled by his ancestors.[64]

The Indian has a natural aptitude for dying well. "Passive fortitude [is] the virtue of the Indian warrior; and it was the glory of the Aztec, as of the other races on the North American continent, to show how the spirit of the brave man may triumph over torture and the agonies of death." Even the once "craven" Montezuma and the once "unmanned" Atahuallpa recover their spirit in time to die like true Indians. Manco's wife also dies properly under torture, and Indians leap from the tops of towers to avoid slavery under the conqueror.[65]

However clearly the Indians deserved "our sympathies" in the reflective passages, Prescott's allegiance was again with the Europeans in the narratives of battles. Treachery and "stratagem" were the common weapons of Indian warfare and diplomacy; the Indian was "a wily foe" addicted to "wily tactics"; even the noble Manco, once he had begun to fight Pizarro, became "crafty." "Secrecy and silence" were almost as much a part of the American Indian "as the peculiar color of his skin." At the same time, embattled Peruvians, though fighting for their country, were capable of "fiendish exultation." Watching "with gloomy satisfaction" a battle among their conquerors, they descended from the mountains "like a pack of wolves" after the battle was over.[66]

For Prescott as well as Parkman the ethics of warfare are absolute, and the fighting Indian can rarely measure up to them except in single combat. In such a situation the best he can do is to die "like a Roman," as does one noble Peruvian who refuses to be captured by Spaniards who want very much to take him alive. Even in the open battles on the plains or on the flat top of a pyramid, where he can rarely do better than show a willing spirit, the Indian usually demonstrates his racial inferiority not only by losing but also by his behavior. In groups the Indians form "a multitude," "a torrent," "clouds," "swarms," "dark lines," "dense masses," "countless multitudes." Under the Spaniards' resolute attacks and superior science, the Indian masses are "seized with a panic" or with "superstitious awe," or they are "filled with consternation." The descriptions of these battles suggest, as Parkman's battle rhetoric implies, that there is something unfair about "entangling" the enemy in streets and "narrow lanes," or in "mountain fastnesses," from which rocks can be rolled down on him. The nobler method is to fight on an open field. The rhetorical odds are against the savage because of his superiority in numbers, his methods of fighting, his obedience to passion rather than discipline. Even when they fight courageously, a "mob of barbarians" have little chance for praise in the account of a battle with "the Christians," for if they do not stand "petrified with dismay," they sound "their hideous war-shriek" and rush "impetuously on the Christians." The eloquence, the resolution, the discipline, and the coolness of the European rarely fail in these conflicts with savage "passion":

The barbarian, when brought into contact with the white man, would seem to have been rebuked by his superior genius, in the same manner as the wild animal of the forest is said to quail before the steady glance of the hunter.[67]

In the battles of Mexico and Peru Prescott naturally found many opportunities for the Gothic emphasis of the other histories. Here, with the presence of "frantic priests" and smoking human hearts; with "the wild, barbaric minstrelsy of shell, atabal, and trumpet"; with the sublimely terrible heights of mountain and pyramidal temple as battle scenes—here the most impressive battle scenes are inevitably Gothic. The most symbolic of these grand battles was fought by Christians and Mexicans on the "aerial battlefield" of the great temple's summit in Mexico City—a flat area interrupted only by the Aztecs' sacrificial stone and the "two temples of stone," one of which was dedicated to each religion. Emphasizing the height and the fact that the whole population of the city watched from below, Prescott built his picture of this scene toward the religious symbols, and completed it with a view of the Indian priests, who, "running to and fro, with their hair wildly streaming over their sable mantles, seemed hovering in mid air, like so many demons of darkness urging on the work of slaughter!" In this sublime arena, from which there was no escape but victory or death, the savage's military "science" was on trial as well as his religion. Since the Aztecs outnumbered the Spaniards two to one, "it seemed" as though "brute force" was certain to defeat "superior science." But of course the Spaniard's "science" and equipment were as superior as his religion, and the best that could be said for the Aztec was that he fought to the death with "the courage of despair." The climax of the sublime scene was the burning of the sacrificial temple, "the funeral pyre of Paganism."[68]

Despite the "swollen tide of passion" that could control his mobs, the dissension that ruined his resistance to the Spaniards, despite his "Oriental" faults and his cruelty, his craftiness, his idolatry, and his materialism; the savage's virtues and his fate entitled him to sentimental treatment. In war he rarely received this sympathy until after his defeat or after the slaughter and pillage had begun; but, especially in Peru, his "patient industry," his enlightened treatment of defeated tribes, his respect for their religion, and his indifference to the value of gold were a rebuke to the gold-lusty conquerors. For all his faults, moreover, the Inca Atahuallpa was perceptive enough to rebuke papal pretension as explained by a "monk"; his eyes "flashed fire, and his dark brow grew darker" during the explanation of Catholic theology and Spanish supremacy, and he told Father Valverde that the Pope " 'must be crazy to talk of giving away countries which don't belong to him.' "[69]

It was the Indians' pathetic fate, however, that most clearly deserved sentimental contemplation. They were robbed of their wealth, consigned to slavery, murdered like "herds of deer." In both Mexico and Peru their civilization was not only superseded but virtually destroyed; the ruin was astoundingly rapid—one generation accomplished the work in Cholula, and in Peru the few years of Pizarro's presence sufficed. Except for his introduction to Christianity, progress was made at the Indian's expense; nor was he expelled or allowed to escape, as were other Indians, the Moors, and the Jews. "He was an alien in the land of his fathers." The fall of Montezuma and of Atahuallpa foreshadowed the ruin of their race, and Prescott emphasized the distance and suddenness of the descent. The facts of such demises were themselves sufficiently melancholy, but Prescott also stressed the emperors' own sense of melancholy. Wounded by his own people, before whom he had degraded himself, Montezuma "resolved to die," and Prescott insisted that he died of spiritual as well as physical wounds; again the dying Indian leader became "a stately tree, the pride of his own Indian forests," but this tree was "the first" rather than the last "victim of the tempest." As "the sad victim of destiny," he was like the Peruvian people who lived on under the Spaniards: "a lonely outcast in the heart of his own capital!" The "refinement" of Atahuallpa, who was condemned to die "the death of a vile malefactor," was "the more interesting that it was touched with melancholy." With his pathetic death began the fatal quarrels of the conquerors.[70]

5

Prescott's concluding remarks on Montezuma compare him to Louis XIV, not only as an " 'actor of majesty,' " but because of the "deep" stain of "bigotry" on his character, a bigotry that led him "to forego his nature."[71] The comparison is not unique, for it suggests a relationship between primitive and civilized opponents of progress that Bancroft and Parkman also exploited. With varying thoroughness, all three historians worked out the affinity of Catholic and infidel. Except for the Jew, each infidel group had fought against progress, and all, including the Jew, were portrayed as materialistic. Whether "enthralled" by Nature or sunk in Oriental indulgence, the infidel was too obedient to his senses.

Whatever their concessions to the spiritual intent behind Catholic material symbols, Parkman and Prescott drove this point right through the heart of the central "fault" in Catholic worship. The distinction between the spiritual and the material was "lost on" Indian and zealot alike. Both Catholic and North American Indian had an unhealthy reverence for "relics of mortality"; the Catholic and all Indians suffered from "superstitious credulity." Because of its overwhelming appeal to the senses, Prescott believed that Catholicism provided its missionary to the Indians with "some decided advantages" over his Protestant competitor; in fact, Parkman said, Catholicism "was the only form of Christianity likely to take root" in the Indian's "crude and barbarous nature." The priestcraft of Aztec, Inca, and Moor; the Aztec's and Inca's monasteries and convents; the Aztec's "confessional" and his "fasts and flagellations"—these similarities strengthened the connection. From mutual susceptibility to materialism, the relationship extended even to national traits. All the infidels were "crafty," and French trapper and Peruvian alike became licentious as soon as they were released from the control of paternalism. The Jesuits, experts in "dissimulation," were "amazed at the depth" of Indian "duplicity."[72]

Many of these resemblances are, of course, superficial. But the superficial likenesses were intended to suggest the underlying affinity. Historians who dramatized the march of humanity in "natural" and racial terms were happy to show that antiprogressives of every sort were basically sensual.[73] Parkman had the advantage of a theater in which Catholic and infidel interests could be merged, and he often exploited his opportunity by uniting priest and pagan on his stage. He portrayed the Indian and Catholic allies not only to emphasize contrasts of splendor and squalor, but also to demonstrate the consanguinity of antiprogressive forces. The very first tableau in his history—the conjuration of New France's "departed shades"—cast "a fitful light" on "lord and vassal and black-robed priest, mingled with wild forms of savage warriors, *knit in close fellowship on the same stern errand."* With both savage and priest, both fiend and ghost, located in a dark forest setting, Parkman thus achieved the alignment of diabolical forces that Cotton Mather had formerly arranged. But even when the subject is a splendid army gathered under the noble Montcalm, the same moral prevails; in the fight against progress, "the brightest civilization" joins forces with "the darkest barbarism." The "scholar-soldier Montcalm" is therefore obliged to accept as ally "the foulest man-eating savage of the uttermost northwest."[74]

There is a major difference, however, between the infidel's and the Catholic's devotion to the Past. The infidel's devotion to the Past is pathetic. When he fights by the rules, not only his courage, but even his loyalty to the Past is noble. Although he stands against progress, he follows his nature, and he often defends a subordinate natural law that can be superseded only by the law of progress. The racial inadequacy that binds him to this inferior law—that denies him a future—leaves him only one noble choice: to oppose progress courageously. Since his extinction or ruin is inevitable, and since the agents of his ruin are sometimes unscrupulous, he is a pitiable casualty of progress. The historians' sentimental contemplation of the infidel's fate sometimes underscores the injustices of unnatural tyranny. As the sufferings of William of Orange and Washington remind the American reader that he is the beneficiary of progress, the infidel's fate reminds him of the mortality of nations. By inspiring an "honorable compassion," it also reminds him that he is a man of "humanity."

3

THE ACHIEVEMENT

History as Romantic Art

CHAPTER VII

The Conquest of Mexico

In the conquest of Mexico Prescott found the ideal subject not only for the romantic historian but for his own particular talents. Both the conventions to which he was committed and his own artistic limitations—his prose style, his inability to portray complexity of character or to emphasize precise detail—required a grand subject, confined in time, that would allow him to concentrate on broad traits of personal and "national" character, on spectacular scenes, and on a simple theme. Although these limitations caused literary and interpretative faults in *The Conquest of Mexico*, it is an impressive work of art, and a large part of its success depends on Prescott's skillful use of romantic conventions.

I

The great virtue of *The Conquest of Mexico* is its brilliant design. Of its seven books only the last, a biographical epilogue on Cortés, contains important structural weaknesses, and some of these are virtually inseparable from corresponding advantages. In the first six books, ending with the conquest, Prescott arranges the events, aligns the characters, and controls the point of view so skillfully that he achieves the "unity of interest" that he considered essential to good history.

The primary source of this unity is, of course, Prescott's concentration on his hero's progress toward a single goal. Even if one were to consider only the broadest outline of the action, one would have to admire Prescott's division of the narrative (after his introductory book) into five books, or acts.[1] In the first half of the narrative he traces a straight line along which Cortés marches steadily upward from anonymity to nearly complete control of a strange, hostile empire. Then, at the very center of the drama, he slides Cortés down along an even steeper line that leads, at the middle of the fourth act, to the verge of ruin. From this dramatic crisis the line rises just as steeply, and at the end of the fourth act Cortés stands ready to attack the empire again. In the last act the whole pattern is retraced more rapidly. Despite minor setbacks (one very nearly costs him his life), Cortés rises almost to victory; then he is dropped to his lowest position since the original fall; and at last he rises to complete victory.

It is in the union of theme and structure, however, that Prescott's skill is most impressive. Convinced that he should think of his story as "an epic in prose, a romance of chivalry," he designed it to support a fundamentally simple theme: the inevitable ruin of a rich but barbarous empire through its inherent moral faults; the triumph of "civilization" over "semi-civilization," of Christianity (however imperfectly represented) over cannibalism; the triumph of Cortés' "genius," "constancy," and resourceful leadership over Montezuma's "pusillanimity" and "vacillation," and then over Guatemozin's noble but savage devotion to a doomed cause. Every one of the first six books illustrates this theme, and in every book—even in his expository introduction—Prescott makes his organization emphasize some aspect of it. The crucial differences between the two cultures, as he sees them, are differences in character, leadership, and religion, and he builds every book toward a crisis, or turning point, somewhere near its center, which depends on one or more of these distinctions.

The introductory book on "The Aztec Civilization" establishes the romantic atmosphere and the moral basis for the conquest. The theme of this book is the combination of "refinement" with savage brutality, and in establishing this theme the central chapter is the third, on Aztec religious institutions. Relying from the very first page on the Oriental comparison, Prescott repeatedly suggests the fatal combination in his descriptions of exotic scenery, of the emperors' pomp, and of Aztec imperialism; but in the first half of the book he arranges his description of Aztec achievements to culminate in the Aztecs' most "elevated" religious conceptions. The turning point of the book and the most emphatic statement of the theme come immediately afterward, in Prescott's discussion of priests, sacrifices, and cannibal feasts. The Aztec priests' influence, he says, was even worse than that of the Spanish Inquisition; he describes the sacrifice in a brilliant tableau; and when he announces that the delicately served cannibal feast was a unique combination of "refinement and the extreme of barbarism" (I, 79)* the inescapable limits of Aztec civilization are clearly established. In the succeeding chapters of the book, on intellectual achievements, economic life, and domestic manners, the Aztecs regain some of their lost respect, but Prescott requires one to see all their progressive accom-

---

* Volume and page numbers in parentheses refer to the three-volume edition published by Lippincott and Company, Philadelphia, 1860.

plishments within the limits to which their "barbarous" religion restricted them. Even as he praises their best achievements he iterates his theme briefly in each chapter, and he reserves his conclusion for a description of Tezcuco, "the Athens of the Western World" (I, 173), on which the Aztec conquerors have had a blighting influence.

In the books on the conquest itself each of these turning points is an episode in the narrative.

The dominant theme of the second book, "Discovery of Mexico," is the resolute enterprise of the knight-errant, whose "life was romance put into action." (I, 217.) The central turning point comes with the first actions of Montezuma, who lacks the knight-errant's virtues and represents the fatal weakness of his empire. Prescott uses the first five chapters to reveal the character of Cortés, the representative hero, and to bring him as far as he can come without waiting for Montezuma's reactions to his intrusion. By this time the narrative has established not only Cortés' representativeness and decisiveness, but also his remarkable conversion from irresponsibility to constancy and reliability. (I, 245–46.) Then, as the Spaniards await Montezuma's reply to Cortés' first message, Prescott turns to Mexico; and his introduction of Montezuma, ending with an indecisive answer that "reveals, at once, both his wealth and his weakness" (I, 317), presents him as Cortés' anthesis: in the decline of his personal character, in his luxury, and in his "fatalism." From here on the narrative tallies increasing evidence of Cortés' resolute leadership, balanced regularly by examples of Montezuma's vacillation.

Thus Prescott's organization as well as his rhetoric emphasizes the interaction of character and destiny. At the beginning of the narrative Cortés' remarkable transformation typifies that of the progressive man; and the bold decision by which he begins his expedition in defiance of his superiors reveals that, although "selected by Providence," he himself "gave the direction to destiny." (I, 252–53.) At the center of the narrative Montezuma's personal decline typifies that of the reactionary, who is demoralized by excessive power and terrified by the prospect of change. He, too, assists destiny, by his mistreatment of conquered nations and by his "fatalism" itself. Once the two representative men have been introduced in this balanced way, the rest of the book works out the contrast in action. Montezuma's weak response to Cortés' first message provokes an even more decisive reaction, and the tempo of contrasting action quickens until Cortés, at the end of the book, burns his ships and thus displays an almost unprecedented confidence in his destiny.

In "March to Mexico," the third book, Prescott continues to play Cortés' strength against Montezuma's weakness until Montezuma is forced to welcome the conquistadors to Mexico. Here again the central crisis turns on individual character and religion. But Prescott gives these added force by transforming even the geographic facts into an artistic justification of his theme. With each major Spanish advance the scenery changes, and the character and "refinement" of the natives change accordingly; and with each Spanish success Montezuma's conduct changes.

Thus every major stage of the Spaniards' advance confronts them with a different aspect of Indian character. Moving from the lush *tierra caliente* to the wild mountains of Tlascala, they meet a "rude republican" army (II, 92) that will not admit them to the city until it has been defeated three times in open battle. Then, having defeated Montezuma's Tlascalan enemies, on whom the emperor has counted to destroy them, the Spaniards are invited to "refined" Cholula, situated on a richly cultivated plateau, where Montezuma, on the advice of his oracles, hopes to ruin them by deceit.

It is in this "Holy City of Anahuac" (II, 8), where there are more temples, more processions and sacrifices, more beggars and priests than anywhere else in the country, that the crisis occurs. Warned of the conspiracy, Cortés orders a retaliatory massacre, and the "effeminate" Cholulans call on their gods to destroy him. The Spaniards, however, destroy the gods, and in the face of this outrage Montezuma's oracles are dumb. With the Spaniards moving unharmed toward Mexico after victories over both savage and refined Indians and after desecrating his gods, Montezuma, trembling, sends a mission to welcome them. The last two chapters of the book describe their march over the most sublime mountains of all and down into the gorgeous valley of Mexico, where the people combine the qualities of rude Tlascalan and refined Cholulan. (II, 92.)

"Residence in Mexico," the fourth book, is symmetrically designed to bring Montezuma to his lowest degradation before the Spaniards and Cortés to the height of his power, and then abruptly to drop Cortés down the long slide that leads to his expulsion from the city. Here again the crisis turns on religion. The steady decline and rise of Montezuma and Cortés, respectively, culminate at the center of the book, when Montezuma gives the Spaniards "great heaps of gold" (II, 201) and tearfully swears allegiance to Spain. But the representative cavalier cannot stop here. Cortés extorts Montezuma's permission to dedicate a Christian chapel on the great Aztec temple, and Prescott contrives brilliantly to use this religious provocation as the beginning of Aztec rebellion. He depicts the scene of the first mass there as an incongruous tableau, with Christian and infidel "side by side," mingling their religious songs. "It was an unnatural union," he says, "and could not long abide." (II, 210.) The Aztec people are so infuriated that within a day the Spaniards, who have planned to begin prospecting for gold, must prepare instead for a siege. As this crucial fifth chapter ends, moreover, Prescott shows Cortés receiving bad news of his Spanish enemies, and through the second half of the book Cortés is fully occupied with avoiding complete ruin—threatened first by his own countrymen and then by the enraged Aztecs. The book ends with a tense scene in which the Spaniards, prepared for a wild attack, hear the terrible roar and see the massive numbers of oncoming Aztecs.

The central division of this book is underscored by Prescott's control of chronology. Just when he stops portraying Cortés' response to opportunity and begins to stress his reaction to adversity, he finds new leaders to contrast with his hero. But he refuses to digress from the events in Mexico until Cortés' position there has changed; until Cortés has also learned that a Spanish force has set out to replace him. Following the technique of Cooper and Scott, Prescott uses this point of suspense as the transition to a summary of events in Spain and Cuba. For the rest of the book he sets Cortés' brilliant leadership against the fumbling of Spaniards—enemies and friends alike. Cortés defeats the enemies, but in his absence from Mexico the slight chance he has had to pacify the Aztecs is spoiled by the rashness of his faithful lieutenant in the city. Prescott informs the reader of this blunder only when Cortés learns of it, and then he follows Cortés on the forced march back to the capital.

In "Expulsion from Mexico," the fifth book, Prescott reverses the structural principle of Book IV. Here the fortunes of Cortés continue to decline until his greatest moment of peril, halfway through the book, and then they rise steadily until he reestablishes himself in Tezcuco, prepared for his last campaign against Mexico. The theme of the book is his fidelity, through the greatest adversity, "to himself." (II, 413.) To support the theme Prescott uses Byronic rhetoric more repetitiously than in any other part of the history, and he also builds the first half of his book toward a crisis in which Cortés can rely on nothing else but himself. In the midst of a losing battle which the tired Spaniards must fight without guns against a vast Indian army, Cortés' "eagle eye" sees the languid Indian commander in a litter near by. Charging him instantly and knocking him out of his litter, Cortés demoralizes the Indian army and saves his own. (III, 399–400.) Thereafter he continues to combine genius with good luck until his arrival in Tezcuco

at the end of the book, and the parallel to Book IV is clarified by his acquisition of men, ammunition, and horses from his Spanish enemies.

In the death of Montezuma and the behavior of his people, this book
also describes a decisive change among the Aztecs: the triumph of their
savagery over their refinement. Prescott dramatizes the transformation by
describing the Aztec people consistently from the Spanish point of view,
from which they appear as a wild mass, and by arranging his narrative so
that Montezuma's final disgrace and his death appear to be stages in the
death of refinement. In each of the first two chapters he relies heavily on
the natural imagery that he always applies to embattled savages and Moors,
and he concludes each of these chapters with a sentimental essay on Montezuma. The method produces a beautiful fusion of structure and theme,
for these chapters lead to the *Noche Triste*: with the refined emperor dead,
the way is prepared for the most unrestrained outburst of savage passions,
and it is clear that the Aztecs will now fight to the death. In the last chapter
of the book, moreover, Prescott introduces the resolute new emperor and
demonstrates that both armies are now stronger than when Cortés first
occupied Mexico. Thus he sets the stage for a war of extermination between civilized man and barbarian.

"Siege and Surrender," the final book on the conquest, epitomizes Prescott's skill in unifying theme and organization. While retracing the narrative pattern of the entire history, Prescott's arrangement of the decisive
campaign intensifies all the basic contrasts between Spaniard and Aztec;
it gives the crucial position again to religion; and, through remarkably
skillful pacing of the action, it facilitates a drastic change in tone toward
the Aztecs.

By devoting the first half of the book to Cortés' isolation of Mexico from
her allies, Prescott makes the very sequence of events intensify the nonreligious contrasts. As Cortés moves methodically around the lake, taking
town after town, his "scientific" strategy stands out clearly against the
Mexicans' reliance on inexhaustible numbers. In almost every town, moreover, his political skill then capitalizes on the weak "moral" basis of the
Mexican empire. The section concludes, appropriately, with his most brilliant political and scientific feats—his disposition of a conspiracy against
his life by his own men, and the launching of his prefabricated brigantines
on the lake.

Although he does not ignore these important contrasts in the second
half of this book, on the siege and destruction of Mexico, Prescott's organization of that section gives the greatest prominence to Aztec religious

defects. Toward the climax of the history the reversals of fortune that have characterized the entire narrative follow one another more closely, and the heights and depths become more extreme. In each of these last changes—in the last Spanish and Mexican victories before the turning point, at the turning point itself, and in the destruction of the city—Aztec religion dominates the action. The climax occurs after the final Aztec victory, when the Spaniards, having watched sixty-two of their comrades being led up the temple to be sacrificed, see their Indian allies disappear "silently . . . before the breath of superstition" (III, 157), because the Mexican oracles have promised victory within eight days. Prescott opens his account of the destruction of the city by recalling the prophecy and criticizing the priests' error in specifying so short a time. (III, 161.) Because the eight days have passed, many of Cortés allies return to help him, and then his final plea for a surrender that will at least save the city from ruin is rejected at the insistence of Mexico's priests. (III, 169–70.)

The conventional changes in tone toward the Indians follow closely changes in the intensity of action. Always at a rhetorical disadvantage when fighting as an enraged "mob," the Aztecs appear at their worst during the sacrificial ceremonies just before the climax. Then, as the action declines, they become eligible for the sentimental treatment always accorded to vanquished "races." Although they manage to make several more, furious attacks, Prescott describes all of these very briefly, and he concentrates on the Mexicans' weakness and horrible suffering. Their "ferocity" is now pathetic; their resistance, impotent. In the closing battle scenes their resistance is almost completely passive, and their vigorous enemies—reluctant Spaniard and eager Indian—hack away at an inactive mass. To conclude the action of the history, Prescott emphasizes their passiveness in a series of pathetic tableaux: of the defiant people "huddled" together awaiting slaughter, of Guatemozin standing among the ruins of his empire, and of the survivors' "melancholy evacuation" just before the narrative ends with a Spanish procession of mass and thanksgiving.

Within this basic design there are several recurrent patterns that enrich it and illustrate the theme. Perhaps the simplest of these is Prescott's use of his conclusions, in both the larger and smaller narrative units, to emphasize the continuity of action. Each of the first four narrative books ends as a prelude to greater action, and, especially in the two books on Cortés' first march to Mexico, chapter after chapter ends with his departure on another leg of his mission. This device sharpens the sense of movement that is so important to an epic in prose; in the books on Cortés' forward movement, moreover, it emphasizes his resolution and the relentlessness of his advance; and, in the sections describing his expeditions to avert threatened disaster, it accents both the need for his presence and the difficulty of his task.

A more important pattern which enhances both "interest" and theme is that of recurring spectacular scenes. The sublime landscapes, vast battle scenes, and splendid processions that appear regularly from beginning to end of the narrative maintain the large scale essential to an epic in prose; most of them also illustrate the theme and the unity of romance and history. Prescott's most effective method is visual; from the first embarkation of Cortés' little fleet to the final evacuation of Mexico by the Aztecs, one can trace the course of the narrative through a succession of grand pictures.

Perhaps the most impressive example is Prescott's use of the Mexican temple, or *teocalli*. This is the one major symbol in the history. Its pyramidal structure epitomizes the Oriental comparison; it represents one of the finest achievements of Aztec material ingenuity; its sacrificial stone, its "hideous" gods, and the "smoking hearts" offered to them (II, 149) typify the brutality of Aztec religion. Introduced dramatically at the turning point of the first book, it dominates scene after scene through the rest of the history. In its sanctuaries the Spaniards see "richly gilded" carvings and gold and silver hearts, along with "smoking" human hearts and "gore" that stains the walls. Standing on its summit, beside Montezuma, Cortés gains his closest view of the Aztec empire in its greatest power; standing there a year later, he sees the city in ruins. There, too, while the Spaniards are insecure "guests" in the city, holding Montezuma as a hostage, a Spanish chapel and an Aztec sanctuary stand at opposite ends, suggesting the temporary equilibrium of the two powers; there, in a portentous battle before their expulsion, the Spaniards slaughter a superior Aztec force and light "the funeral pyre of paganism" (II, 328); there, at the climax, sixty-two Spaniards are sacrificed in full view of their comrades. And finally, on the site of the ruined *teocalli*, the Spaniards build the largest cathedral in Mexico, burying the original stones in the ground as a symbolic foundation.

Such grand scenes gain structural importance through Prescott's recurrent, though not exclusive, use of the Spaniards' point of view. Periodically throughout the history, the sights that they see, when presented from their point of view, illustrate the immense odds against them. A major unifying device in each of the first two narrative books is Prescott's regularly spaced description of their first view of each major region—first from a distance and then as they enter the main city. And periodically thereafter he describes their entrances and exits from their point of view, comparing them with one another—when Cortés marches through the ominously silent streets of Mexico toward the end of Book IV, when he tries to escape on the *Noche Triste*, when he returns to Tlascala for the first and second times in Book V. With similar regularity the Spaniards' point of view enables Prescott to depict the Aztecs' vast but vague numerical superiority—when the Spaniards see them attacking at the very end of Book IV, when Cortés rides over a ridge and sees an Indian army spread over the valley at Otumba, when he sees the "flood" of retreating Spaniards and pursuing Aztecs rushing toward him in the last Mexican victory before the conquest. Just before the climax, moreover, the Spaniards' point of view allows Prescott to dramatize their feelings as they see their comrades led round the sides of the temple to the sacrificial stone at the summit. It is largely because of this point of view that he succeeds in highlighting the most lurid features of Aztec religion in his picture of the last Aztec triumph.

A third important pattern is the rhythmic succession of crises that Cortés must face from his entrance on the scene until his death. Even more successfully than Parkman's volume on La Salle, in which the rhetoric is so remarkably similar to Prescott's,[2] *The Conquest of Mexico* traces a hero's course from difficulty to difficulty. Regularly balancing the narrative of his victories are the periodic demands of his men to abandon the idea of conquest and return to Spain or Cuba; and Prescott follows each of these internal crises with an account of Cortés' skillful eloquence or political shrewdness. Less frequent, but still regularly balancing his problems with Indian enemies, are his periodic difficulties with Spanish enemies; and Prescott illustrates these recurring historical facts with periodic scenes that portray Cortés in meditation and summarize his difficulties.

Down to the eve of victory, moreover, these problems grow increasingly complex. The administrative difficulties come to include not only restraining some of his impetuous officers but also managing his Indian allies. The result is that Prescott keeps his hero walking always on the edge of ruin; and the succession of dilemmas makes forward movement seem imperative. In several desperate military situations Cortés resolves to march out and meet the superior enemy rather than await an attack; and throughout the history Prescott stresses heavily the central political fact of the expedition: only complete success will save Cortés from punishment for the illegality of his adventure.

The sole artistic value of Prescott's debatable epilogue, "The Subsequent Career of Cortés," seems to me to be its completion of this last pattern.[3] There is no rest for the representative cavalier, and he wants none. Despite Prescott's fear that the book was too "tame," it follows the pattern of endless striving from crisis to crisis down to the day of the hero's death. Cortés must still be everywhere at once, and the troubles that dominate this book take him on a "dreadful march" to Honduras (III, 279), a dangerous return voyage to Mexico, and two voyages back to Spain. During the latter of these, while awaiting royal justice, he joins an expedition against Algiers, on which he is shipwrecked; and at his death he is preparing to return to Mexico for more exploration of Western coastal waters.

The basic fault of this book, the weakest of the seven, is not so much its tameness as its compression. Covering the twenty years in little more than one hundred pages, it reveals the weaknesses in Prescott's selective standards more clearly than do the five books on the conquest, which tell the story of a two-year expedition to a single goal. Prescott's announced purpose is to give the reader "a nobler point of view" from which to "study" Cortés' character, by portraying him as colonial administrator, agricultural experimenter, and nautical explorer. (III, 274-75.) But the accounts of these activities are extremely superficial, and conventional sentiment repeatedly supersedes the announced purpose—not only in Prescott's preoccupation with crises, but in his accounts of the fate of Cortés friends and enemies, and of the reward given to Cortés' mistress, Marina. In these passages Prescott seems to forget the small scale to which he has set this book, and the result is a diffusion of emphasis in which only the trials of Cortés remain distinct.

2

In characterization as in structure Prescott's best achievement is in the broad alignment. Stationing his characters along the line from savagery to extreme formality, he succeeds in making the conventional distinctions an integral part of the historical action and an asset to his theme. Although this achievement has its price in distortions and in shallow perspective, the basic arrangement is historically sound and aesthetically true.

I have already demonstrated how skillfully Prescott builds the character of Montezuma and that of Cortés into the structure of his first three acts, and how well he takes advantage of the fiery Guatemozin's accession before the final campaign. He uses all the other characters in much the same way. The basic method is not to characterize in depth, but to display character types along the line of action and to contrast the types repeatedly, either explicitly or through the order of the action. In displaying types, moreover, Prescott often uses a pictorial method and conventional rhetoric. The result is a kind of panorama in which the characters assume poses associated with their typical action but lacking sharp detail.

There are two sets of virtuous and defective characters, the Spaniards and the Indians. Prescott requires one to see them along an axis that displays progressive or "natural" virtue at one pole, "savage" virtue at the other, and corruption clustered near the center. There are more gradients on the Spanish than on the Indian side of the center, but the major divisions on the two sides balance each other. Cortés and Guatemozin, "the last of the Aztecs" (III, 286), stand at the poles; the intriguing Governor of Cuba and the Bishop of Burgos face the sinister Aztec priests, "the Dominicans of the New World" (I, 82), at the center; and at the halfway point on the respective sides, where the corruption of luxury and self-interest begins to predominate, stand the Spanish officers and men sent out to replace Cortés, and the emperor Montezuma. Close to Cortés are his most reliable officer and his good-hearted priest, both of whom have fewer faults than the hero but lack his "comprehensive genius" (III, 275); close to Guatemozin are the chiefs who rebuke Montezuma and die with passive bravery.

The conventional contrasts work all along the line of action, all along the line of characters. Cortés must often recall his wavering men to their opportunity and their duty; Cortés perpetrates a massacre which, though morally dubious, is politically brilliant, and a few weeks later one of his lieutenants orders a massacre which is politically stupid. Cortés' original men, having learned through self-denial and excellent leadership to emulate his daring, defeat a larger, better-equipped Spanish army that has been corrupted by comfort and self-indulgent leadership; and on the *Noche Triste* they fight bravely along with their leader while their greedy former enemies are weighed down by excessive quantities of Aztec treasure. Among the Indians one sees two chiefs die silently at the stake while their emperor sits in chains, and then one sees the emperor thank Cortés for his release from the chains; one sees the collaborator Ixtlilxochitl jeered by his Tezcucan countrymen who resist the Spaniards until hopelessly defeated.

In the over-all narrative these historically documented contrasts are artistically valuable because all of them tend to delineate minor characters who would otherwise be less distinct, and because all of them help, at the same time, to clarify the theme. Repeatedly, moreover, a minor character's conventional trait, abstracted from a particular incident, helps to define the most valuable traits of the hero and the "natural" quality of his mission. The genius of Cortés is successfully defined not so much by those rhetorical passages in which Prescott discusses it as by the succession of incidents and by the array of characters from whom he is distinguished.

The most effective example among the minor characters is that of Narvaez, the officer sent out from Cuba to replace Cortés. The brief battle between the two Spanish forces is decided almost exclusively by differences in leadership. Apparently having little evidence for a full portrait of Narvaez, Prescott stresses the trait most clearly revealed by the battle itself: Narvaez prefers comfort to viligance, and underestimates his enemy. In short, this is a Mexican parallel to George Washington's victory over the Hessians. Prescott shows Cortés preparing his smaller force to attack during a severe storm; next he depicts Narvaez retiring for the night in his comfortable quarters; and then the decisive attack comes. A few words on the "softening" effect of an easy colonial life suffice to make the characterization sharp, for the action itself illustrates the personal contrast, and self-reliant, natural merit triumphs once more over inferior leadership depending on the letter of the law. (II, 254–67.)

With the two major characters as well, Prescott's best achievement is in unifying action, scene, and the conventional aspects of the theme. The progressive hero, originally aimless and irresponsible, is transformed by opportunity and follows thereafter a dedicated, resolute course; he is the energetic, self-made man, responding equally well to opportunity and adversity, and finally building success out of ruin. He is destiny's darling. His antagonist, the victim of destiny, is corrupted by power, luxury, and "superstition," and irresolute reaction only precipitates his inevitable decline.

As these qualities rise out of specific incidents and scenes and fit into the general structure, they represent the best of Prescott's art. His finest technical achievement is in the recurrent images of the two representative men.

A large majority of Prescott's pictures of Montezuma show him standing motionless or moving reluctantly toward some melancholy destination. From the beginning one sees him *receiving* news of Cortés, the protagonist, and one almost never sees him acting on his own initiative. Immersed in an atmosphere of ruin suggested by Prescott's description of the "tangled wilderness" that "now" overruns the splendid palace grounds,

Montezuma watches lavish entertainments, reluctantly listens to the petitions of his subjects, and drinks great quantities of a cloying beverage. (II, 124.) Then, when the action of the fourth book begins, one sees him quietly guiding the Spaniards through the temple, remaining to do penance after Cortés has insulted the gods, agreeing from his own throne to become a hostage in Spanish quarters, sitting in chains as his attendants try to relieve the pressure of his irons, and finally swearing allegiance to Spain. These images culminate in his last grand scene, when he stands on high and tries to persuade his enraged people to let the Spaniards leave in peace. Struck down by one of his own people, he embodies the stately refinement that savage passions destroy. One sees him, at last, literally supine, resolved to die.

The characteristic image of Cortés, on the other hand, depicts him in energetic motion: riding onward and upward toward Mexico, charging in battle after battle, tumbling idols down the sides of a temple, riding on forced marches to avoid disaster, crossing a steep canyon to attack Indians in a natural fortress, addressing his men eloquently, pacing his quarters at night while his men sleep. When one does see him in a stationary pose, as when he sits exhausted after the *Noche Triste*, he is usually contemplating future action, and in at least one tableau his pose is implicitly aggressive: at his first meeting with Montezuma he tries presumptuously to embrace the sacred emperor as an equal.

Except for some of the scenes of nocturnal reflection, which are imposed in stilted language on the action, all of these images rise out of documented actions. Along with the unpictured narrative of Cortés' achievements, they demonstrate the value of Prescott's basic method. Few of them are sharply detailed, yet they reveal the most important characters in poses that illustrate not only the theme but also the most important events down to the time of Montezuma's death. Prescott's deployment of his characters throughout the story of the conquest achieves the same double goal, and it therefore remains an admirable example of historical art.

But the method is also costly. Although the types are admirably suited to the historical facts and the theme, they are types only. For all their clarity in illustrating the basic conflict, they reveal nearly blank faces when one tries to examine them closely. They are ill suited to the portrayal of complex motivation, of complex character. They do not allow graceful qualification. These limitations weaken the portrayal of both Montezuma and Cortés, the two men whom Prescott tries to portray in detail, and they produce some distortion in the action itself.

The portrait of Montezuma is marred, of course, by the confusion of Prescott's double standard for savages, but the confusion is compounded by the unique prophecies of Aztec religion. Anyone acquainted with the double standard might expect Prescott to stress Montezuma's intrigue when describing his early resistance to Cortés, and then to judge his placid acceptance of the Spaniards by the standards of Indians who resisted to the death. What is surprising—and most damaging—is Prescott's careless treatment of Montezuma's belief that the Spaniards represented the "white gods" whose advent had been prophesied. Montezuma's puzzling behavior justifies some doubts that he consistently believed in the Spaniards' divinity.[4] Yet Prescott does not even raise the question. Without suggesting that the belief wavered, he follows the peculiar course of condemning Montezuma's "pusillanimity" and then attributing it to the belief that the Spaniards were indeed divine agents. (See, for example, II, 75.)

Whatever the justice of this procedure, which seems to be based on an unexplained distinction between superstition and religion (II, 350), it certainly confuses the characterization. Following the pattern of contrasts, Prescott wedges Montezuma so firmly between the decisive Cortés and the resolutely hostile Aztecs that he fails to display clearly the religious aspect of Montezuma's motivation, even though his own judgment requires him to do so. In the narrative Montezuma's religious motivation stands forth clearly only in those incidents which precede the Spaniards' arrival in Mexico—incidents that highlight timid vacillation, human sacrifices, and deceit. This portion of the characterization ends when Montezuma, in a "paroxysm of despair" (II, 57), secludes himself to fast as the Spaniards approach the city. Once the Spaniards have arrived, however, the sinister behavior that they expect of Montezuma never occurs; not only does he treat them graciously and faithfully, but his religion prompts him to as many courageous as "pusillanimous" actions.[5] Faced with this evidence, Prescott seems to forget the Aztec prophecy. Especially in the crucial episode of Montezuma's "incredible" capture in the palace, he restricts the psychological context almost exclusively to "honor," "pride," and "courage"; and he uses secular language to motivate all of Montezuma's actions in this scene. Only after having declared, in a reflective paragraph, that Montezuma should have fought to the death, does he allude to fate, and even then he uses Montezuma's belief in fate to explain his loss of "courage." (II, 166–68.)

Although Prescott's emphasis in this scene is unconvincing, the most important fact to notice here is that he himself does not finally believe in it. Twice more before Montezuma disappears from the history Prescott asks the reader to be charitable because the emperor's strange submissiveness was "less" the result of "fear than of conscience." (II, 198, 343-44.)

Thus, without underestimating the difficulty of portraying so strange a character, one must find Prescott's Montezuma out of focus. Unable either to doubt the religious sources of Montezuma's conduct or to examine it outside the frame of conventional Indian courage and patriotism, Prescott cannot achieve a coherent portrait. When the simple formula of emasculating decadence seems to him inadequate, he relies on feeble qualification which, instead of deepening the conventional portrait, only blurs it.

The same kind of defect weakens the portrayal of Cortés. In him Prescott sees such a combination of admirable and blameworthy traits that at beginning and end he emphasizes the idea of paradox. Yet in the narrative Cortés' unconventional traits and motives have little functional importance. Prescott describes several cruel actions and mentions some unheroic motives, but these become indistinct under the intense light that he concentrates on the conventional heroic qualities: lofty ambition, constancy, self-reliance, courage, leadership. When Cortés' actions reveal cruelty and avarice, Prescott regularly subordinates these traits to other qualities (such as firm discipline or strategic brilliance), or he remarks that other Spaniards were more cruel and avaricious. Whether or not this latter method is too lenient, it too often allows Prescott to exclude the unheroic qualities from his explanation of Cortés' behavior. By concentrating on how the historian ought to judge cruel actions themselves, Prescott avoids dealing with cruelty as a trait of his hero; by highlighting constancy as the main trait and ambition as the main motive, he obscures one's view of avarice as a lesser trait or motive. He may imply in his reflections on one episode that Cortés has no "humanity" (II, 177), but in a dozen narrative passages he highlights Cortés' sensibility. Since the narrative does not make the reprehensible traits a harmonious part of the characterization, one is left at the end with a combination of "incompatible traits." (III, 352 ff.)

The rigidity of the conventional pattern also forces Prescott into careless inconsistency. Confronted with Bernal Diaz' statement that it was the officers and not Cortés who first suggested capturing Montezuma in his own palace, Prescott uses Cortés' habit of command as his main argument against Diaz (II, 160, n. 3); but later on he reverses this argument completely in order to show that the officers and not Cortés were responsible for a disaster. (III, 136, n. 1.) Again in the epilogue, moreover, he says that the officers and men virtually forced Cortés to torture Guatemozin during the search for hidden treasure. (III, 234.)

With both major characters, then, Prescott is willing to qualify his judgments. But his adherence to the conventional pattern sometimes distorts his interpretation of specific actions, and it prevents him from making unconventional motives a coherent part of his characterization.

The same kind of weakness affects Prescott's portrayal of the Aztec people and their "priests." One can hardly condemn his revulsion against human sacrifice and cannibalism or his conclusion that these customs precipitated the ruin of Mexico. Certainly the need for sacrificial victims encouraged the Mexicans' imperial wars and aggravated their relations with conquered peoples. In the Spanish campaign itself, moreover, the Aztecs lost several opportunities to delay the conquest—and even an easy chance to kill Cortés—simply because they were obliged to save captives for the sacrifice. But although Prescott exploits these facts skillfully, his commitment to the conventional attitudes hinders his efforts to qualify the mass characterizations. He insists that sacrifice and cannibalism debased the national character, but his faithfully presented evidence of "civilization" often outweighs the evidence by which he tries to justify the prefix "semi." (See, for example, II, 135–39.) Although the Mexicans' military tactics and religious rituals were, respectively, savage and brutal, Prescott offers no evidence besides the customs themselves that they debased character.

With the priests, whom he portrays as Gothic figures "flitting" wildly about in certain battle scenes, Prescott has little trouble until the last section of the narrative, when they advise Guatemozin never to surrender. Their influence on this decision should suffice to demonstrate the religious cause of the destruction of Mexico. But Prescott cannot let this fact alone show the inevitability of the catastrophe. After reporting their irrefutable arguments for refusing to surrender, he impugns their motives without offering any evidence for doing so, and he thus weakens his already exaggerated portrayal of them. (III, 169–70.)

3

The triumph of excellent design over faulty detail is nowhere clearer than in Prescott's prose style. In *The Conquest of Mexico* it is often his organization, his control of the narrative, or his conception of a scene—rather than brilliant rhetoric or precise description—that contributes most to the effectiveness of a passage. Both the faults and the virtues of his style account for this fact, and many passages succeed in spite of serious defects in the prose itself.

This is not to deny that *The Conquest of Mexico* contains passages of faultless rhetoric or description. But Prescott's stature as a great stylist has been exaggerated by modern critics, who have usually cited only his best passages or ignored stylistic faults in others that are memorable.[6] Even J. B. Black, whose study of eighteenth-century historians compares Prescott unfavorably to Robertson, overlooks characteristic faults in the fine paragraph that he cites from *The Conquest of Mexico*, and he praises Prescott's style without qualification.[7] This generous procedure prevents an adequate appreciation of Prescott's art, for it not only fails to discriminate but neglects the relationship between merits and defects.

The main virtues of Prescott's style are its graceful balance, its frequently stately cadences, and its clarity. Modest but substantial merits, these qualities are extremely valuable in the history. They suggest judiciousness, and in many appropriate passages they provide what Prescott called "elevation."[8] They are well suited to expository summary, to the grand procession, to the spectacular scene. In many sections, moreover, they call one's attention to the structure of the narrative, to the orderly sequence of paragraphs, rather than to details within the paragraph. The skillfully meshed, graceful sentences move the narrative so well that one may often overlook all but the most distracting faults within the sentences.

Although adequate illustration of this judgment would require the quotation of an entire episode, three paragraphs should suffice to clarify it. In the Spaniards' first penetration to the center of Mexico during the final campaign, they had to fight their way slowly along a causeway intersected by several canals, at each of which the retreating Mexicans destroyed the bridge and made a stand. Prescott's seven-page account of this battle is controlled by two simple devices that are largely responsible for its success. Every one of his twelve paragraphs is constructed to emphasize the alternation between forward movement and pause or retreat. And, beginning with the Spaniards' entry on the main street, he emphasizes pictorial views looking toward the central objective, the square of the temple, where the decisive action occurs. It is the movement toward this square, with the clear suggestion of what that movement cost in a whole day's battle, that distinguishes the account. The representative passage begins with the vista opened to the Spaniards as they arrive on the main street, and it ends with their view of their objective. They have just come off the causeway after having taken and filled in the last of several breaches in it.* (III, 111–13.)

[1]The street, on which the Spaniards now entered, was the great avenue that intersected the town from north to south, and the same by which they had first entered the capital. [2]It was broad and perfectly straight, and, in the distance, dark masses of warriors might be seen gathering to the support of their country-

---

* I have numbered Prescott's sentences for later reference.

men, who were prepared to dispute the further progress of the Spaniards. [3]The sides were lined with buildings, the terraced roofs of which were also crowded with combatants, who, as the army advanced, poured down a pitiless storm of missiles on their heads, which glanced harmless, indeed, from the coat of mail, but too often found their way through the more common *escaupil* of the soldier, already gaping with many a ghastly rent. [4]Cortés, to rid himself of this annoyance for the future, ordered his Indian pioneers to level the principal buildings as they advanced; in which work of demolition no less than in the repair of the breaches, they proved of inestimable service.

[5]The Spaniards, meanwhile, were steadily, but slowly, advancing, as the enemy recoiled before the rolling fire of musketry, though turning, at intervals, to discharge their javelins and arrows against their pursuers. [6]In this way they kept along the great street, until their course was interrupted by a wide ditch or canal, once traversed by a bridge, of which only a few planks now remained. [7]These were broken by the Indians, the moment they had crossed, and a formidable array of spears was instantly seen bristling over the summit of a solid rampart of stone, which protected the opposite side of the canal. [8]Cortés was no longer supported by his brigantines, which the shallowness of the canals prevented from penetrating into the suburbs. [9]He brought forward his arquebusiers, who, / protected by the targets of their comrades, / opened a fire on the enemy. [10]But the balls fell harmless from the bulwarks of stone; while the assailants presented but too easy a mark to their opponents.

[11]The general then caused the heavy guns to be brought up, and opened a lively cannonade, which soon cleared a breach in the works, through which the musketeers and crossbow-men poured in their volleys thick as hail. [12]The Indians now gave way in disorder, after having held their antagonists at bay for two hours. [13]The latter, jumping into the shallow water, / scaled the opposite bank without further resistance, / and drove the enemy along the street towards the square, / where the sacred pyramid reared its colossal bulk / high over the other edifices of the city. (III, 111–13.)

Although far better than the worst prose in the history, these typical paragraphs not only illustrate the merits but also suggest the defects of Prescott's style. The conception and general construction are admirable, for the order of each paragraph reflects the basic qualities of the action, advance and pause, and each of the three pictures stresses one kind of difficulty that delayed the Spaniards' advance. The balanced length and rhythm of elements in the compound and complex sentences often underscore the changes in action, as in the second sentence, the entire second paragraph, and the eleventh and thirteenth sentences. Although the succession of subordinate clauses in the third sentence threatens to escape Prescott's control, his skillful use of subordinate clauses allows him to provide a good deal of information without impeding the narrative.

The rhythms of this prose also require attention. Phrase, clause, and sentence consistently end with a firmly stressed word, emphasizing the almost orotund symmetry. Moreover, although the length of rhythmic elements is properly varied, Prescott often uses a pentameter line to intensify battle action, as in the series of five that I have marked in the last sentence, and he sometimes makes this line regularly iambic. With one exception (end of sentence 3) he also makes the most euphonious lines those which describe the most vigorous action, as one can see in the sharp contrast between the rhythm of the second sentence and that of the line describing the missiles hurled from the rooftops.

Yet Prescott's sense of rhythm and balance often leads him into trouble, as one can see even in this successful passage. Although the heavy alliteration of the first two paragraphs is sometimes appropriate (as in the letters I have italicized in the second paragraph), the alliteration in the first paragraph shows a marked failure to discriminate. Perhaps unintentionally alliterated, the succession of five heavily stressed plosives (italicized in sentence 2) puts these unpoetic words in grotesque contrast to the excessively poetic "already gaping with many a ghastly rent"—an unquestionably intentional flight which soars conspicuously above the rest of the language. Surely, moreover, the "storm" of missiles is "pitiless" largely because Prescott wants to alliterate with "poured," a word that has already weakened the "storm" metaphor; and the phrase "on their heads," which leaves the next clause at least momentarily dangling, would have been deleted by a writer less frequently tempted to write by rhythmic phrases rather than individual words. In the same careless way Prescott gives the stone rampart a "summit" in the next paragraph because he is thinking more of rhythm and sibilance than of precise meaning.

Neither these faults nor the awkward shifts to the passive voice in each of the first two pictures ruin the passage, but they do illustrate the basic defects in Prescott's prose. The central weakness is inadequate attention to detail, a surprising insensitivity to precise meaning. The result is often no worse than an annoying verbosity that tempts one to substitute a word for a phrase; but if such tautologies as "gifted with a truer foresight into futurity" (II, 421) are fortunately rare, they reveal the extremes to which Prescott could be led by this kind of carelessness. The fault is most damaging in his imagery.

A writer who describes a "tempest of missiles . . . which fell thick as rain" (II, 302-3) has stopped visualizing the image itself. Much of Prescott's imagery, though it is seldom so weak as this example, issues from the same defective principle. The majority of his figures are so conventional that they might just as well have come from his reading—or from a list of figures in a handbook of rhetoric—as from his own comparison of figurative and literal action. Often, therefore, they do not accomplish what Prescott warned himself that figures must do; they do not "make [the narrative] *clearer, or stronger.*"[9]

In the many battle scenes the conventionality of the imagery is not in itself the main flaw. When they make the reader visualize a specific action the worn metaphors can still be serviceable. When Cortés, for example, standing on the causeway, first hears and then sees his army being chased toward him by an immense Indian force, the familiarity of the "torrent" image does not vitiate the impact, for Prescott skillfully requires one to see the action from Cortés' point of view. (III, 143-44.) And, in the same way, the conventional natural imagery with which Prescott describes his Indians is often forceful despite its triteness, because it is relevant to his theme and appropriate to the Spaniards' point of view. (See I, 443; II, 315.)

For each of these figures, however, Prescott employs at least one that does weaken the passage in which it appears. Monotonously repetitious in his battle imagery, he makes tempest or torrent, current, tide, or flood soak almost every battle scene. Often, he uses his trite images as substitutes for concrete description. Often, too, he prefers trite metaphorical phrases to single, literal verbs; and his habit of using rather elaborate similes often produces a trite figure at the end of a literal description that is already sufficiently clear and forceful. Sparks of courage kindle in bosoms, and sparks of hope die away in bosoms (II, 56); men in trouble imagine themselves standing on the brinks of dark and yawning gulfs; armies and cities lie buried in slumber (I, 433); buildings are wrapt in flames (III, 58), and news spreads like wildfire or on the wings of the wind; in the still watches of the night many an anxious thought crowds on the mind of Cortés (I, 433); Indians huddle together like herds of frightened deer (II, 24); passions are fanned into a blaze (II, 287), and an annunciation of bad news falls like a knell upon the ears of the Christians (II, 332); a restless eye roves round the battlefield, becomes, in the next paragraph, an eagle eye, falls on its desired object, and then lights up with triumph (II, 399); the stoutest hearts are often filled with dismay (II, 394); brows darken (II, 289), and wounds rankle deep in bosoms (II, 291); brigantines, ready to be launched on the bosom of a lake, emerge, at last, on its ample bosom, and make the hero's bosom swell with exultation (III, 77, 88); missiles carry desolation through the ranks (II, 324), and cavaliers repeatedly plunge headlong into the thickest of the press; Spaniards hew down Indians as easily as the reaper mows down the ripe corn in harvest time. (II, 24.)

One should recognize, of course, that most of these figures, along with others which Prescott used regularly, were accepted as ordinary expressions in the prose of the time, and that at least some of them were not regarded as figures to be analyzed for accuracy or consistency. Prescott's physical handicap provides an even more important explanation; his terrible eye trouble, which denied him that experience of precise observation on which the best imagery is based, also led him to compose some entire chapters in his head before writing, and to warn himself repeatedly against looking back over too much of his manuscript before proceeding with his composition. He wrote at his noctograph, trying to refrain from looking at the page, and when his manuscript had been copied for him, he left a large part of the revision to his friend W. H. Gardiner. Indeed, he once enjoined himself not to worry too much about details of composition, for his own revision or Gardiner's would correct nice faults.[10]

But however much these facts may explain, however much they may temper one's judgment of Prescott, they cannot alter the defects. Even if he had not criticized these very faults in his notebooks and in his biography of Charles Brockden Brown,[11] Prescott's history would have to stand by itself. In so far as the tradition in which he was writing sanctioned these faults, it was a faulty tradition.

The effects of Prescott's insensitivity to language appear regularly throughout the history, often tainting otherwise excellent passages. Many of the sentences are marred by what Prescott himself called vague "epithets." Sometimes the heightened rhetoric, especially in battle scenes from which specific detail is omitted, seems merely stilted; sometimes the diction is inconsistent or awkwardly elevated.[12] In passages describing strong sentiment, Prescott often displays an awkward lack of restraint—not only by using trite language that diffuses instead of intensifying the particular sentiment, but also by saying too much. Occasionally, his inclination to conventional phrasing leads him to say something that he could not possibly believe.[13]

Even some of the great moments, the most memorable scenes, in the history include such faults. The portrait of Montezuma sitting in chains is unforgettable because of its place and meaning in the narrative, because Prescott displays a fine sense of pictorial grouping, and because he knows how to use one essential detail. But the flaws of his language—cliché, abstract, unnecessary simile, and repetitious or unnecessary telling—show

up clearly when one examines the picture. I have italicized those words
that might well be omitted or replaced.

Montezuma was speechless under the infliction of this last insult. *He was like
one struck down by a heavy blow, that deprives him of all his faculties.* He offered no resistance. But, though he spoke not a word, low, ill-suppressed moans,
from time to time, *intimated the anguish of his spirit.* His attendants, *bathed
in tears, offered him their consolations. They* tenderly held his feet in their arms,
and endeavoured, by inserting their shawls and mantles, to relieve them from
the pressure of the iron. But they could not reach the iron which had penetrated
his soul. He felt that he was no more a king. (II, 172–73.)

Prescott's moving descriptions of the *Noche Triste;* of Montezuma's fatal
attempt, from the palace roof, to calm his people; of Cortés' return to silent,
hostile Mexico after the expedition against Narvaez—all contain similar
defects. They are memorable, and our literature would be the poorer without them; but they are superior to their defective parts.

Because of this combination of skills and stylistic faults, and because of
the nature of his subject, Prescott's most remarkable achievements in the
history are the general scenes so important to its structure. It is the tableau,
the sweeping panorama, the grand procession, that most often compels one's
admiration. For the same reasons his presentation of battle settings is usually more impressive than his account of the battles themselves. Neither his
style, his inclination to choose generalizing epithets, nor the scarcity of
detailed information permitted him to write his best prose in his circumstantial descriptions of violent action. In almost all the battle scenes the
quality of his description declines as he moves closest to the specific action
and as the amount of imagery increases. The best battle scenes are those in
which he minimizes his imagery (as in the passage quoted above) or those,
such as the *Noche Triste,* in which the importance of the event and his concentration on specific sounds and broad pictures of the scene overcome
serious faults in the language. (See, for example, II, 23–25.)

One should not conclude from this analysis that there are no passages
of consistently good prose in the history. Although it would be difficult to
find a section of fifteen or twenty pages that is not damaged by some of
the faults which I have discussed, Prescott achieves many fine passages of
clear exposition. The least defective of these are the descriptions of quiet
action, such as the Spaniards' first entry into Mexico, and of such factual
subjects as Montezuma's way of life. In these sections Prescott does not seem
to feel obliged to elevate his language, and the grace and clarity of his ordinary prose are not offset by excesses in rhetoric. Moreover, his most successful rhetorical passages usually describe scenes that allow his rhythm and

the sounds of his words to emphasize slow rather than rapid motion. Prescott's style, like Hawthorne's and Irving's, is better adapted to the tableau than to vigorous action.

Prescott's first description of a sacrificial ceremony, in his introductory book, illustrates the principle. A captive, surrounded with splendid luxury from the day of his selection as a victim, must give it up on the last day:

As the sad procession wound up the sides of the pyramid, the unhappy victim threw away his gay chaplets of flowers, and broke in pieces the musical instruments with which he had solaced the hours of captivity. On the summit he was received by six priests, whose long and matted locks flowed disorderly from their sable robes, covered with hieroglyphic scrolls of mystic import. They led him to the sacrificial stone, a huge block of jasper, with its upper surface somewhat convex. On this the prisoner was stretched. Five priests secured his head and his limbs; while the sixth, clad in a scarlet mantle, emblematic of his bloody office, dexterously opened the breast with a sharp razor of *itztli*,—a volcanic substance, hard as flint,—and, inserting his hand in the wound, tore out the palpitating heart. The minister of death, first holding this up towards the sun, an object of worship throughout Anahuac, cast it at the feet of the deity to whom the temple was devoted, while the multitudes below prostrated themselves in humble adoration. The tragic story of this prisoner was expounded by the priests as the type of human destiny, which, brilliant in its commencement, too often closes in sorrow and disaster. (I, 76–77.)

This scene epitomizes Prescott's romantic art. The contrast between splendor and horror, a common romantic device, emphasizes the theme of the history; the height of the stage, another romantic quality stressed at the beginning and end of the scene, adds to its effect; the priests' moral foreshadows the doom of Mexico itself. As in Hawthorne's more famous tableaux, the silence and the hint of a silhouette, as the pageant winds round the temple and as the priest reaches toward the sun, reinforce the picture's symbolic quality. One should notice, too, that Prescott makes the transition from sweeping movement to horrible detail by presenting the Gothic image of the priests; and that he direct's one's attention again to the large scene, to the multitude, by the priest's act of raising the heart to the sky, and then flinging it down. The cadences and the sounds of individual words ("as the sad procession wound up the sides"; "a huge block of jasper") intensify the melancholy atmosphere.

In this kind of picture, in his deployment of characters along a scale appropriate to both historical fact and romantic conventions, and above all in his brilliant organization, Prescott achieved a masterpiece despite the inescapable limitations of his method and his language.

CHAPTER VIII

The Rise of the Dutch Republic

As the conquest of Mexico suited Prescott's conventional theories and individual talents, the Dutch rebellion against Philip II suited those of Motley. Although it posed serious structural problems, this story, too, centered on the conflict of two irreconcilable "races," political systems, and religions, and Motley believed that the conflict had aided all democratic progress. The Dutch rebellion also offered abundant material for Motley's skill in portraying cruel, treacherous, and merely contemptible characters, and for his skill in describing grotesque and horrible events. In the Dutch patriots' endurance through innumerable defeats, innumerable executions, and recurrent pillage he found ideal evidence that liberty was indestructible. In the letters of Philip II and others he found signed confessions of treachery and secret murder—crimes committed against rebellious heretics and loyal Catholics. In the Dutch hero he found a sixteenth-century Prince who not only had defied alien, "ecclesiastical tyranny" but had upheld against his own people the nineteenth-century ideals of religious freedom and federal unity.

Out of these materials Motley built a history which, though at times singularly exasperating, represents a major literary achievement. *The Rise of the Dutch Republic* does suffer from the romantic methods that account for much of its success, from the vehemence of Motley's antipathy to "ecclesiastical tyranny," and from his failure to construct it as tightly as Prescott had built his masterpiece. But it is distinguished by superb scenes that dramatize its grand theme, by a remarkably brilliant gallery of historical portraits, and by some of the finest narrative prose in American literature.

I

Despite all its advantages, Motley's subject alone sufficed to prevent him from achieving Prescott's kind of structural triumph. Motley could not build his narrative on the geographical advance, retreat, and return of his hero. William the Silent, indeed, had begun his campaign not by marching resolutely toward the enemy, but by fleeing the country. He had never defeated a major Spanish army in the field. And his heroic struggle, far from ending in victory, had ended with his assassination. During the thirty years covered by Motley's history, moreover, the complex religious and political changes within the Netherlands and the intricate negotiations with several other governments had been just as important as the battles, and Motley was obliged to include them in his narrative. Yet the majority of battles and conferences alike had, in themselves, decided little. The Dutch patriots had succeeded rather by enduring than by winning a clear military or diplomatic victory; even at the time of William's death, Motley's concluding event, they had achieved neither a peace settlement nor any definitive geographical decision. The two provinces of Holland and Zeeland had declared their independence, but the war continued for another twenty-five years before the republic of seven provinces was defined, and for still another thirty years before their independence became secure.

In the face of these difficulties Motley followed Prescott's example and organized *The Rise of the Dutch Republic* dramatically. After his "Historical Introduction," he divided his narrative into six "Parts": a dramatic prologue,[1] and five acts corresponding to the terms of the five governors whom Philip II had sent to the Netherlands during this period. The prologue, "Philip II in the Netherlands," prepares the stage admirably. Opening with the abdication ceremony at which Charles V gives his native Netherlands to his "foreign" son, it introduces many of the main characters, foreshadows the betrayal that awaits several of them, describes a "petty" war in which the Pope and the Kings of France and Spain betray one another, and closes with Philip's ominous departure from the Netherlands. The first act, "The Administration of Margaret, Duchess of Parma," reveals the basic conflict and leads to the verge of inevitable war. Philip's intensified persecution of Dutch heretics provokes many of the lesser Dutch nobles to demand that he honor his oath to respect their constitutional privileges; William the Silent and other great nobles try desperately to resolve the conflict; but then the Dutch people explode into action. Margaret, forced to grant concessions, revokes them at the first opportunity and imposes loyalist garrisons on all the towns, but Philip nevertheless sends a Spanish army to "crush" the country that has already been "subjugated." (II, 82.)* The act ends as this army marches toward the Netherlands, and William must at last commit himself to rebellion.

---

* Volume and page numbers in parentheses refer to the three-volume edition of *The Rise of the Dutch Republic*, published by Harper, New York, 1856.

In the second and third acts (Parts III and IV) the Dutch people are
are reduced to "sublime desolation," but the patriot cause survives because
of a few timely successes, the oppressors' stupid economic policy, and the
death of Philip's third governor. This accident near the center of the third
act enables the unpaid Spanish troops to mutiny, and their pillage of Antwerp—"the Spanish Fury"—provokes all Dutch classes and religious fac-
tions to demand the expulsion of the Spanish troops. Before Philip's new
governor-general can arrive, the Dutch have won virtual control of the
entire country, and their fortunes continue to rise through most of the
fourth act. They achieve their greatest success just before the climax, when
William wins an alliance with England and unites all the provinces under
the "New Union of Brussels." But immediately afterward the patriot
armies are crushed at the battle of Gemblours, and the final act of the drama
is one long denouement. According to Motley, the battle of Gemblours has
permanently divided the Netherlands, and his fifth act dramatizes the inevitable sequel. Again on the defensive, the patriots are occupied with mini-
mizing their political and military defeats until the drama ends with William's assassination.

Thus Motley had to invert the chart of action that Prescott had traced
in *The Conquest of Mexico;* in *The Rise of the Dutch Republic* progressive
fortunes decline, rise, and finally decline. This arrangement seriously weakens the structure, for Motley's drama lacks an appropriate conclusion. At
the end the basic conflict, the struggle for religious and political liberty remains unresolved. Liberty survives in the Netherlands, but the concluding
events do not even dramatize its precarious survival. Apparently aware of
this problem, Motley tried to solve it by concentrating on the secondary
issue of Dutch national unity, by insisting that William's death had elimi-
nated the last dim hope of union; yet he had to admit that the final separation had not been completed until the fall of Antwerp in the following year,
and he could neither make William's assassination a dramatic substitute for
that event nor establish a clear connection between the two disasters. (III,
615–16.) William's assassination, moreover, does not follow dramatically
from the major scenes that precede it, or from the climax; it is an isolated
episode, a historical accident.

But if the course of Dutch fortunes and the final incident of the history
prevented Motley from completing his drama as effectively as he had begun
it, they gave admirable support to his central theme. His story of those
thirty years of bloodshed proclaims two complementary "laws": that liberty
and religious truth, always indestructible, are invincible when defended by

a brave, energetic people; and that in such a conflict tyranny, however powerful, inevitably defeats itself, because its methods and its men are as unnatural as its ends. To this theme the rarity of patriot victories becomes a distinct advantage, for the power of the drama lies in the struggle against overwhelming adversity. The most terrible defeats do not destroy liberty, and tyranny's most crushing victories lead only to frustration.

The structural importance of Dutch suffering is apparent from beginning to end. Motley's atavistic Introduction reviews the Netherlands' centuries of struggle against massive forces, and his drama traces a course of fruitful suffering under Spanish oppression. As Prescott's conquistadors had done, Motley's patriots move from crisis to crisis, but here the majority of crises turn against the progressive forces. In spite of rebel successes the gory evidence of Dutch suffering accumulates steadily through 1,700 pages until the representative hero, who has already lost most of his property in the cause, loses his life. Using spectacular catastrophes to dramatize the principle, Motley demonstrates that the patriots' difficulties and the horrors they endured increased with time. From the terrors of the rejuvenated Inquisition and the sack of a few recalcitrant Dutch towns in the first act, he moves to the vindictive tyranny of the Duke of Alva, whose ubiquitous "Blood Council" seems to carry bloodletting to its extreme. But Alva's successful siege of Harlem, where Dutch liberty is driven to its original "lair," is still more gruesome; his unsuccessful siege of Leyden, still more bloody. The Spanish Fury, in the third act, accomplishes new refinements of individual brutality and new records of slaughter and destruction; and Alexander Farnese's reduction of Maestricht, in the last act, is the most destructive battle of the entire history.

This accumulation of gore helps, of course, to characterize Spanish tyranny as well as Dutch endurance. Although he recognized the danger of tedious repetition (III, 196), Motley was determined to paint a complete picture of tyranny, and he tried to convert the immense bulk of his material into an artistic advantage. However awkwardly they sometimes impede his narrative, the scores of disingenuous proclamations, inconclusive conferences, cynical economic proposals, and treacherous letters of Spanish officials add great power to this gross picture. Alternated as they are with innumerable pictures of cruel actions, they assume the shape of almost superhuman evil. Horrible dramatic scenes in Gothic settings, plain entries from a ledger of payments to an executioner, grotesque pictures of Spanish leaders in unnatural situations—not only the concrete detail but the cumulative number of such facts reveals a picture of Gothic horror. With the heavy weight of vast, documented evidence Motley stamped Philip's government of the Netherlands as the type of all tyranny. (II, 314.)

For working out this picture in historical and dramatic terms Motley
had the advantage of royalist characters whose individual traits seemed
appropriate to both the course of events and Spanish policy during their
respective administrations. Although he used the persistence of cruelty
and deception through all five administrations to demonstrate that tyranny
remains essentially the same under varying disguises, he made the governors
themselves represent different aspects of tyranny, corresponding to the
different masks that events led Philip II to present to the Netherlands. Each
of the first four administrations fails, and the fifth does not succeed completely; the end of each of the first four acts, therefore, emphasizes a personal failure.

Religious oppression and sly deceit stand forth most clearly in the first
act, in which the Dutch government is dominated by the Iagoesque Cardinal Granvelle; here the personal drama focuses on Granvelle's secret calumny of the "great" Dutch nobles; on the mutual deceit of Granvelle and
the regent, who "stab fiercely at each other in the dark" (I, 447); and on
Philip's intrigues with each of these agents against the other, while all three
unite to promise false concessions to the Dutch. When these traits and
policies have failed to destroy heresy, Philip removes both Margaret and
Granvelle, who have lost his confidence and that of the Dutch people, and
resorts at last to total oppression.

Philip's next agent, the Duke of Alva, wears no mask at all, but reveals
to the Netherlands the bare face of tyranny. He violates every Dutch constitutional privilege, condemns the whole nation to death (excepting by
name "a few" individuals), levies an incredible tax on every single business
transaction; and when, having finally lost Philip's confidence, he sneaks
out of Amsterdam without paying his personal debts, he recommends that
every city in the country be razed. Portraying him as the nearly mad incarnation of despotism (II, 178–79), Motley calls this Part of the history one
of the most "finished" pictures ever recorded of a "perfect tyranny." (II,
503.)

With the failure of Alva total oppression disappears from the history,
and so, for the moment, does the strong Spanish character. Motley opens
his third act by announcing that Philip has "again" turned to "the mask
and cothurn," sending "a grave and conventional personage . . . to perform an interlude of clemency." (II, 513.) The "mediocre" Grand Commander, Requesens, pursues the war but offers pardons and abolishes Alva's

Blood Council. His relative colorlessness suits Motley's purposes, for it is Philip's failure and the absence of leadership that are to be emphasized in this act. Requesens' efficient military strategy nearly succeeds, but his death on the eve of victory encourages the Spanish troops to reward their King's niggardliness with mutiny. Aimless, indiscriminate military force then takes over, terrorizing and ruining the richest city in Europe. In this furious sack of Antwerp Motley symbolizes the ultimate evil of pure military force in the Spanish troops, who discard "even the vizard of humanity" and behave like fiends. (III, 111–12.)

Even the freedom of fiction could not have given Motley a more ideal Spanish leader for his fourth act than history gave him in the last "crusader of chivalry" (III, 145), Don John of Austria. The hero of Lepanto, whose barren victory there offered a neat contrast to William's fruitful defeats; the "romantic hero," whose chimerical designs on the English throne invited comic comparisons with his real difficulties in the Netherlands; the hot-blooded cavalier, yearning to fight but helpless without any army to lead against the enemy—here was the perfect governor for Motley's section describing the greatest rebel successes of the entire history. This type of the popular, debonair hero illustrates the hollowness of the tyrant's kindness. Knowing that the people foolishly love him, he tries to reconcile them to Philip; secretly, however, he advises Philip to treat them severely, and he soon proclaims the Council of Trent in the Netherlands. But he is a pathetically inept intriguer, and he fails more completely than any other Spanish governor. Betrayed by his suspicious half-brother the King, and outwitted and humiliated by the Dutch, he is still begging Philip for specific instructions when he dies, broken in health and spirits, the victim of Dutch perseverance, his own folly, and his half-brother's tortuous policy.

In Alexander Farnese Philip finally happens on a perfectly qualified governor. Hero of the decisive battle of Gemblours, Alexander combines the military skill and intriguing art that are the tyrant's most effective weapons against a divided country. Since he knows whom to bribe and how to bribe them, he capitalizes on all the Dutch weaknesses, and Motley insists that no one but William could have prevented him from conquering the northern provinces. His character and administrative skill enable the Spaniards to regain the offensive, to succeed at last in killing William, and (though Motley reserves this achievement for his *History of the United Netherlands*) to recover the southern provinces permanently.

Besides giving historical order to Motley's portrait of tyranny, the course of Dutch fortunes also enabled him to build his theory of progress into the

structure of his history; for both his hero's character and the events dramatize the progressive function of the representative man. William's life is a
"Christian epic." (III, 616.) He progresses morally, politically, and intel-
lectually, and Motley uses his growth to emphasize the development of the
rebellion. Throughout most of the first act, while William is still a loyal
Catholic working to reconcile King and people, the incipient rebellion is
encouraged by irresponsible nobles, whose futile threats and gestures damage the cause. Then, after the people's impulsive movement toward Protestant liberty has failed and Philip has moved to crush them, William accepts
sole leadership of the rebellion. At this point, when he can "find no one
to comprehend his views," he stands entirely alone. For the rest of his life
he marches, as the representative hero should march, in advance of his age.
Committed to religious freedom, in which neither Calvinist nor Catholic
believes, he works for toleration even though he sometimes has "no one to
lean on but himself" (II, 486–87); and he succeeds at least in curbing the
persecution of Anabaptists and Catholics. He achieves his greatest political
and moral success in the new Union of Brussels, when he unites the whole
country on a basis of religious toleration.

But he cannot maintain this eighteenth-century constitution with the
inadequate men and against the overwhelming circumstances of the sixteenth century. When the Catholic nobles sell themselves, one by one, to
Spain; when he is forced to support a treacherous French duke for the
crown; when his disconsolate brother feels compelled to leave the Netherlands and his brother-in-law commits treason; William must stand once
again completely alone. The best he can do is to strengthen the "burgher"
class for its future republican duties and solidify the union of the two most
determinedly independent provinces. At his death the republic and liberty
survive, and their tenuous survival is the measure of his success.

Clearly, then, Motley's method combined exposition and personal drama.
Individual characters bear the burden of his narrative. He achieves his most
effective organization when he can make their conflict typify the broader
action while he brings in the people for grand, symbolic scenes. Therefore,
although interesting characters and individually brilliant scenes abound
throughout the history, its most effective units are the prologue and the first
two acts. Crammed though they are with expository material, they combine
personal drama and popular action in strategically placed scenes to emphasize both the continuity of events and decisive changes.

As the prologue opens, Charles V enters the scene of his abdication on the arm of William of Orange; as it closes, the enraged Philip II publicly insults William just before leaving the Netherlands. Through the battles of St. Quentin and Gravelines, moreover, the prologue reveals the character whose "tragedy" forms the central personal drama of the first two acts: Lamoral, Count of Egmont. Egmont's heroic but barren victories in these battles not only typify the Dutch people's futile expenditure of loyalty and blood in Philip's service; they also provoke the jealous enmity of Alva, who will one day behead Egmont as a traitor, and they establish Egmont as a popular Dutch hero.

Between this high moment of his career and the moving scene of his public decapitation, Egmont's romantic tragedy serves Motley as a major unifying device—defining varied political groups, dramatizing the essential traits of the most important characters, and illustrating the theme. William, of course, is the one consistently accurate political navigator, but Motley uses Egmont's impulsive tackings to define William's almost imperceptible course. Too rash in the early days of jocular protest against Granvelle, Egmont is seduced by the King's flattery, and he soon becomes too vigorous in enforcing the royal punishment, too credulous of royal promises. His example teaches William, as Motley intends it to show the reader, the consequences of critical loyalty to Philip; and William's futile efforts to save him culminate in a moving scene just before William flees the country. Besides assuring his own death on the scaffold, Egmont's refusal to escape leaves William at last completely alone.

Through letters and scenes, Egmont's story also dramatizes the most sinister deceit of Granvelle, Margaret, Philip, and Alva. Then, after the fine, climactic scene in which he is arrested while guest of honor at Alva's own table (II, 123-25), Egmont becomes "a colossal emblem of the condition in which the Netherlands were now gasping." (II, 178.) By arresting and trying him, Alva and Philip have gone beyond violating Dutch constitutional liberties; they have ignored the privileges of the Order of the Golden Fleece. Since the Holy Roman Emperor himself fails to convince Philip to try Egmont according to the rules of the Order, Egmont's trial proves that "law and order were now abrogated throughout the land"; and Motley takes advantage of the fact that "the last act" of Egmont's tragedy is precipitated by William's first counterattack in the northern provinces. (II, 179.)

In the final scene of this tragedy, "emblem" and people meet at last. The three thousand Spanish troops whom Alva has ordered to control the mob cannot "restrain them from tears and from execrations," or from dipping "their handkerchiefs in the blood, to be preserved . . . as ensigns of revenge." (II, 208.) From the "graves" of Egmont and Horn, Motley insists, sprang a daily intensifying, universal hatred for Alva. (II, 211.)

Not only here, but in the first act as well and on two strategic occasions later in the second, the facts allow Motley to balance his complex tale of representative characters by dramatizing popular action. He first animates the Dutch people just after the noble Beggars have implicitly threatened the Regent. First he describes the "field preachings," vast gatherings of crudely armed but peaceful folk to hear Protestant ministers outside the walls of towns all over the country. Against these relatively placid scenes, then, he sets a more violent example of spontaneous action: a remarkable series of Gothic scenes in which smaller mobs of nocturnal marauders gut dozens of the most beautiful churches in the country. It was through the iconoclasts, Motley says, that "the religious war, before imminent, became inevitable." (I, 573.) Besides provoking Philip's vengeance, this outburst also forces the three great nobles to define their positions. Between a chapter on Horn's failure to suppress the heretics and the concluding chapter in which Egmont helps the government to crush them, Motley uses another popular uprising in Antwerp to display William in his finest hour as the only man who can control the people. William, entirely alone and unarmed, dissuades a Protestant mob from rushing out of Antwerp against the government troops, and then, in a scene that dramatizes all the people's divisions and their relationship to their representative leader, he prevents a battle for which Catholics, Calvinists, and Lutherans inside the city have already pitched their camps. (II, 64–72.)

Again in the second act popular action clarifies personal conflicts and dramatizes decisive changes. After William's first two invasions have failed, Alva's monstrous tax provokes legal resistance in the estates and passive resistance among the people. When William's allies desert him once again, the Dutch merchants simply close their shops rather than pay Alva's tax; and just as Alva sentences eighteen merchants to be hanged in their doorways, a popular force of wild "sea-beggars" takes the city of Brill, securing the "foundation" of the Republic. This scene sets off a revolution throughout Holland and Zeeland, and it begins the decline of Alva. He succeeds in taking Harlem, but the people's heroic resistance—dramatized repeatedly in Motley's account of the seven-month siege—makes the victory too costly. From this point on, Alva encounters a series of reverses until his ignominious departure, and the government is bankrupt when he leaves.

In the last three Parts of the history Motley was able to dramatize popular action in several more grand scenes—the siege of Leyden, the Spanish and French "Furies" at Antwerp, and the destruction of the Antwerp citadel by ten thousand citizens of all classes. But he could not give these scenes the same structural value that he had given those of his first two acts. After the siege of Leyden, the story itself becomes more fragmentary. Diplomatic and internal problems become more complex,[2] and Motley defines them less clearly. The connections among separate events become less clear. And the weaknesses in Motleys' selective standards do more damage.

The basic trouble, then, is not that Motley's powers fail, but that his subject itself highlights faults which have appeared, only less prominently, in the preceding sections. Consider, for example, the vagueness of his religious statistics. Although clearly apparent throughout the history, this understandable deficiency does not seriously weaken his narrative of the development of the rebellion. For if he cannot give the precise ratio of Dutch Protestants to Catholics, he can at least demonstrate that thousands were executed, that thousands attended the "field preachings," that mobs desecrated Catholic churches, and that three religious armies once pitched camp for a battle in Antwerp. Interlocked with the personal drama of the great nobles, these scenes suggest the magnitude as well as the nature of the conflict.

After the death of Requesens in the third act, however, Motley must describe two important reversals in the religious alignment, and he is unprepared for the occasion. Having ignored the religious statistics for five hundred pages, he cannot prepare the reader for the universal revulsion against all Spaniards without admitting that Catholicism "had, of late years," grown rapidly enough to win half the people in the country. (III, 56.) This sudden announcement is astounding, for nowhere in the preceding act, which consistently emphasized Alva's oppression of Catholics and Protestants alike, has Motley given any reason for a revival of Catholicism. Indeed, the loathing for foreign tyranny that now, "at last," infuriates all the people is exactly the feeling that Motley has said they expressed eight years before. (See II, 116–17, 285–86; and I, 271.) Even though his dramatic skill and his moral preoccupations have led him into this difficulty, he might still avoid the confusion by analyzing the changes more carefully. But he disposes of the subject in a paragraph, less space than he devotes to William's second marriage. (III, 56.)

The same kind of confusion follows from Motley's vague and inconsistent use of economic statistics. His excellent analysis of Alva's preposterous tax, capping as it does the evidence of Alva's tyrannical folly, demonstrates his awareness that economic causes are important. But this very dramatic success leads historian and reader into a trap. Having read that grass grew in Dutch streets during Alva's administration (I, 147) and that Requesens did nothing to revive prosperity, one learns with surprise that, at the time of the Spanish Fury, Antwerp was still "the richest city in Europe"—that it had "flourished more freshly than ever" in the midst of Dutch miseries. (III, 96.) And even after Motley has blamed the Spanish Fury for the permanent decline of Antwerp as a commercial center, he describes its prosperity once again when narrating the French Fury that attacked the city a few years later. One fails to find in this history a clear picture of either wealth or poverty. Motley's standard for defining one or the other seems to fluctuate according to his moral and dramatic purpose, for he does not account for changes.[3]

But the most damaging fault in Motley's history is his repetitiousness. It is this quality, far more than his well-known partisanship or his inconsistencies, that makes some parts of the work so exasperating. Proceeding though it does from his moral intention, the basic fault is an organizational weakness. Motley has good literary and moral reasons for heaping up evidence of the tyrant's deceit, but it is hard to see any justification for his steady repetition of moral judgments. In portraying Charles V, Philip II, and Granvelle, he can seldom resist the obvious ironic comment even after overwhelming evidence and his own previous remarks have made the moral perfectly clear. (See, for example, I, 206, 426–27, 475–76.) He often presents the evidence of deceit by summarizing the sinful example as he introduces it, then quoting extensively from the hypocritical document, and at last repeating his judgment. In a few episodes, moreover, he repeats the same moral several times in virtually the same words. His otherwise excellent chapter on the iconoclasts is thus marred by eight assertions within twenty pages that these mobs, unlike Spanish conquerors, stole nothing and hurt no human beings; and the language (at one point in two successive paragraphs) is so nearly identical that he seems to have forgotten his previous paragraph.[4] The moral distinction, important to Motley's theme, seems valid, but the repetition is extremely offensive.

These serious faults do not ruin the broad outline of the history, but they often obscure it. As Motley reports the details of each exchange in fruitless negotiations (III, 12–18); as he iterates the heavy irony of Dutch popular tributes to Charles V (I, 206); as he paints a large portrait of a *femme fatale*

who does not influence the events of his drama (III, 225-27); as he dramatizes the detailed actions of the Duke of Anjou and Archduke Matthias—
at such times, though aware that these details are relevant, one loses sight
of the broad movement of the history. Motley develops his theme admirably
and makes excellent use of some dramatic scenes, but the immediate relationship of some parts to his narrative whole is unclear.

2

Motley's great strength lies in characterization. As I have already demonstrated, he built the conventional distinctions firmly into the structure
of his history and made them reinforce his theme. But his success extends
much further than this. Although he relied on types, although he used
personal contrasts even more explicitly than Prescott had used them, although his technique and his partisanship led him inevitably to distort—
Motley saw acutely and painted precisely the features of individual character. His portraiture excels Prescott's because of the very large number
of people whom he depicts in sharp detail.

In aligning his characters, Motley modifies Prescott's arrangement but
follows the same basic principles. Instead of polarizing the virtues of two
embattled civilizations, he consistently opposes the best of the one to the
worst of the other. For *The Rise of the Dutch Republic* does not culminate
in a decisive battle between the finest representatives of the conflicting
nations, and Motley's Spaniards have no particularly national virtues. The
chief antagonists in this history come as close to representing absolute good
and absolute evil as any opponents since Cotton Mather's Devil attacked
the Puritans. Yet Motley does portray virtues and defects on both sides of
his battleline, and he repeatedly uses the faults of both groups to define the
character of his hero. He balances the two groups by placing the subtle
tyranny of Philip II at one extreme and the "savage" demagoguery of some
rebels at the other. He builds a pyramid of characters, with William of
Orange, the perfect hero, at the top. Down one side he deploys the royalists,
with Philip at the base; down the opposite face he stations the patriots—
with the rash Beggars, the wild iconoclasts, some of the "savage" Beggars
of the Sea, and the treacherous demagogues grouped near the base.

Among the Dutch as among the Spaniards, almost all of these distinctions help to clarify not only the individual characters but the developing
action. During the first two acts, for example, Motley concentrates on distinguishing William from the rebellious Beggars and from such loyal opponents of Granvelle as Egmont; and in the last two acts, after the republic

has been founded, he sets William against the "Malcontents," Catholic nobles who want to subvert the republic, and against the jealously provincial burghers and the "demagogues" Imbize and Ryhove. (III, 378.) Even among the minor characters the varying types appear at appropriate moments in the drama. If Peter Titelmann, a "grotesque yet terrible goblin" (I, 332), typifies clerical agents in the days of Granvelle and the Inquisition, John Sarrasin, an "indefatigable monk" who is "delicate, noiseless, unscrupulous" (III, 395-96), represents Spanish policy in the last act, when Alexander is systematically bribing the Malcontents.

It is not these techniques, however, that explain Motley's remarkable success. His finest achievement lies in his brilliant use of circumstantial detail to depict these conventional characters. Like Prescott, he often uses a pictorial method, but he is much more precise than Prescott. The specific action, the revealing letter, the visual peculiarity—all of these stand forth so clearly in *The Rise of the Dutch Republic* that reality merges with convention, supports allegory. Although perfect justice would require a more sympathetic representation of Philip II's motives and his less reprehensible traits, Motley records enough unquestionably deceitful and cruel actions to mark him as the type of "consummate" tyranny (II, 314), whether or not one wants to insist that Philip's taste for art was a virtue. Philip is angered by the *"clemency"* of a cruel decree issued by his Regent (II, 97); he orders Dutch theologians and lawyers to find a way to remove the "glory" from heretics' executions without diminishing their "sufferings," and he substitutes "secret drowning" for "public burning." (I, 466, 474-75.) Long after he has condemned every person in the Netherlands to death, he proclaims a general amnesty which, as Motley carefully notes, pardons nobody but those who have committed no crimes; and then he swears before a notary that he cannot be bound by his offer because he has made it under duress. (II, 5, 298.)

In Motley's portrait of Philip, as in the whole gallery of villains, the very detail that sometimes causes an annoying repetitiousness is what makes the characterization memorable. Occasionally, indeed, Motley offers a new horrible fact just when it seems that no new kind of detail is possible. Philip's "murder" of Baron Montigny, for example, seems to offer nothing new, for Count Horn, Count Egmont, and Montigny's own brother have already been betrayed and executed in violation of several laws. But as Motley proceeds one sees the importance of this episode in characterizing Philip. It demonstrates the great King's love of deception for its own sake, his inveterate affection for the minutiae of intrigue. Having worked out every particular of a fantastically elaborate scheme to convince everyone that the prisoner has died of a fever, Philip not only deceives his own bride,[5] but forces Montigny himself to become "an accomplice in the plot." (II, 308.) By providing for the number of memorial masses that will be paid for with a small part of the victim's confiscated estate, he also arranges "the mode" of Montigny's "passage through purgatory." (II, 309.) His final action in this affair is to scribble a marginal note admonishing his secretary "that we should always express favorable judgments concerning the dead." (II, 313.)

Of the forty-odd characters to whom Motley imparts a memorable individuality the most striking are the villains and others whom he criticizes. From their own papers he selects quotations that depict them as clearly as their portraits. Viglius, the collaborating state councillor, adopts the motto *"vita mortalium vigilia,"* and the narrative reveals that "the vigils had all been for Viglius" (III, 207–8); Philip makes an error of more than half a million ducats, and in his own favor, in estimating the royal accounts (I, 293); Alva tells Philip that the Blood Council is necessary because "the men of law only condemn for crimes which are proved" (II, 137); Granvelle writes letters in language that resembles Iago's; Don John complains to Philip that liberty is a "contagious disease" (III, 309); and in a proclamation requesting Dutch obedience, Philip claims to be both a "brooding hen and the prodigal's father, a range of impersonation hardly to be allowed him even by the most abject flattery." (II, 461.)

When Motley calls this last mixture of figures "very grotesque," he offers the key to most of these letters and to the documented pictures that illustrate them in his history. The opening portrait of Philip reveals, beneath a "broad forehead, and blue eye, . . . [a] heavy, hanging lip, with a vast mouth, and monstrously protruding jaw." (I, 104.) And one of the last pictures of him in this history shows him receiving a formal visit from the corpse of Don John, which he has brought in three sections to Madrid, and which has been stuffed, wired together, and dressed formally for the interview. (III, 361.) Between these two pictures Motley hangs a large exposition of grotesques. The glutton Charles V, retired to a monastery, spits out pronouncements of "savage bigotry" while ingesting "surfeits of sardine omelettes, Estramadura sausages, eel pies, pickled partridges, fat capons, quince syrups, iced beer, and flagons of Rhenish, relieved by copious draughts of senna and rhubarb, to which his horror-stricken doctor doomed him as he ate." (I, 132.) The "hysterical" Queen Mary announces that she has already borne Philip's son, although she is not even pregnant. (I, 138.)

The Duke of Alva, who has "almost literally been drinking blood for seventy years," postpones death during his last illness by drinking milk "from a woman's breast." (II, 497.) And Don Carlos, far from being a proper hero for romance, has a figure "as misshapen as his mind." (II, 237.) The Duke of Anjou, whose falseness prompts French wits to remark that a two-faced man needs two noses, stands, at the moment of his inauguration as the Dutch protector, "below the middle height, puny, and ill-shaped. His hair and eyes were brown," Motley says, "his face was seamed with the small-pox, his skin covered with blotches, his nose so swollen that it seemed to be double." (III, 527–28.)

Although Motley relied solely on Dutch sources for some of his grotesque pictures, many others came from Spanish sources, and the private letters of the subjects often support the same kind of inference. The grotesque painting and imagery extend, moreover, to the most savage rebels as well as to Spanish villains. In a war of absolutely antithetical principles there were bound to be some Dutchmen who fought as cruelly as Spaniards and who deviated as widely as Catholic "fanatics" from the true principles of William. When the documents permitted, therefore, Motley highlighted fantastic detail in scenes of Dutch activity and pictures of Dutch leaders, simultaneously illustrating the inhuman hatred bred by religious war and providing a grotesque background for the portrait of his humane, truly Christian hero. In some of his general scenes he was able to depict ragged Dutch freebooters parading in the splendid priestly robes that they had taken from a captured cathedral; in others he could reveal Dutch atrocities, as when a rebel commander nailed a Spanish heart to his ship's prow and invited his men to sink their teeth in it. (II, 366.) And in such characters as William de la Marck, the Dutch admiral, he found portraits with which to complete the fantastic, allegorical picture. This "wild, sanguinary, licentious noble, wearing his hair and beard unshorn, according to ancient Batavian custom, until the death of his relative, Egmont, should have been expiated, [this] worthy descendant of the Wild Boar of Ardennes, this hirsute and savage corsair seemed an embodiment of vengeance." (II, 350.)

The range of defective character exposed by Motley's attention to precise detail is as remarkable as the number of striking pictures and quotations. Beside the grotesque stands the comic, the ridiculous. The Archduke Matthias, a figurehead whose greatest achievement has been to "escape from Vienna in his nightgown" (III, 305–6); the pedantic state councillor Viglius, who tries to find "the exact path between right and wrong" (I, 353); the petty Malcontents who have a priest jailed for impugning their motives after they have "sold out the liberty of the Celtic provinces" (III, 406–9);

and the pathetically misplaced bastard Don John, to whose resignation the Dutch reply by asking him to make sure that his successor is of legitimate birth (III, 258–60)—all these are comic figures whom Motley uses to fill out his broad panorama of particularized villainy and folly.

With these and two dozen other sharply focused portraits of reactionaries, Motley achieves an unforgettable characterization of tyranny in action. The petty and pretentious as well as the vicious; the paid, superstitious assassin as well as the misguided, brave crusader; the subtle Cardinal as well as the pedantic state councillor; the vigorous, hot-tempered Emperor as well as his cold, lethargic son; the rigid fanatic and the flexible opportunist—each of these stands forth with such remarkable clarity that the heroic and virtuous characters seem less distinct.

William of Orange, the "statue of spotless marble" that Motley sets against this background, lacks the sharply individual features of these lesser men. Motley's metaphor is apt not only because of the "sublimity" of the contrast, but also because William, through most of the history, appears as a grand *figure*. His self-sacrifice, his advanced principles, and his political incorruptibility give him "colossal stature" (II, 242), especially in the innumerable contrasts that place his conduct against the base actions of others. But many of these incidents show him not acting when others act. He remains calm when others act rashly; he repeatedly declines bribes when others scramble for them; he fails to draw the enemy into open battle; and in his most vigorous scene he does not charge in the manner of a Cortés but holds his horse in as he quiets an angry mob. Despite his eloquence and his occasionally shrewd generalship, one never sees him swinging an "immense two-handed sword" in the manner of Alexander Farnese. (III, 370.) His strength lies in his firm endurance; his achievement, in gaining victory through "a long series of defeats." (III, 267.) He is "watchful William." (III, 203.)

Since this basic image of William accords with the facts and illustrates the theme, it need not be faulty. Anyone would agree, moreover, that deliberately ordering the knife put to every throat in a captured city is a more distinctly memorable action than ordering that Anabaptists be spared; Alva's worst actions, therefore, were bound to be more sharply impressive than William's best. The trouble is that Motley misses important opportunities to reveal the person beneath the heroic figure, and that some of his efforts to move closer to William do more harm than good. As his attempts to keep the statue spotless lead him into ethical inconsistencies,[6] so they lead him to use the emptiest, most generalized rhetoric at times when he might show real feeling instead of telling about conventionally prescribed feeling.

He tries to make William seem more active by having him "seize the swift occasion by the forelock," but his inability to find any events to justify this phrase leaves William standing with a fistful of hair. (III, 55 ff.) Instead of concentrating on real emotion or omitting the subject entirely, he says that William was "neither dismayed nor despondent" after the most brutal, discouraging defeat of the war. His first announcement that William has been converted to Lutheranism comes, without elaboration, in a subordinate clause (II, 69); and later on, to introduce his equally unanalytic announcement that William has turned Calvinist, he declares, in the face of his own more complex evidence, that William's sole motivation in all these years was faith in God. (II, 490.)

At its worst, this technique of characterization is unconvincing, contradictory, sentimental, and it occasionally causes ludicrous stylistic blunders. At its best, it leads one away from the particular individual to the conventional figure. If Motley had not glossed over William's failure to protect his eldest son before fleeing the Netherlands, if he had dramatized the Prince's confusion in the face of military frustration or defeat, if he had not accepted at face value every one of William's apologies for diplomatic miscalculations, he would have achieved a more human and a more convincing portrait. As it is, he always maintains a reverent distance from the statue, and his excesses in portraying William do more damage than does his one-sided portrayal of Philip II. For the most extreme examples of the latter focus on indelible, documented fact, while the former tend to diffuse into generalizations as misty as the atmosphere in which Motley says William's "form dilates." (II, 242.)

This is not to say that Motley's characterization of William fails completely. One cannot read the history without being convinced of William's greatness. But Motley succeeds here because of the cumulative record of his hero's fidelity to humane principles and because of the contrast provided by the specific villainy of others, rather than by his efforts to characterize William intimately or to generalize on his greatness. When he quotes a Calvinist aide's criticism of William for failing to see the difference between Catholic and Protestant persecution (III, 206-7); when he reprints Don John's complaint that "the people here are *bewitched* by the Prince of Orange . . . and take no resolution without consulting him" (III, 203); when he reprints the notorious ban denouncing William "as an enemy of the human race" and offering pardon and a title to any criminal who might assassinate him (III, 493); he does more to impress William's virtues on the reader than when he himself expounds them.

3

As one might infer from Motley's successful portrayal of villains, he relies on a bold, clear prose that not only expounds but exposes. Like Prescott, he often uses balanced constructions, but here the stresses are heavier, the antitheses sharper, and vigorous judgment stands implicit in almost every line. Solidly based in the specific, moreover, Motley's indictments and exposés gain force as they proceed. For the repetition of subjects and sentence patterns, the carefully placed short sentences, the thumping, often alliterative stresses of balanced cadences in parallel constructions, the strong verbs, the periodic emphasis, and the relentless logical analysis that mingles fact and judgment give much of his prose an irresistible momentum.

When he attempts, for example, to demonstrate why the Inquisition was "the great cause of the revolt," Motley insists, first of all, that the distinctions among papal, episcopal, and Spanish inquisitions "did not, in the sixteenth century, convince many unsophisticated minds" that the institution was good "in any of its shapes."[7] Proceeding then to the Spanish Inquisition, he sweeps in one long paragraph from a hammering statement of its unearthly irresponsibility to a specific analysis of its legal processes and extralegal devices:*

[1]It was a court owning allegiance to no temporal authority, superior to all other tribunals. [2]It was a bench of monks without appeal, / having its familiars in every house, diving into the secrets of every fireside, judging, and executing its horrible decrees without responsibility. [3]It condemned not deeds, but thoughts. [4]It affected to descend into individual conscience, and to punish the crimes which it pretended to discover. [5]Its process was reduced to a horrible simplicity. [6]It arrested on *suspicion*, tortured till con*fession*, and then *punished* by *fire*. / [7]Two witnesses, and those to separate facts, / were sufficient to consign the victim to a loathsome dungeon. [8]Here he was sparingly supplied with food, / forbidden to speak, or even to sing—to which pastime it could hardly be thought he would feel much inclination—and then left to himself, / till famine and misery should break his spirit. / [9]When that time was supposed to have arrived he was examined. [10]Did he confess, and forswear his heresy, whether actually innocent or not, he might then assume the sacred shirt, and escape with confiscation of all his property. [11]Did he persist in the avowal of his innocence, two witnesses sent him to the stake, one witness to the rack. [12]He was informed of the testimony against him, but never confronted with the witness. [13]That accuser might be his son, father, or the wife of his bosom, for all were enjoined, under the death-penalty, to inform the inquisitors of every suspicious word which

---

* I have numbered Motley's sentences for later reference.

might fall from their nearest relatives. [14]The indictment being thus supported, the prisoner was tried by torture. [15]The rack was the court of justice; the criminal's only advocate was his fortitude—for the nominal counsellor, who was permitted no communication with the prisoner, and was furnished neither with documents nor with power to procure evidence, was a puppet, aggravating the lawlessness of the proceedings by the mockery of legal forms. [16]The torture took place at midnight, in a gloomy dungeon, dimly lighted by torches. [17]The victim—whether man, matron, or tender virgin—was stripped naked, and stretched upon the wooden bench. [18]Water, weights, fires, pulleys, screws / —all the apparatus by which the sinews could be strained without cracking, the bones crushed without breaking, and the body racked exquisitely without giving up its ghost, was now put into operation. [19]The executioner, enveloped in a black robe from head to foot, with his eyes glaring at his victim through holes cut in the hood which muffled his face, practiced successively all the forms of torture which the devilish ingenuity of the monks had invented. (I, 323–24.)

This remarkable passage typifies Motley's finest prose. Here even his well-known indignation becomes a literary advantage. Although the analysis characteristically overlooks the similar practices of some other courts of the time, it does not focus on legal process or torture until the unique irresponsibility, the unusual punishment, and the court's primary interest in "thoughts" have been established. And if it seems to rely unfairly on the conventional bogey of "devilish" monks who employ "familiars," one should notice that the other-worldly power and concerns cited at the beginning of the passage, and the fiendish picture of the executioner at the end, support the imagery. Indeed, the movement from thought-control, through a "mockery of legal forms," to the fierce Gothic picture and appalling physical sensation of the last four sentences epitomizes the relationship, so important to Motley's success throughout the history, between general principle and concrete fact.

Of the rhetorical qualities in this passage, the only one that requires further analysis here is the remarkable control of rhythm and diction. The importance of sentence length, parallelism, and antitheses to this effect should be obvious, but Motley's acute sense of sound demands closer attention. His alliteration, so prominent throughout this description, varies sufficiently (as in sentence 6) to avoid monotony, but the kind of sounds that it most often emphasizes adds considerable power to the description and force to the judgment. The large majority of his alliterative consonants, pounding home the inexorable cruelty of the evil agency, are fricatives, plosives, dentals, hard c's, almost rolling r's and blunt b's. The monosyllables, too, often gain emphasis from these sounds, and they sometimes appear at the end of a climactic series or a ringing antithesis (6, *fire;* 11, *rack*). When these sounds are combined in the individual words and the incremental combination of onomatopoetic verbs of the eighteenth sentence, the description reaches a startlingly powerful climax.

One further rhythmic skill should be noticed: the variation not only of sentence length but of flowing, longer lines with series of shorter elements that place extremely heavy stress on an early and a late syllable. The second sentence, for example, begins with a flowing line of iambic pentameter (though with an inverted first foot) with three heavy stresses of which the last is the strongest, and in the series of participial phrases that follow Motley stresses the first syllable of each verb more vigorously than any other except the last accented syllable of each phrase. In the seventh sentence, just after the most forceful series of short phrases so far, he turns again to fluid iambic pentameter, and after this sentence comes to a forceful stop he begins the next with a flowing line of blank verse before the short pair "forbidden to speak, or even to sing." The same arrangement, though more complexly worked out, strengthens the climactic eighteenth sentence.

These qualities give Motley's prose an admirable versatility. The same rhetorical skills expose the brutality of Charles V's "edicts," the deception in the Moderation of 1566, the procedures of the Blood Council, periodic acts of alleged amnesty, and the insincerity of dozens of characters. The predominant tone of these analyses is indignant, but Motley's forceful, balanced, repetitive style serves equally well for other tones and subjects. Along with his close attention to the language of the documents, it gives unusual force to his skillfully placed, revealing quotations. (I, 341; II, 137, 295; III, 258–59.) If it communicates his amazement, even in the third volume, at the extent of treachery (III, 197, 392), it also conveys his sense of grim comedy when he delineates the pathetic frustration of Don John, the time-serving of Viglius (I, 353; II, 295), the contemptible treason of Anjou. (III, 561–70.) Motley's forceful diction and rhythm function well in active scenes of gory horror; his antitheses and cumulative summary, in pictures that emphasize contrast.[8] And, with the heaviest alliteration omitted and some of the blunt emphasis removed from the short sentences, the same techniques give unusual distinction even to his ordinary exposition. Some of the best prose in the history combines narrative and analysis, as in his description of the Inquisition, but simply in order to clarify rather than to judge.[9]

That acute perception which is revealed so clearly in Motley's characterization helps also to distinguish his style, and one can see its value in his imagery. He once advised Oliver Wendell Holmes to burlesque trite figures in "The Autocrat,"[10] and his own practice demonstrates his sensitivity to the meaning of his figures. He does not always avoid the conventional metaphor, but he almost never fails to maintain consistency, and he regularly chooses figures that are directly relevant to the specific action: the ubiquitous familiars of the Inquisition who dive into the secrets of conscience, or the puppet that mocks legal forms. Again and again, moreover, he picks up a metaphor from the documents and extends it in his own narrative.[11] And he repeatedly describes the behavior of characters in imagery inspired by their own professions. Thus the misplaced soldier Don John "marches from concession to concession" in his diplomacy (III, 259); Alva looks narrowly at the world "through the loop-hole of the fortress in which Nature [has] imprisoned him for life" (II, 179); and Cardinal Granvelle, when asking Philip for additional property, approaches him "with the whine of a mendicant." (I, 426–27.) The Spanish troops, far from home but living with their women and children, form "a locomotive city . . . , permanently established on foreign soil. It was a city walled in by bayonets, and still further isolated by the impassable moat of mutual hatred." (II, 543–44.)

This close attention to detail is especially valuable in vivifying the conventional. As Motley recognized the language of Iago in some of Granvelle's letters, he saw "something alert and snake-like"—the Dutch historian Bor had called it *"een fel gesicht"*—in the portrait of Alexander Farnese (III, 371), and he based much of the diabolical imagery that controls his portrayal of tyranny on similarly factual evidence. (II, 110–11, 255.) In the beautiful Gothic cathedral at Antwerp he noticed not only the "upward tendency" of the spire and the "tall columnar trunks," but the "prismatic lights and sepulchral shadows" cast on the floor by their "branches" and their "fantastic" fruit. (I, 554.) Then, as the "shadows of night" deepened the "perpetual twilight of the church," he was able to focus on a group of "furious iconoclasts [who] clambered up the dizzy heights, shrieking and chattering like malignant apes, as they tore off in triumph the slowly-matured fruit of centuries." (I, 562.) Even a conventional priest gains individuality through this careful control of figurative language. As the Prior of St. Vaast carries Alexander's bribes among the Malcontents throughout Artois, Motley's rhythm and imagery catch his movement and make him into an unusually successful type, while colorful paraphrase (and, later, quotation) conveys his individual reality:

With the shoes of swiftness on his feet, the coat of darkness on his back, and the wishing purse in his hand, he sped silently and invisibly from one great

Malcontent chieftain to another, buying up centurions, and captains, and common soldiers; circumventing Orangists, Ghent democrats, Anjou partisans; weaving a thousand intrigues, ventilating a hundred hostile mines, and passing unharmed through the most serious dangers and the most formidable obstacles. Eloquent, too, at a pinch, he always understood his audience, and upon this occasion unsheathed the most incisive, if not the most brilliant weapon which could be used in the debate. It was most expensive to be patriotic, he said, while silver was to be saved, and gold to be earned by being loyal. (III, 396.)

"Flitting about" in the fish-market, "blithe and busy as usual when storms were brewing," this brave, unscrupulous character, "whose golden opinions had irresistible resonance," represents the triumph of the conventional. In the brief description of the counterrevolution that he led in Arras, culminating in "a series of terrible Rembrandt-like night pieces"— nocturnal executions in a howling storm—Motley demonstrates the value of his method. This priest is comically unique but conventionally deadly, and the combination of incremental summary and precise individual example, of historical, diabolical, and Shakespearean imagery with documented Gothic scenes of death, functions beautifully to dramatize the final effort of liberty in the "Celtic provinces." (III, 396–404.)

But despite its effectiveness in narrative, summary, judgment, and picture, Motley's prose has its faults, and his use of the conventional does not always produce a rhetorical triumph. One has only to recall some of his statements about William in order to see what can happen when he moves the conventional sentiment or language too far away from specific fact. When Motley says that "Prerogative was weary, Romanism was weary, Conscience was weary, the Spirit of Freedom was weary, but the Prince of Orange was not weary" (II, 454), his repetition emphasizes the almost ludicrous extravagance of the comparison; and the same principle applies when William seizes the swift occasion by the forelock. The fundamental weakness is a lack of restraint. The enthusiastic sense of participation that allowed him to talk of "pitching into" Philip and Alva, to allude bitterly to his own unhappy diplomatic experience when narrating the mistreatment of a diplomat in his *Barneveld*, and to write with such magnificent indignation of particular treacherous acts has inevitably bad effects not only on his judgment but on his language.

The vituperative diction that mars portions of *Barneveld* is much less prominent in *The Rise of the Dutch Republic*, but no one can read this history without suspecting that Motley found some personal catharsis in "the romantic agony"[12]—in the very horrors he deplored, the very curses he reprinted at length (I, 69–70), the violent diction he often chose. Although it seems to me that both the literal facts and the imagery of a "rank" forest justify the figure, one can see the tendency clearly in his picture of the iconoclasts who shriek and chatter like malignant apes. And when he says that Alva rejected a plea for clemency even though "it came from the lips of tigers, dripping with blood" (II, 240), there is no question about his excessive shrillness. As his passion moves him to repeat too many judgments and to overemphasize obvious irony, so his sense of forceful language and rhythm often leads him to excessive alliteration, excessive reliance on pairs, excessive rhetorical questions and contrasts in diction; occasionally, too, his enthusiasm causes him to construct overwrought metaphors.[13]

These lapses in taste occur more frequently in the Introduction than elsewhere in the history. In that section, which compresses the events of centuries into less than a hundred pages, Motley establishes the romantic wildness of both geological and human development, and he tries to establish the immense scale of the conflict. From the opening paragraphs describing the "slime" with which three rivers formed "oozy islands" on "the dunes and sandbanks heaved up by the ocean," he resorts often to similar diction. He fills his pages with "wild, chaotic, sanguinary scenes" (I, 28); with "groveling" and "bestial" people (I, 67–68), "foul" crimes, and "hovels" built "under the wolfish protection of little potentates." (I, 26.) In these pages he resembles Carlyle rather than Macaulay. Cramming many of his sentences with too much frenzied sentiment, too many adjectives, too many alliteratives and ponderous metaphors, he sometimes produces an overwhelming, exhausting effect. The foundations of the frozen North are opened, the waters prevail, but the ark of Christianity floats upon the flood. As the deluge assuages, the earth returns to chaos, the last pagan empire is washed out of existence, but the dim, groping, faltering, ignorant infancy of Christian Europe has begun. (I, 19.) Later, the genius of Liberty, conducted by the Spirit of Commerce, descends at last to awaken mankind from its sloth and cowardly stupor. (I, 26.) At one crisis, "A sudden spasm of liberty gives the whole people gigantic strength." (I, 49.) And when "imperial and papal persecution" continues "its daily deadly work with such diligence as to make [the country's survival] doubtful" (I, 80), one begins to doubt the desirability of plodding on.

Even in the Introduction, however, these faults are a small price to pay for the richness of Motley's best prose. His description of Luther, for example, relies on his most frenzied language, but in that paragraph he retains control of his diction and his rhythm. Beginning with images taken from the "moderate" pleas of Erasmus, he turns the conventional storm imagery into an apt, original figure and makes his own rhythm and Luther's concern with the Devil convey the fierceness of the man and the excitement of the time. I have italicized Erasmus' metaphors.

Meantime the man, whose talk is not of *doves and owls,* the fierce physician, who deals not with *ointments and cooling draughts,* strides past the crowd of gentle quacks to smite the foul disease. Devils, thicker than tiles on house-tops, scare him not from his work. Bans and bulls, excommunications and decrees, are rained upon his head. The paternal Emperor sends down dire edicts, thicker than hail upon the earth. The Holy Father blasts and raves from Rome. Louvain doctors denounce, Louvain hangmen burn, the bitter, blasphemous books. The immoderate man stands firm in the storm, demanding argument instead of illogical thunder; shows the hangmen and the people too, outside the Elster gate at Wittenberg, that papal bulls will blaze as merrily as heretic scrolls. What need of allusion to events which changed the world—which every child has learned— to the war of Titans, uprooting of hoary trees and rock-ribbed hills, to the Worms diet, the Peasant wars, the Patmos of Eisenach, and huge wrestlings with the Devil? (I, 76–77.)

Clearly, then, Motley knew how to make the best of his talents and of the imperfect attitudes and conventions with which his own temperament, Unitarian Boston, and romantic literature had supplied him. One must often wish that both his aesthetic and his moral judgment had been more consistent. But in passages such as this one, in his sharp characterizations, his precise scenes, his lucid analyses, and his dramatic construction of a great historical episode, one must recognize the achievement of a master. It will not suffice to distinguish between his historical and his literary achievement, for as the two are closely related in his failures, they have equal parts in his successes.

CHAPTER IX

Montcalm and Wolfe

Montcalm and Wolfe, published more than forty years after *The Conquest of Mexico* and almost thirty years after *The Rise of the Dutch Republic,* represents the culmination not only of Parkman's history of *France and England in North America,* but of his long career. It seems at first, therefore, to be the least clearly "romantic" of all the major histories. By 1884 some of the more obviously conventional language had gone out of fashion. Even the ageless Bancroft, having brought his history down to 1789, was preparing to condense his twelve-volume work into six volumes from which much of his "nauseous grandiloquence"[1] would be removed—and Parkman had learned to minimize the tritest of his own rhetoric. The impression is strengthened, too, by Parkman's emphasis on geographical precision and by his increased reliance on letters and journals to carry parts of his narrative. But the impression is misleading. In theme, in construction, in characterization, and even in style, Parkman's masterpiece stands squarely in the New England romantic tradition, and both its merits and its defects need to be examined in that context.

The subject itself offers a perfect conclusion to Parkman's work. In one decisive conflict it brings together all the racial, moral, and natural forces depicted in his earlier volumes.[2] The issue is decided in action by a mortal battle between the two most admirably representative soldiers of France and England; in principle, by the torpid corruption of the worst representatives of "Absolutism" and the "vigorous" patriotism of the best representative of Liberty. Unstable Indians, sought as allies by both sides and "hounded on" at times by intriguing Catholic priests, vacillate, murder indiscriminately, and at last choose to help the country most clearly opposed to their own true interests. Furthermore, this first major European war to originate in America begins with a frontier skirmish that introduces the hero of the American Revolution, and it also makes the Revolution inevitable. It opens the West to colonization; it ruins France as a world power; it establishes Britain as the "mother of nations" and Prussia as the foundation of modern Germany. (II, 409–14.)* By thus giving immense

* Volume and page numbers in parentheses refer to the two-volume edition published by Little, Brown and Company, Boston, 1893.

political significance to the volumes that dramatize the results of Parkman's major themes, it deepens the meaning of his entire series.

Parkman recognized these advantages, and he used them to achieve a remarkable literary feat. Without the help of great prose, without achieving a single great characterization, he wrote the most completely successful of all the romantic histories. He controlled masterfully a much more complex narrative than *The Conquest of Mexico*, and avoided the worst of Motley's interpretative errors. And although he failed to control his inadequate rhetoric when faced with certain kinds of character and scenery, he exploited his documents, his precise sense of place, and the point of view to give events and some characters an immediacy that is rare in any general history.

I

Although Parkman did not divide *Montcalm and Wolfe* into books with separate titles, he did give it a clearly dramatic structure, which invites subdivision into a prologue and five acts. The prologue (chaps. 1–6) introduces "the combatants," states the theme, and moves to the departure of French and British armies for America. The first act (chaps. 7–10) follows Braddock's and Shirley's unsuccessful campaign against four French objectives. Act II (chaps. 11–17) moves from Montcalm's successes to the fall of Newcastle's government in England; Act III (chaps. 18–23), from the accession of Pitt to the "brink" of Canadian "ruin" after the loss of Fort Duquesne; Act IV (chaps. 24–28), from Wolfe's appointment as commanding general to the fall of Quebec; and the last act, to the Peace of Paris.

This arrangement enabled Parkman to combine the structural advantages of Prescott's and Motley's best works while avoiding their faults. Provided with an even better historical climax than Prescott's, he had also a definite conclusion that followed from it, and he needed no biographical epilogue. Although he had no single hero on whom to focus, the rise and fall of progressive forces enabled him to begin in failure, as Motley had done, and then to move through a series of setbacks and partial successes to the climax on the Heights of Abraham.

The beauty of this structure, however, lies less in Parkman's recognition of neatly placed crises than in the usefulness of these divisions to his conventions and his theme. He regarded this battle of "past against future," "united few" against "divided many," "moral torpor" against "moral vigor," as a test of principles, institutions, and national character. He had little doubt that France's failure in all three of these had caused her to waste the heroism that had been lavished on New France, and he designed *Montcalm and Wolfe* to dramatize the importance of those faults. Each of his major divisions is based not only on important events, but on contrasts in character that represent the essential contrast.

The prologue demonstrates through character and action that both countries are "weak in leadership" (I, 180–81) and that neither knows its own true interests. If the "effeminate libertine" king of France can give political control to "Jane Fish" Pompadour (II, 44), the "dull, languid" England of 1750 is capable of trusting Newcastle. Especially in his prologue, Parkman establishes a balance between such characters, and, after beginning with a discussion of France and England, he extends this symmetry to America. There the jealous niggardliness of English colonial legislatures almost negates good leadership, and it becomes more damaging, for the moment, than the "heartless" fanaticism of French missionaries and the corruption of Canadian officials. As he turns from Europe to America and from the site of Pittsburgh in the West to Acadia in the East, Parkman can therefore set French "celerity" (I, 143) against English slowness; he can show that England temporarily lost the West because the provincial assemblies hindered Washington and Dinwiddie while the Canadian government encouraged Fathers Piquet and Le Loutre to foment Indian war. In the last chapter of this section he returns to Europe to focus once more on Newcastle, "a fantastic political jobber" (I, 179), and on Madame de Pompadour during the mutually deceitful preparations for war.

This entire section has a comic quality, for Parkman dramatizes the inefficiency, corruption, or villainy of all the "combatants": France, England, Canada and the British colonies. In his last chapter, moreover, he quotes satirical anecdotes from Horace Walpole's *George II* and Smollett's *Humphry Clinker* to illustrate Newcastle's incompetence, and he declares that at this time neither army had a great general. It is against this background that the naval phase of the European fighting begins—with a treacherous British attack on a French ship—and the stage is prepared for the "gallant bulldog" (I, 220), General Braddock.

The first act curtain rises on Braddock, whose march to Fort Duquesne opens a four-point campaign against French positions, and in peacetime. This action begins in foolish inefficiency and ends in disgraceful retreat. Braddock's stubbornness,[8] the provincial assemblies' stinginess, and Dunbar's cowardice leave the frontier completely unguarded. (I, 233.) True to his principles of balanced contrast, Parkman turns then to Acadia, where

the faults of French character are equally costly. Vergor, the French com-
mandant at Beauséjour, is a corrupt political appointee, whose cowardice
offsets the fanatical vigor of Father Le Loutre. He surrenders even before
the British have placed their cannon (I, 250–51), and Le Loutre's aggressive intrigues gain nothing but suffering for the Acadians, whom the
British feel obliged to expel. In the rest of this act Parkman follows the
same principles, showing that in the attack on Crown Point British leadership caused a "failure" that was "disguised under an incidental success"
(I, 313) and that all the British faults combined to defeat the fourth part
of the original plan. (Chap. 10.) At the end British fortunes approach
their nadir as the incompetent Loudon and Abercromby take over the
army, and the French send murdering Indians all along the frontier. After
one brief glimpse of Washington standing almost alone against this invasion (I, 333–34), Parkman devotes the last pages of this act to the Quakers'[4]
opposition to appropriations for defending the frontier. And in this British
crisis the French accidentally find their best leader.

Here Parkman has deliberately passed by the declaration of war and
Montcalm's victory at Oswego in order to give the French hero a more
emphatic position and to avoid interrupting his account of the four-point
British campaign. Montcalm, representing the best of French nobility,
dominates Parkman's second act, but Parkman takes care to magnify his
virtues by setting them against the French weaknesses that destroy New
France. Opening this act in Europe with the formal declaration of war,
Parkman sets the manly Frederick against Maria Theresa and Madame
de Pompadour, whose "infatuated" policy neglects Canada; only then does
he introduce Montcalm, who owes his appointment to the unwillingness
of any court favorites to accept "a command in the backwoods." (I, 356.)
Before dramatizing Montcalm's victories, Parkman also uses his arrival in
New France as the occasion for describing Governor Vaudreuil, the boast-
ful, jealous, indecisive provincial whose faults will prove so important at
the climax. The action occurs in this context. Montcalm destroys Oswego
while the British ministry delays assigning a new commander; and when
Loudon (the choice of Newcastle) does come, he proves incompetent. In
spite of the difficulties presented by Vaudreuil, Montcalm and his "man-
eating savages" also destroy Fort William Henry, because Loudon has
foolishly drawn British troops off the mainland for an abortive attack on
Louisbourg. After these French successes, however, Parkman uses Montcalm's letters during the ensuing "winter of discontent" to give his first
full report of Canadian official corruption. As he entitled his opening chap-

ter "Montcalm," he names his concluding chapter for the "sinister" In-
tendant, Bigot. By focusing here on this colossally representative pecu-
lator, he reveals Canada's "desperate" financial condition and prepares at
the same time for the accession of William Pitt.

The critical third act restores England and France to a temporary balance and then swings toward the inevitable result. In the opening chapter
on Pitt, Parkman returns again to Europe for his most energetic picture
of Frederick—the incarnation, here, of indomitable Will. (II, 38–39.) Then,
as "silken" King Louis dismisses the best two French ministers, the English middle class, sick of Newcastle, find in Pitt "a leader after their own
heart." Parkman considers this change so important that he compares
Pitt's influence to that of Nature: "as Nature, languishing in chill vapors
and dull smothering fogs, revives at the touch of the sun, so did England
spring into fresh life under the kindling influence of one great man." (II,
46.) Under Pitt's "robust impulsion" tough British sailors, who resemble
Motley's Beggars of the Sea, win a series of naval victories, and in the
first action of Pitt's three-point attack on New France the "ardent" General Wolfe (II, 58) helps to take Louisbourg.

But even in this grand British victory one can see the balance of the
two powers. This is the kind of battle Parkman loves, for besides occur-
ring in a sublime natural setting, it reveals the best qualities of both countries. The officers and men on both sides of the walls prove to be good
fellows, and the British win only by overcoming a "gallant defence." (II,
75.) Save for an accident, moreover, the same kind of battle might have
occurred at Ticonderoga, when Vaudreuil's inexplicable delay left Montcalm "to defend himself as he could" (II, 87) against an army led by
Lord Howe—a "Lycurgus" more responsible than any other man for breaking down the rivalry between English and American officers. But in an
action between two groups who are both lost in the dense forest, Howe is
killed. Abercromby, a compromise relic of Newcastle's government, leads
his fine army of 15,000 men to ruin. (II, 97.)

Montcalm's great leadership thus capitalizes on his one chance to win,
but despite Abercromby's "poltroonery" (II, 114) a largely colonial British
force takes Fort Frontenac, another army reopens the West by taking Fort
Duquesne, and the third act ends on "the brink of [Canadian] ruin." (II,
164.) Montcalm, increasingly harried and disgusted by Vaudreuil's jealousy and the corruption of his associates, is abandoned by the French court.
It is his own letters during the winter of 1758–59 that tell most of the story.
"We will save this unhappy country or perish," he says near the end of the
act. But Parkman assigns the final speech (a vain boast) to Vaudreuil.

The fourth act curtain rises on Wolfe, for Parkman has decided to devote the entire act to the decisive battle for Quebec. Having reserved Wolfe's portrait and biography for this position, he is able to reveal the triumphant "spirit" just before Wolfe's greatest achievement. He brings Wolfe to Quebec, dramatizes the siege and the failure of Wolfe's first assault on the city, and then, as Vaudreuil boasts vainly once again, turns to the methodical Amherst's failure to mount a diversionary attack after capturing Niagara. This device accomplishes more than an increase in suspense, for it offers another contrast in character, and it demonstrates that Wolfe must now rely on himself alone if he wants to take Quebec before winter.

The climax, one of the best-known episodes in our literature, needs no rehearsal here, but one must notice that Parkman takes advantage of every opportunity to make it depend on the fundamental contrasts that are so important to his theme. Wolfe's only hope lies "in the composition of Montcalm's army" (II, 260), and although the "difficulties" of the assault seem "insurmountable," Wolfe's own indomitable spirit is aided by something more than chance. Captain of the slovenly guard at the point where Wolfe climbs the heights is none other than Vergor, the coward of Beauséjour, who has been acquitted of misconduct there only because Bigot and Vaudreuil have interceded for him. Vaudreuil, moreover, fails to send Montcalm the necessary reinforcements after the British have been discovered. And Montcalm himself indulges his French "impetuosity" (II, 293) in attacking the firm British line. In this crucial battle, on the other hand, it is British "discipline" that wins, as the silent Redcoats hold their fire until the shouting French have rushed into confusion. At last, with Montcalm dying and Wolfe dead, Vaudreuil shamefully abandons Quebec, only to be persuaded too late that it might be defended. "The funeral of Montcalm" (who is buried in a shell-hole under a chapel) becomes "the funeral of New France" (II, 310); and at the end of this act Vaudreuil tries to save himself by "belittling [Montcalm's] achievements and blackening his name." (II, 317.)

Even the short fifth act, though it chronicles the decline of action, depends on conventional contrasts of character. Parkman raises the curtain on quiet scenes that depict not only the ruin of Quebec but the virtues of English troops, whom French nuns call "the most moderate of conquerors." (II, 330.) British "humanity" rescues a dying French soldier and the deed is rewarded by a warning of surprise attack; then a temporary French victory allows Indian converts to "murder, scalp, and mangle" most of the English wounded (II, 313, 351); and soon afterward a British commander prevents his unconverted Indian allies from scalping French prisoners. General Amherst, mobile at last after a ponderous start, is an ideal representative of the methodical British strength that would eventually have crushed New France in any case; and he also represents British moral indignation when he denies the Montreal garrison "the honors of war" because of "the infamous [Indian] barbarities" tolerated by French officers throughout the war. (II, 373.) As the American action ends, moreover, Parkman allows New England ministers to pronounce the final speeches: on future prosperity and the conversion of the wilderness from a trapper's paradise to "the glory and joy of the whole earth." (II, 379.)

Nor can the drama end before the Canadian peculators have been tried or before Pitt and Frederick have fought their battles to the end. Telescoping the European war as he has throughout the history, Parkman focuses on the two heroes in his last chapter of action—as Frederick barely avoids destruction and as George III's tyrannical jealousy forces Pitt, the people's "representative," to resign. (II, 387–91.) It is by bringing these two titans to rest that Parkman restores Europe to the moral lassitude of 1750. Although British armies and navies still feel "the impulsion" of Pitt's "imperial hand" and "the unconquerable spirit that he had aroused," the government is returned to "weak and unwilling hands." (II, 400.) And Frederick learns to restrain his insults and to live at peace with new tyrants. (II, 399.) Thus, before Parkman issues his final challenge to American leadership, he has painted his two exhausted heroes as examples: Frederick, deserted by England, but fighting on and rewarded at last "as by a miracle"; Pitt, carried to Parliament to thunder one last protest against an excessively generous peace treaty.

It is against these images, and the more remote ones of Montcalm and Wolfe, that Parkman's last challenge must be read. His demand that democracy give the world "types of manhood as lofty and strong" as those of other systems does not pay mere "lip-service"[5] to progress. It concludes a history organized from beginning to end around contrasts that demonstrate his implicit faith in conventional ideas of progress.

Parkman's organization, then, is remarkably economical. While he exploits the genuinely dramatic arrangement that the course of the war invited him to fashion, he uses his characters with equal skill. Far from being embarrassed by the lack of a dominant hero for the entire history, he repeatedly brings forward the right man at the right time, dramatizing the merits and defects of both countries at appropriate moments of victory and defeat. Nor does his final evaluation of French and British institutions prevent him from sympathizing with both sides, for he does not need to deal directly with the absolute moral cleavage that divides Motley's history, and he has within the French lines a hero from whose pathetic, thoroughly moral point of view he can reveal the worst effects of bad government. This last technique serves him especially well during the winter after each of Montcalm's campaigns—an occasion for filling in the narrative with the observations on Canadian society and official corruption that Montcalm wrote during the long months in Montreal and Quebec. In this way Parkman describes the society without seeming to interrupt his narrative of military action, and he uses the same kind of device to provide important information about the English colonies. Besides making his military narrative reveal the complex relationship between colonial legislatures and governors, he often advances his narrative by using contemporary journals that illustrate the manners of provincial soldiers, the methods of recruiting, the perils of life on the frontier.

Parkman's acute awareness of geography also affects his organization. Besides arranging his acts so that he can summarize European events at the beginning or end of every one of them, he keeps always before the reader some sense of the vast continent for which the two nations fought. His first paragraph on America emphasizes the "boundless interior" controlled by the French posts from Canada to Louisiana (I, 20), and his final paragraph on France points out the "two island rocks . . . that the victors had given her for drying her codfish." (II, 410.) In the drama that he enacts between these opposite pictures he moves periodically from western to eastern campaigns while centering most of the action in the recurrent battles along the short line from Albany to Montreal. Regularly, moreover, he takes the reader inside a raiding party or an army—often as it marches over wild country that has already been "won" by one side or the other— and he thus communicates a sense not only of immediacy but of the terror and futility of military conquest in the forest. (II, 14-15.) The first British success at Crown Point and Montcalm's victories at Oswego, Fort William Henry, and Ticonderoga are all equally barren. Soon after each one of them the scene becomes a "wild solitude" again. (See, for example, I, 416, 513.)

2

The characterization in *Montcalm and Wolfe* needs little detailed analysis beyond what I have already said here and in earlier chapters, for its chief literary value lies in the skill with which Parkman built the conventional contrasts into his dramatic structure. Although he chose to tell the story in only half the space that Motley had used in *The Rise of the*

Dutch Republic, he was obliged to portray almost as many characters, and most of them were well known even through American histories before he started to write *Montcalm and Wolfe*.[6] Like Prescott, moreover, he was interested in the influence and experience of the individual character without having either the desire or the ability to communicate more than the broad outlines of a few traits. For these reasons, and because he had no dominant hero, he did not devote as much space to any one person as Motley and Prescott had given to each of several figures. He relied on concise summaries and action itself to portray most of his cast, and for the few characters whom he considered most important he employed more of the conventional rhetoric and more extensive quotations from their letters. If these techniques prevented him from achieving more than one distinguished portrait, they also spared him the worst distortions of Motley and Prescott, and they focused attention on his theme and the developing action. Only when he trusted his most "elevated" rhetoric did the method fail him.

The line of characters projected in *Montcalm and Wolfe* includes nearly every type to be found in the romantic histories. Vigorous English, French, and American aristocrats represent the natural, the normal; Wolfe, Pitt, Howe, Montcalm, and Washington stand at the center. To their right extends a row of increasingly less natural characters: the sturdy governors Dinwiddie and Shirley; the typical generals, from Braddock the "bulldog" and Amherst the slow mover to the competent French officers and the incompetent Loudon and Abercromby; the fanatical priests and the dishonest Canadian officials; and, at the extreme, Newcastle, George III, Louis XV and his Pompadour. On the left the file includes fewer distinct individuals, but the progression from Rogers "the woodsman" to the few good Indians and the crowds of "man-eating savages" is perfectly clear.

In arranging this line, Parkman concentrates on economy. Like Prescott, he often fixes the attitude of a character in a single incident or a few words and then lets the contrast indicate his significance, but most of these sketches are much more precise than Prescott's, because Parkman offers more detailed evidence. In one paragraph, for example, he uses the action and the documents themselves to characterize a British sailor who resembles Fenimore Cooper's Long Tom Coffin, and to dramatize the cleavage between ordinary Englishmen and Frenchmen. Parkman's only descriptive words about this man who is to bring Wolfe's fleet up the Saint Lawrence are those that introduce him as "an old sailor named Killick, who despised the whole Gallic race, and had no mind to see his ship in charge of a Frenchman." Everything else depends on the order of the paragraph and the words of a contemporary journal. When the captured French pilot, who has "'gasconaded'" at the beginning of the paragraph, insists that no French ship has ever attempted the passage without a native pilot, Killick promises "'to convince you that an Englishman shall go where a Frenchman dare not show his nose.'" He navigates the strange channel casually, joking along the way, and as the French pilot lifts "'his eyes to heaven with astonishment and fervency,'" Killick declares that the Thames is often much more dangerous than this part of the Saint Lawrence. The quotations come from Captain John Knox's journal, but Parkman uses them efficiently to introduce a type and to foreshadow the distinction between French and British soldiers that will be so important on the Heights of Abraham. (II, 204-6.)

When he does rely more exclusively on his own words for such a contrast, Parkman usually avoids the more elaborate rhetoric of conventional characterization and relies instead on simpler, though equally common terminology. At the moment when several Indian tribes are to be persuaded to desert the French, he introduces the brave Moravian Frederick Post as the antithesis of both good and bad Jesuit missionaries. Characterized by "simplicity of character, directness, and honesty"—all the reverse of traits in Parkman's Jesuits—"Christian" Post represents Protestant self-reliance. He is "a plain German, upheld by a sense of duty and a single-hearted trust in God"; he has married a "converted squaw"; and he has tried to teach the Indians "peace." He goes to the suspicious Delawares "alone, with no great disciplined organization to impel and support him, and no visions and illusions such as kindled and sustained the splendid heroism of the early Jesuit martyrs." (II, 144.) After this introduction, Parkman allows the action and Post's journal to complete the characterization. He himself intrudes only to add a few lurid words on the Indians' ferocity and to reinforce the French-British contrast with a simple narrative fact. While Post is urging peace on the Indians, a French officer arrives in their village and asks them to attack a British army. (II, 147-50.)

This kind of technique and emphasis also succeeds in Parkman's portrayal of more important characters, from Braddock to Montcalm. But as the scale increases the quality of Parkman's interest and the limitations of his technique are more clearly defined. Even for Montcalm, to whom he gives more space than to any other character, Parkman sketches the typical pose very quickly, and he uses a minimum of conventional language— almost all of it abstract—to do so. Having announced Montcalm's appoint-

ment just after one of his most vehement denunciations of the French
court, Parkman writes a brief biographical sketch that makes the facts
emphasize conventional types. His first two paragraphs frame Montcalm's
own youthful statement of personal goals between the demands of a "pedantic" tutor that he write a better hand, and a report of the grotesque fate
of Montcalm's brother, who died at the age of seven because "his preco-
cious brain had been urged to fatal activity" by the pedant's "exertions."
Montcalm's goals themselves express the essence of Parkman's own desires:

"First, to be an honorable man, of good morals, brave, and a Christian. Secondly,
to read in moderation; to know as much Greek and Latin as most men of the
world; also the four rules of arithmetic, and something of history, geography,
and French and Latin *belles-lettres,* as well as to have a taste for the arts and
sciences. Thirdly, and above all, to be obedient, docile [to my parents]. . . .
Fourthly, to fence and ride as well as my small abilities will permit."

Then, between two paragraphs that outline Montcalm's "more wholesome
growth" and reprint some statements expressing his love for his family
and his chateau, Parkman offers one more descriptive statement about
him: "He was pious in his soldierly way, and ardently loyal to Church
and King." (I, 356–59.) To complete the "scholar-soldier's" portrait, Parkman troubles only to summarize his military injuries and to paint him as
Governor Vaudreuil must have seen him when Montcalm arrived in New
France: Vaudreuil "saw before him a man of small stature, with a lively
countenance, a keen eye, and, in moments of animation, rapid, vehement
utterance, and nervous gesticulation." (I, 366.)

From this point until his death the portrait does not change. Montcalm
is the "impetuous" scholar-soldier. His piety, his loyalty to Church and
King, his nervous energy, and his affection for his family become clearer
as one reads frequent quotations from his letters; by the same means Parkman communicates Montcalm's disgust with corruption and with having
to employ savages, and his intense loneliness in Canada. His letters and
the action, then, reveal some of his deepest feelings, and the characterization
succeeds. But both the visual picture and Parkman's own analysis are
frankly abstract. The success of the characterization depends not, as in
Motley, on precise analysis or precise pictures, but on skillful arrangement
of detailed action and documents to reveal a few typical traits.

Thus Parkman's interest centers less on the complexity of individual
character than on a few qualities relevant to his own situation and to his
conventional interpretation of the war. He seems, moreover, to concentrate
primarily on communicating a sense of the character's experience, and on

a particular kind of experience. From Frederick Post and a nameless pioneer "buried in the woods . . . in an appalling loneliness" (I, 334–35) to Frederick the Great and Montcalm and Wolfe themselves, he focuses repeatedly on lonely effort in the midst of terrifying danger, overwhelming physical difficulties, incompetent support, implacable enemies. He communicates these and other qualities most effectively when he stays close to the documents and the specific fact and when he uses his least inflated language.

When he turns to Pitt, Frederick, and Washington, however, the inadequacy of his rhetoric becomes more damaging, for in these characterizations he must stand farther away from the documents, and the kind of pose in which he wants to display these men persuades him to use an energetic language that often escapes his control. Parkman's forceful rhythm, his occasionally consistent imagery (II, 42), and the energy of the historical characters save him from complete failure in these passages, but trite, inconsistent imagery, and shoddy diction repeatedly betray him. If Pitt consistently hurls down lightningbolts in one paragraph, he becomes in the next a tower of strength that turns contemptuously from the tricks of politics and throws itself on the people's patriotism and public spirit. This crisis, moreover, has occurred just after England has been dragged into the Continental war because of an apple of discord, while her great ally (Frederick) was reaping a full harvest of laurels. Then an event takes place pregnant with glorious consequence: the reins of power fall into the hands of William Pitt. Pitt's heart that beats in unison with all that is British finds responsive throbs in every corner of the vast empire. (II, 40–43.) Later, Frederick holds the invading hosts at bay, but then the end seems near. He cannot be everywhere at once, and while he stops one leak the torrent pours in at another. He continues to fight with smiles on his lip and anguish at his heart, with cool and stubborn desperation. But his cup is not yet full. (II, 387–88.) Pitt, meanwhile, cannot stay in power, for besides incurring the dislike of George III he has ridden roughshod over men far above him in rank. But he holds to his purpose regardless of the gathering storm. (II, 391–92.) His fall, when it does occur, is like the knell of doom to Frederick, around whom the darkness grows darker yet and to whom not a hope seems left; when as by a miracle the clouds break and light streams out of the blackness. (II, 398.)

These lines cast some doubt on the judgment that Parkman's prose style is rarely equalled in American literature for "precision and energy and hard grace"; that of all the romantic historians he was "incomparably the best writer."[7] Although the faults cannot be blamed entirely on the kind

of characters that provoked them,[8] they usually occur when Parkman expresses strong feeling—his own or that of his characters. In moments of
extreme crisis for his Byronic heroes his diction becomes extremely unre-
liable. Just as a crucial test of La Salle's endurance and a Northern defeat
in the Civil War had led Parkman to write two of the worst paragraphs
he ever published,[9] so in *Montcalm and Wolfe* his worst passages describe
Frederick and Pitt; and his diction also betrays him in some of Wolfe's
moments of decision. When he says, "Here was Wolfe's best hope. This
failing, his only chance was audacity. The game was desperate; but, intrepid gamester as he was in war, he was a man, in the last resort, to stake
everything on the cast of the dice" (II, 210), his combination of short sentences, heroic rhythm, and periodic construction only calls attention to the
triteness of his figures. When he describes the battle itself, however, his
quotations and his intense interest in the facts and the experience help him
to avoid this kind of error.

One must conclude, then, that Parkman's best method of characterization was to reveal conventional contrasts by combining factual and unpre-
tentious, abstract language with documents and with a careful arrangement of the action. He simply did not have Motley's talent for conveying
visual images of character. Even his famous portrait of Wolfe, against
which he placed a reproduction of the painting (II, 184), displays his tritest
language at just the moment when descriptive art demands more original
phrasing. I have italicized the imperfect words:

His face, when seen in profile, was singular as that of the Great Condé. The
forehead and chin receded; the nose, slightly upturned, formed with the other
features the point of an obtuse triangle; the mouth was by no means shaped to
express resolution; *and nothing but the clear, bright, and piercing eye bespoke
the spirit within.* On his head he wore a black three-cornered hat; his red hair
was tied in a queue behind; his narrow shoulders, slender body, and long, thin
limbs [arms] were *cased* in a scarlet frock, with broad cuffs and ample skirts
that reached the knee; while on his left arm he wore a band of crape in mourning
for his father, of whose death he had heard a few days before.

If one places this picture beside Motley's portrait of Elizabeth, Henry of
Valois, the Prior of Saint Vaast—or even beside the portrait of Macaulay
that Motley sent in a letter to his wife—one sees a sharp contrast. From
Macaulay's profile Motley turns to a frontal view:

The face, to resume my description, seen in front, is blank, and as it were badly
lighted. There is nothing luminous in the eye, nothing impressive in the brow.
The forehead is spacious, but it is scooped entirely away in the region where

benevolence ought to be, while beyond rise reverence, firmness, and self-esteem, like Alps on Alps. The under eyelids are so swollen as almost to close the eyes, and it would be almost impossible to tell the color of those orbs, and equally so, from the neutral tint of his hair and face, to say of what complexion he had originally been.[10]

Parkman's abstract picture of Montcalm excels his picture of Wolfe, for it does not pretend to do more than it actually accomplishes. His characterization is most impressive when he describes a Braddock, a Bigot (II, 24), a Post, a Vaudreuil, in action.

3

If the weakness of Parkman's prose lies in his most self-consciously heroic diction and his trite imagery, its great strength comes from his acute sense of specific place and specific fact, and from his brilliant control of the pace of his narrative. In spite of his embarrassing faults, Parkman was indeed a good writer. Much of his prose does have a "hard grace," but his most "energetic" prose is often his least precise. His best prose is his ordinary exposition, his least pretentious narrative—those relatively unadorned passages which, dominating most of the two volumes, communicate social information, analyze the opposing nations' arguments (I, 124–25), prepare the reader carefully for a particular action, bring the reader inside one camp or another; those passages which, by joining specific fact to general action, give the narrative its admirable order.

One can see the value of this kind of prose by examining Parkman's account of a single battle, Sir William Johnson's defeat of Baron Dieskau on the site of Fort William Henry. Parkman approaches the action by describing not only the terrain but each of the two armies. Since this is the first battle involving New England militia, he wants to describe Johnson's "crude" army with some care, while remaining true to his principle of narrative economy. He chooses, therefore, to depict the army as it waits nervously for supplies. He begins with a paragraph on some of the colonial officers, including future heroes of the Revolution, and then he describes the men:

The soldiers were no soldiers, but farmers and farmers' sons who had volunteered for the summer campaign. One of the corps had a blue uniform faced with red. The rest wore their daily clothing. Blankets had been served out to them by the several provinces, but the greater part brought their own guns; some under the penalty of a fine if they came without them, and some under the inducement of a reward. They had no bayonets, but carried hatchets in their belts as a sort of substitute. At their sides were slung powder-horns, on which, in the leisure of the camp, they carved quaint devices with the points of their jack-knives. They came chiefly from plain New England homesteads,—rustic abodes, unpainted and dingy, with long well-sweeps, capacious barns, rough fields of pumpkins and corn, and vast kitchen chimneys, above which in winter hung squashes to keep them from frost, and guns to keep them from rust. (I, 291.)

This paragraph illustrates Parkman's most effective description. He does not paint a detailed picture, but instead names significant objects. The short sentences that set the one uniform against daily clothing; the moderate alliteration, the repetition, the simple diction, and the forceful rhythm gained from balanced constructions and periodic emphasis—these function as well as *farmers, plain homesteads, rustic abodes,* and the final picture to emphasize the naturalness of the men. Some of the objects and statements, moreover, clearly suggest a double significance. The contrast between "fine" and "reward" suggests the niggardliness and lack of concert that Parkman has just been deploring in English colonial legislatures; the quaint devices carved on the powder horns with jacknives imply both rude individuality and the boredom of waiting in camp; the guns above the chimneys suggest self-reliance and constant preparedness for danger.

But the full value of this paragraph becomes clear only as one sees its place in the narrative. Parkman stays with Johnson's force until it has finally moved to Lake George, and then, as the British sentries are posted, he turns to the French army. He establishes the moral contrast simply by paraphrasing Baron Dieskau's order telling the Indians "not to amuse themselves by taking scalps till the enemy is entirely defeated, since they can kill ten men in the time required to scalp one." And he drives home the point by quoting from a letter of Dieskau's:

"They drive us crazy," he says, "from morning till night. There is no end to their demands. They have already eaten five oxen and as many hogs, without counting the kegs of brandy they have drunk. In short, one needs the patience of an angel to get on with these devils; and yet one must always force himself to seem pleased with them." (I, 297.)

This idiomatic translation of Dieskau's letter exemplifies the great merit of Parkman's narrative technique. His short sentences name things and concentrate attention on the participant's point of view, stressing the problems of a competent officer faced with difficulties beyond his control. Since the Indians' irresponsibility is the main cause of Dieskau's eventual defeat

(I, 305), their inferiority to the New England farmers has particular significance here, and Dieskau's allusion to devils justifies the imagery that Parkman himself applies to fighting savages. It is through the Indians, moreover, that Parkman, in the next sentence, again sets his narrative in motion.
Reluctant even to "go out as scouts," they finally do bring in an English
captive whose "patriotic falsehood" persuades Dieskau to march against
the British.

The same kind of technique leads one to the action itself. Since the first
engagement is a French-Indian ambush that drives the English back to their
camp, Parkman follows the French and Indian army to the "snare," leaving
them only after he has stationed "a Canadian or a savage, with gun cocked
and ears intent," behind "every bush." (I, 300.) Then, having created the
desired suspense, he uses English documents to place the reader inside the
vanguard who march into the trap. He dramatizes both Johnson's "complete misconception" of the size of the French force, and the eloquent
warning of the Mohawk chief Hendrick, the noblest Indian of the entire
history, against marching out to meet the French. And he quotes from the
hasty letter of a New England officer who will be killed in the ambush.
(I, 301–2.)

After this remarkable preparation neither the skirmish nor the decisive
battle requires "elevated" prose. One sees "some sign of an enemy"
through "the sharp eye of old Hendrick," and the firing begins "at that
instant." With a fine sense of drama Parkman recognizes that the best way
he can suggest the suddenness of injury or death is to rely on flat statements
of fact: "Hendrick's horse was shot down, and the chief was killed with a
bayonet as he tried to rise. [Colonel] Williams, seeing a rising ground on
his right, made for it, calling on his men to follow; but as he climbed the
slope, guns flashed from the bushes, and a shot through the brain laid him
dead." (I, 302–3.)

When he comes to the climax of the ensuing battle, Parkman achieves
an artistic triumph by combining all these methods, for he concentrates
once again on Dieskau. At the moment when an attack would surely have
succeeded, the "French Indians" and Canadians had refused to obey, and
some of the Indians had then been "driven off by a few shells dropped
among them." With plain statement and Dieskau's own words, then,
Parkman impels one to look more closely at the particular action and its
meaning than any of the other historians can manage to do:

At length Dieskau, exposing himself within short range of the English line,
was hit in the leg. His adjutant, Montreuil, himself wounded, came to his aid,

and was washing the injured limb with brandy, when the unfortunate commander was again hit in the knee and thigh. He seated himself behind a tree while the Adjutant called two Canadians to carry him to the rear. One of them was instantly shot down. Montreuil took his place; but Dieskau refused to be moved, bitterly denounced the Canadians and Indians, and ordered the Adjutant to leave him and lead the regulars in a last effort against the camp.

It was too late. Johnson's men, singly or in small squads, were already crossing their row of logs; and in a few moments the whole dashed forward with a shout, falling upon the enemy with hatchets and the butts of their guns. The French and their allies fled. The wounded General still sat helpless by the tree, when he saw a soldier aiming at him. He signed to the man not to fire; but he pulled the trigger, shot him across the hips, leaped upon him, and ordered him in French to surrender. "I said," writes Dieskau, " 'You rascal, why did you fire? You see a man lying in his blood on the ground, and you shoot him!' He answered: "How did I know that you had not got a pistol? I had rather kill the devil than have the devil kill me.' 'You are a Frenchman?' I asked. 'Yes,' he replied; 'it is more than ten years since I left Canada'; whereupon several others fell on me and stripped me. I told them to carry me to their general, which they did. On learning who I was, he sent for surgeons, and, though wounded himself, refused all assistance till my wounds were dressed."

Here Parkman comes almost as near as Mark Twain and Stephen Crane to the kind of plain statement in which Ernest Hemingway describes violent action. Dieskau does not, like Frederic Henry, put his hand into the hole where his knee has been, but one sees his helplessness just as clearly; not only the picture of the man sitting down, but the numerous blunt sentences and the naked, monosyllabic statement of fact suggest the incoherence and awful tension of the action. As Dieskau's position suffices to reveal his helplessness, so his point of view, his first-hand report, and Parkman's blunt assertion of other facts ("The French and their allies fled.") communicate the meaning of the episode.

Although Parkman concentrates his simplest language in these climactic paragraphs, scarcely a line in the twenty-six-page chapter departs from the relatively simple diction and plain statement that make them so admirably effective. Throughout the chapter Parkman subordinates rhetoric to fact, and his selection and placement of facts—from the description of Johnson's soldiers to Johnson's restraint of the Mohawks who want to torture Dieskau—express his judgment much more effectively than his few figurative efforts can express it. Indeed, the only two inadequate lines in the entire chapter are a trite metaphor personifying a brook (I, 300) and another describing Johnson's reward. (I, 315.)

It is through these methods that Parkman gives so much of his narrative an immediacy rare in any of the other romantic histories. His thorough research allows him to use the journal of James Smith, a prisoner at Fort Duquesne who watched nine hundred French and Indians prepare and depart for the attack on Braddock's army (I, 210–11); his personal knowledge of the battle sites enables him to describe both the natural setting and the fortifications before he moves in close to the action;[11] his economical, factual language and his skillful use of quotations enable him to offset the disadvantages of conventional rhetoric and of his frequent inability to choose precise graphic language. If the conventional imagery fails him when he says that "Braddock showed a furious intrepidity. Mounted on horseback, he dashed to and fro like a madman," he achieves an unforgettable impression when he describes Braddock lying "among the bushes, bleeding, gasping, unable even to curse." (I, 219, 220.)

One should not conclude that Parkman's more elaborately rhythmic and figurative rhetoric never succeeds. Although he rarely approaches the heights of either Motley's or Melville's best prose, his more ambitiously pictorial rhetoric does often succeed when he concentrates on the forest as a symbol of ghastly death. Even here he is not infallible, for he may make a "gloomy brook" "gurgle" (I, 300); but his intense fascination for the grim horror of the Nature he professes to love usually impels him to describe it much more honestly. Sometimes, as in the description of Wood Creek,[12] he combines the imagery of upright skeletons, prehistoric bones, and invisible, dangerous ghosts in a series of rhythmic lines that almost fall into blank verse; he repeatedly emphasizes the "chaotic" disorder of the forest in scenes of danger (I, 334; II, 12–13, 95–96, 141); and when Montcalm uses felled, pointed trees and tangled branches for a breastwork at Ticonderoga, Parkman uses them to create a hideous picture at the most horrible moment of the disastrous British attack.

The scene was frightful: masses of infuriated men who could not go forward and would not go back; straining for an enemy they could not reach, and firing on an enemy they could not see; caught in the entanglement of fallen trees; tripped by briers, stumbling over logs, tearing through boughs; shouting, yelling, cursing, and pelted all the while with bullets that killed them by scores, stretched them on the ground, or hung them on jagged branches in strange attitudes of death. (II, 106.)

But if Parkman's sense of the violent terror and beauty (II, 220) of Nature does allow him to write some excellent poetic prose, he relies during most of the history on the more ordinary virtues of order, economy, and forceful rhythm. Even his analytical exposition depends chiefly on these qualities. He manages consistently to fit his analytical passages into the narrative, as when he describes the French and British definitions of Acadian boundaries (I, 123–26) and the disputes between British colonial governors and legislatures. In all these discussions, and in the Introduction as well, his clear, firm prose stresses some kind of contrast; the sentences, though necessarily a little longer than most of those I have cited, retain their graceful balance and vigorous movement; and none of these passages stays long away from specific things. When he explains the extravagant British definitions of British territory, he says that they claimed "every mountain, forest, or prairie where an Iroquois had taken a scalp" (I, 125); when he explains the inconsistency of French claims to the West, he says that after seventy-five years the territory was "still a howling waste, yielding nothing to civilization but beaver-skins, with here and there a fort, trading post or mission, and three or four puny hamlets by the Mississippi and the Detroit" (I, 25); when he describes the gallant "butterflies" of the French court, who "fought as gaily as they danced," he says that "their valets served them with ices in the trenches, under the cannon of besieged towns." (I, 12.)

Parkman's style, then, has the solid merit of his characterization and his dramatic organization. It is rarely brilliant, but it enables him to show his nearly perfect mastery of his subject—to join precise fact and large narrative movement, conventional character and political analysis, individual experience and national traits, in a splendid construction that stands as the most admirable synthesis of all the romantic histories.

CHAPTER X

Conclusion

The New England historians' achievement entitles them to a far more important place in the American Renaissance than they have usually been given. Their fifty volumes on Spanish, Dutch, Franco- and Anglo-American history are not a curious by-product but a central expression of romantic thought in America. They found in romantic conventions a way of giving the Past artistic order and contemporary moral significance. Confronted with real historical characters, they did what any historian who wants to portray individual character is likely to do: they turned to the vocabulary of contemporary literature. That vocabulary allowed them to adapt romantic conceptions of the hero to the values of a liberal, republican society; to concentrate on representative types who had drawn much of their strength from their "natural" relationship with the People. In this terminology the historians also found the means to express the moral drama that the Unitarian, along with most liberal Americans, saw in history. They did not ignore the influence of "forces"—even of economic forces—on history, nor did they ignore the importance of struggle. Almost every one of their works dramatizes that conflict between "artificial" and "natural" principles which they all regarded as the inevitable condition of progress.

Even in Motley and Bancroft this conflict did not mean a decisive battle between absolute good and absolute evil. The historians achieved their greatest success when they dramatized the continuing struggle by portraying a wide range of types—from the "savage" to the sensual reactionary—whose differences might be emphasized by the very organization of the history. When the romantic historian placed Indian, priest, and Catholic king against the progressive hero, he not only reinforced mid-nineteenth-century conceptions of destiny; he clarified the meaning of the "natural," and he prepared for a more convincing resolution of the conflict than historical romancers like Cooper had been able to achieve. For although the historical hero's victory, like that of Cooper's Edward Effingham, represented a compromise between the extremes, the historical hero was real—a

Washington or a Wolfe, whose actual achievements matched the theoretical virtues that Cooper's readers had to accept on faith.

Although their reliance on contrasting types restricted the historians to limited kinds of subjects, it gave their best histories an order and a significance that more recent, "scientific" monographs too often lack. Despite their inconsistencies and their peculiar terminology, their version of moral and historical truth often has an enduring value. The economic, religious, and political errors of Mexico, of Spain in the Netherlands and at home, of France in Canada and England in the colonies, seem as clear to modern historians as they seemed in nineteenth-century America; the romantic historians made the errors memorable by dramatizing them in the context of moral vigor and torpor.

The conventional methods also limited the kinds of traits that might be delineated in the histories. But although they could not suffice to explain individual psychology, they gave Motley's villains, Prescott's Montezuma and Cortés, and Parkman's La Salle and Montcalm a deeper reality than these characters might otherwise have had. To individual portraits, scenes, and incidents, moreover, they gave a human truth that transcends all the obvious inadequacies. The pictures of La Salle amid the wreckage of his last voyage, of Montezuma sitting in chains, of the Prior of Saint Vaast bribing the Malcontents—these are unforgettable not in spite of the conventional ideas, but because of them.

Clearly, then, the New England histories suggest the impossibility of divorcing literary methods from historical theory. Although one might like to know just how deliberately the historians imposed the romantic formulas on the historical record, the question seems unanswerable. The assumptions on which the formulas were based had already pervaded the historians' conception of the Past before they began writing; the assumptions, indeed, had affected each man's decision to write history in the first place, and they had also helped to attract each of them to his particular subject. One cannot separate the New England case against Rome from the literary types in which the case was embodied.

It is precisely because of this relationship that the New England historians belong not on the periphery of the American Renaissance, but at the center. Their histories provide a foundation in documented fact for the tension between form and essence, head and heart, civilization and Nature, that preoccupied so many of their contemporaries. Their three greatest works dramatize that conflict by exploiting the most effective conventions of the period without belying its highest standards of historical research.

NOTES

Notes

1. Bancroft's third volume—with its narrative sections on the Jesuit martyrs and on La Salle, and its long essay on the Indian race—may have influenced Parkman's choice of subject. This successful volume was published in 1840, and Prescott's enthusiastic review appeared in January 1841. Parkman's copy of this edition is in the Harvard College Library. In 1856, when Parkman was hoping to start work on the main body of his subject, he asked Bancroft for bibliographical help, and Bancroft's reply stressed the brilliant literary promise of the subject. Bancroft to Parkman, July 31, 1856, Parkman Papers, Massachusetts Historical Society. (Hereafter Massachusetts Historical Society will be abbreviated as "MHS.")

2. Letter to W. H. Prescott, January 5, 1858; Prescott to President King of Columbia, September 23, 1857. Prescott Papers, MHS. In a plaintive letter from St. Petersburg in 1841, Motley told his wife that he preferred "the profession of diplomacy . . . to any other" and considered himself best fitted for it. *The Correspondence of John Lothrop Motley*, ed. George W. Curtis (New York, 1889), I, 80–81.

3. Two years before he died, Prescott said that he had given up law because of his poor eyes. Letter to George E. Ellis, June 1, 1857, Prescott Papers, MHS. Prescott was embarrassed by his slowness in choosing a useful profession, and his helpful young friends were calling him "the gentleman" by 1820. George Ticknor, *Life of William Hickling Prescott* (Boston, 1864), p. 54, n. 7.

4. *Ibid.*, p. 110. Gardner, Prescott wrote in his Journal, spent "weeks, and I may say months on its careful revision" for style. Notebooks VIII, Prescott Papers, MHS, pp. 73–74.

5. Samuel A. Eliot to Bancroft, October 22, 1818, Bancroft Papers, MHS.

6. See *The Transcendentalists*, ed. Perry Miller (Cambridge, 1950), pp. 157–246.

7. Andrews Norton, *The Evidences of the Genuineness of the Gospels* (3 vols., Boston, 1837–44); *On the Latest Form of Infidelity* (Boston, 1839). Prescott read the *Evidences* carefully and commented in detail in his Notebooks VIII, pp. 22–50.

8. George Bancroft to Edward Everett, September 12, 1818, Bancroft Papers, MHS. Bancroft quotes Kirkland's letter to Eichhorn in his letter to Everett from Leyden, August 5, 1818.

9. Bancroft to Norton, March 9, 1820, Bancroft Papers, MHS.

10. Bancroft told Edward Everett (August 1, 1819): "They have written to me, they would be well content if I abandoned that science [German theology] and attended to any other branch." Bancroft Papers, MHS.

11. 2 vols., New York, 1828.

12. Bancroft to Everett, August 1, 1819. In this letter Bancroft suggested that he might do well to turn his energies to history, since history "has always interested me, suits well with my theology, & I think I could become useful by it."

13. See Bancroft to Norton, October 26, 1818.

14. John G. Palfrey, *History of New England* (4 vols., Boston, 1884). Charles W. Upham, *Lectures on Witchcraft . . . in 1692* (Boston, 1831); *Salem Witchcraft: with an Account of Salem Village* (2 vols., Boston, 1867); and *Salem Witchcraft and Cotton Mather* (Morrisania, N.Y., 1869). Edward Everett, "Life of John Stark," in *Library of American Biography*, ed. Jared Sparks (New York, 1839), I, 1–117. In the preceding generation Aaron Bancroft wrote a *Life of Washington* and Abiel Holmes compiled his *Annals of America*.

15. See Thomas P. Peardon, *The Transition in English Historical Writing, 1760–1830* (New York, 1933), chap. x; and G. P. Gooch, *History and Historians in the Nineteenth Century,* 2d ed. (London, 1920), chaps. i–v.

16. See Bancroft to Prescott, February 10, 1846, Bancroft Papers, MHS.

17. Prescott to Bancroft, n.d.; endorsed "1839." Bancroft Papers, MHS. Amos A. Lawrence to Bancroft, January 10, 1842, Bancroft Papers, MHS. When Everett entered Whig politics, he asked Bancroft to return all his letters. Everett to Bancroft, February 15, 1840, Bancroft Papers, MHS. Cf. his letter of December 28, 1841.

18. Letter to Bancroft, April 3, 1843, Bancroft Papers, MHS. See also Everett's letters of January 2, February 1, and February 28, 1843.

19. The library Bancroft sent home from Germany included the works of Herder and Grimm. Bancroft wrote essays on Schiller, Heeren, Goethe, Herder, and Boeckh for *The North American Review:* "Schiller's Minor Poems," XVII (October 1823), 268–87; "Heeren's *Politics of Ancient Greece,*" XVIII (April 1824), 390–406; "Goethe's Werke," XIX (October 1824), 303–25; "Herder's Writings," XX (January 1825), 138–47; and "Boeckh's *Economy of Athens,*" XXXII (April 1831), 344–67.

20. Letter to George E. Ellis, June 1, 1857, Prescott Papers, MHS.

21. Quoted in Ticknor, *Prescott,* p. 43.

22. Diary (June 28, 1817), Prescott Papers, MHS, p. 117.

23. Letter to Andrews Norton, January 9, 1819, Bancroft Papers, MHS. For an expression of similar sentiment see Bancroft to Prescott, August 17, 1847, in M. A. DeWolfe Howe, *The Life and Letters of George Bancroft* (New York, 1908), II, 20–23.

24. Letter of August 12, 1832, in *Correspondence,* I, 25–26.

25. Prescott, Notebooks IV (February 13 and 20, 1825), pp. 68, 71.

26. Letter to his wife, April 15, 1842, in *Correspondence,* I, 106.

27. "The Polity of the Puritans," *The North American Review,* LXIX (October 1849), 493–94. See also *Morton's Hope* (Boston, 1839), I, 149–50; II, 80–83; and his letter to O. W. Holmes, November 20, 1853, in *Correspondence,* I, 161–65.

28. *A Half-Century of Conflict* (Boston, 1893), II, 258.

29. Motley, "The Polity of the Puritans," *N.A.R.,* LXIX, 493; letter to Holmes, in *Correspondence,* I, 162.

30. Prescott, "Sir Walter Scott" (April 1838), in *Essays from the North American Review,* ed. Allen Thorndike Rice (New York, 1879), p. 45. Cf. Parkman, Diary, Parkman Papers, MHS, p. 1.

31. Letter to George and Georgiana Keats, October 21, 1818, in *The Letters of John Keats,* ed. M. B. Forman (New York, 1935), p. 241.

32. Thomas Carlyle, "Biography," in *Critical and Miscellaneous Essays* (London, 1888), II, 256.

33. Thomas Carlyle, "Sir Walter Scott," in *Essays,* III, 214–15.

34. Letter to Edward Everett, December 29, 1834, Bancroft Papers, MHS.

35. See Peardon, *Transition,* chaps. iv–viii; T. B. Macaulay, "History," in *The Works of Lord Macaulay,* ed. Lady Trevelyan (London, 1866), V, 152–56.

36. Commonplace Book (1820–22), Prescott Papers, MHS, p. 39.

37. Notebooks V, p. 36. Hallam himself apologized in the preface to his *Middle Ages* for having had to write a "political dissertation" rather than a "narrative," and thus for having failed to provide "that circumstantial delineation of events and characters upon which the beauty as well as the usefulness of a regular history so mainly depends." Henry Hallam, *View of the State of Europe During the Middle Ages* (New York, 1887), I, vii.

38. Letter to Prescott, August 17, 1847, Bancroft Papers, MHS.

39. Notebooks IV, pp. 80, 81. On another occasion he resolved not to be "an antiquarian

drudge." Notebooks V, p. 45. Parkman, too, found "the task of exploring archives and collecting documents . . . repulsive at best." Quoted in Charles H. Farnham, *Life of Francis Parkman* (Boston, 1900), p. 331, n. 1.

40. Notebooks V, pp. 34–38.

41. Notebooks X, pp. 54–55.

42. *Ibid.*, pp. 58–59, 61.

43. *Ibid.*, pp. 58–59.

44. *Ibid.*, p. 54.

45. *Ibid.*

46. "Irving's Conquest of Granada," in *Biographical and Critical Miscellanies* (Philadelphia, 1875), pp. 83, 93–94. In discussing the "philosophical" historians Prescott used the same "advocate" image which Macaulay had used a year earlier in the essay on "History," *Works*, V, 154. Cf. Prosper de Barante, *Histoire des ducs de Bourgogne de la maison de Valois, 1364–1477*, 4th ed. (Paris, 1826), I, 2. Barante praised Bancroft's history: see Bancroft's letter to George Sumner, July 29, 1846, Bancroft Papers, MHS. Prescott acknowledges his debt to Barante in the Preface to *The Conquest of Peru* (Philadelphia, 1861), I, xiii–xiv; and in a letter to Barante himself, January 17, 1846, Prescott Papers, MHS.

47. Parkman: "Is this true history, or a romance of Christian chivalry? It is both." Last sentences of the chapter on the founding of Montreal in *The Jesuits in North America in the Seventeenth Century* (Boston, 1893), p. 210. See his treatment of "traditions" in *The Conspiracy of Pontiac and the Indian War after the Conquest of Canada* (Boston, 1892), I, 219–21. See Motley's account of the last meeting between Maurice of Nassau and John of Barneveld, *The Life and Death of John of Barneveld, Advocate of Holland* (New York, 1874), II, 240–41, and especially the long footnote on p. 242; and his *History of the United Netherlands from the Death of William the Silent to the Twelve Years' Truce—1609* (New York, 1888), I, 289–90. Prescott's remarks about the "romance of chivalry" at the head of this chapter should serve as sufficient illustration, but many more can be found in *A History of the Reign of Ferdinand and Isabella, the Catholic* (New York, 1851): I, xliii–xliv; II, 99; III, 135–36. Bancroft asked Dr. Robert W. Gibbes of South Carolina to write a history on Southern topics; despite the difficulty of getting documents in the decentralized South, he argued that "the Southern history is as full of romantic incident as possible, needing only diligence and opportunity . . . to be presented to the world in the most interesting form." Letter to Gibbes (1846, n.d.), Bancroft Papers, MHS.

Prescott told Motley that "the style for history is as different fr[om] what is required by romance as that of a great historical picture is from the scene frankly for a theater." Letter of April 28, 1856, Prescott Papers, MHS. Yet Prescott himself, when writing *The Conquest of Mexico*, compared his descriptions closely with those in Robert Montgomery Bird's *Calavar*, in order to "improve mine thereby." Bird, he noted, "uses Mexican terms of things—w[ith] effect, & notices national peculiarities, of dress and arms—well—& scenery." Notebooks X, p. 89. Motley was pleased to be told by a young girl that his *Dutch Republic* was "just like a novel." *Correspondence*, I, 245.

48. "James Fenimore Cooper" (January 1852), in *Essays from the N.A.R.*, pp. 358–62. Parkman did not believe that many of Cooper's women "breathed," and he criticized them severely in his essay (p. 362). When he praised Cooper *and* Scott for creating "breathing men and women," he presumably alluded to no women but Scott's. Cf. Edward Everett's praise for Bancroft's first volume: "You give us not wretched pasteboard men; not a sort of chronological table . . . —but you give us real, individual, living men and women, with their passions, interests, and peculiarities." Letter to Bancroft, October 5, 1834, Bancroft Papers, MHS.

49. Letter to O. W. Holmes, November 20, 1853. *Correspondence*, I, 164–65 (italics

mine). Bancroft thought Rubens' painting "ugly." Journal (July 10, 1821), Bancroft Papers, MHS.

50. "Scott," in *Essays from the N.A.R.,* p. 24. Bancroft admired in Scott the same qualities praised here (letter to Prescott, September 15, 1848, Bancroft Papers, MHS), but felt that Scott's finest work was his poetry; the battle in "Marmion," he said, "has not been surpassed since Homer."

51. Prescott, "Scott," in *Essays from the N.A.R.,* pp. 25, 35. Prescott spent almost half his essay on Scott's personal character, which he called "probably the most remarkable on record" (p. 34). "The first quality of his character, or rather that which forms the basis of it, as of all great characters, was his energy" (p. 35). Parkman called both Cooper and Scott "practical men, able and willing to grapple with the hard realities of life. Either might have learned with ease to lead a regiment, or command a line-of-battle ship." It is immediately after this statement that he praises their "solid embodiments of living flesh and blood." "Cooper," in *Essays from the N.A.R.,* p. 359. Later in the essay he compares them with "less masculine writers" (p. 362).

52. See Carlyle's letter to David Laing, May 3, 1854, in *Essays,* III, 518. In his review of Bancroft's third volume Prescott said that although Grahame's history is good, a foreigner cannot write *the* history of America. "It is the same as in portrait painting. The artist may catch the prominent lineaments, the complexion, the general air, the peculiar costume of the subject,—all that a stranger's eye will demand; but he must not hope, unless he has had much previous intimacy with the sitter, to transfer those fleeting shades of expression . . . which are revealed to the eye of his own family." "Bancroft's United States" (January 1841), in *Biographical Miscellanies,* p. 284.

53. Rashleigh, who had studied to be a priest, hoped to ruin Diana Vernon by teaching her mathematics, astronomy, and the "casuistry which school-men call philosophy." *Rob Roy* (Edinburgh, 1871), p. 180.

54. *United Netherlands,* I, 14–15.

55. *John of Barneveld,* I, 29.

56. *Ibid.,* II, 240–41 (italics mine).

57. See below, pp. 114–15.

58. *Conspiracy of Pontiac,* I, 202. Cf. Prescott's comment on the portrait of Philip II in *History of the Reign of Philip the Second, King of Spain* (Philadelphia, 1860), I, xxxv.

59. "History," in *Works,* V, 160.

60. December 29, 1834, Bancroft Papers, MHS.

61. *Jesuits,* p. 189.

62. Letter of December 20, 1837, Bancroft Papers, MHS. See *Ferdinand and Isabella,* I, 133.

63. *Essays,* II, 257.

64. *United Netherlands,* I, 318.

65. "History," in *Works,* V, 159. Motley's Elizabeth and his Leicester are both more ridiculous characters than Scott's. Concerned with the theme of royal and national policy rather than with romance, Motley omitted the beauty of Scott's Elizabeth and the pathos of Scott's handsome Leicester.

66. "Cooper," in *Essays from the N.A.R.,* p. 370.

67. Letter to the Abbé Casgrain, October 23, 1887, Parkman Papers, MHS.

68. Bancroft recorded his affected reactions to these "natural" experiences in his journal of the trip, and then he wrote letters describing them to Samuel A. Eliot and Andrews Norton. "I was seized with delight," he wrote in his journal on October 6, 1821; "tho' warm with a long walk, could not but caper & sing or at least cry out the chorus of a rude song, as I passed amidst such beautiful scenes. I danced & spouted & sprang about & might well have been taken

for a madman." To Eliot he wrote: "I have wandered in the narrow valleys while the pitiless shower was beating around me, and the swollen torrents rushing by my feet; I have been at night, aye and in rain too, amidst forests & precipices I hardly know where; and all the while I have felt calm & serene & happy. I never knew till now how beautiful earth is." October 12, 1821. The letter to Norton was written the next day. Bancroft Papers, MHS. One almost pities the anti-"enthusiastic" Norton for his subjection to such passages as these from his protégé.

69. "Peter the Great," in *Essays from the N.A.R.*, pp. 178–79.

70. Letter to his sister, August 8, 1837, Bancroft Papers, MHS.

71. See *United Netherlands*, IV, 75–76; and *The Rise of the Dutch Republic* (New York, 1859), II, 189–90.

72. Notebooks IX, p. 66; Notebooks X, p. 75. In Notebooks IX, p. 73, he warned himself to "be minute in the localities, and everything relating to them, topographical, physical, and historical—transporting the reader to the country, and to the age." For praise of Humboldt and Malte Brun, see Notebooks IX, pp. 16–17, 52.

73. "Cooper," in *Essays from the N.A.R.*, pp. 370–71.

74. See Motley, *United Netherlands*, II, 13; IV, 36. After three pages of general description of the action Motley says, "The tide of battle ebbed and flowed like the waves of the sea, but it would be mere pedantry to affect any technical explanation of its various changes. . . . the very nature of the ground had made artistic evolutions nearly impracticable."

75. Prescott, *Ferdinand and Isabella*, III, 48. Parkman, *Jesuits*, pp. 233–36; *Half-Century*, I, 91. Motley, *Dutch Republic*, II, 301–12. Cf. Bancroft, *A History of the United States from the Discovery of the American Continent* (10 vols., Boston, 1834–74), III, 397–98. Hereafter Bancroft's work will be cited as *History*.

76. See, for example, Parkman, *Jesuits*, p. 375: "On the morning of the fourth of July, when the forest around basked lazily in the early sun, you might have mounted the rising ground on which the town stood, and passed unchallenged through the opening in the palisade. Within, you would have seen [huts]. . . . You followed the foul passageways among the houses, and at length came to the church. . . . Suddenly the uproar of voices, shrill with terror, burst upon the languid silence of the town. 'The Iroquois! the Iroquois!' A crowd of hostile warriors had issued from the forest, and were rushing across the clearing." The inconsistency in mood shows carelessness, and in the excitement of the raid Parkman leaves "you" at the mercy of the Iroquois and then forgets "you." But the purpose is clear. Cf. Motley's description of the betrayal of Deventer to the Spanish, *United Netherlands*, II, 170–71.

77. *Works*, V, 144; cf. Barante, *Ducs de Bourgogne*, I, 2. Barante said that the French genius was remarkably fitted for lively narrative, "où le narrateur . . . donne une physionomie dramatique aux faits qu'il rapport, aux personnages qu'il représente." He used the painting analogy, too, and deplored the historian's appeal to the reader's critical faculties rather than his imagination (*ibid.*, p. 13). Prescott mentions Barante's dramatic analogy in the review of Irving's *Granada* (*Biographical Miscellanies*, p. 93). Cf. Motley, "Goethe," *New York Review*, III (October 1838), 402.

78. Letters to Bancroft: October 17, 1854; and May 1, 1858. Bancroft Papers, MHS. Cf. *Peru*, I, xiii; and Notebooks V, p. 49.

79. *Works*, V, 158.

80. See, for example, *Montcalm and Wolfe* (Boston, 1893), II, 163–66.

81. Prescott to Bancroft, October 17, 1854.

82. Raleigh, for example, referred to Leicester as "sweet Robin." After quoting the phrase as Raleigh's, Motley uses it repeatedly in his satiric portrayal of Leicester's relationship with Elizabeth. *United Netherlands*, I, 478. For another example see *ibid.*, p. 485.

83. Motley, "Goethe's Works," *New York Review*, V (July 1839), 18.

84. *United Netherlands*, II, 91–92, 99.

85. "The Polity of the Puritans," *N.A.R.,* LXIX, 475.

86. Letter to Bancroft, April 16, 1858, Bancroft Papers, MHS.

87. Letter to Motley, April 28, 1856, Prescott Papers, MHS.

88. "Prescott's Ferdinand and Isabella," *Democratic Review,* II (May 1838), 164.

89. *United Netherlands,* II, 96, n. 1.

90. *Ibid.,* I, 348; III, 188. Prescott to Bancroft, December 20, 1837, Bancroft Papers, MHS.

91. Motley, *United Netherlands,* III, 54–55.

92. Notebooks VII, p. 176.

93. Notebooks VIII, p. 89.

NOTES TO CHAPTER II

1. Theodore Parker, "Prescott as an Historian" (March 1849), *The American Scholar,* ed. George W. Cooke (Boston, 1907), p. 184.

2. See Daniel J. Boorstin, *The Lost World of Thomas Jefferson* (New York, 1948), pp. 226–31.

3. See Bancroft's letters to Andrews Norton, October 17 and October 26, 1818; and to Joseph Kirkland, January 15, 1820. See Bancroft's Journal, August 29, 1818, March 28 and May 17, 1819, Bancroft Papers, MHS. John L. Motley, "The Novels of Balzac," *N.A.R.,* LXV (July 1847), 86–87, 108; *United Netherlands,* III, 514. Bancroft expressed the same idea in his essay on Goethe; and William Charvat has pointed out the similarity to Howells' comments. The concern with evil in human nature was sound for a German writer, Bancroft said, "but in the United States, thanks to the venerated sanctity of domestic attachment, the book [Goethe's *Elective Affinities*] would be thrown aside with incredulity as a false and dangerous libel on human nature." William Charvat, *The Origins of American Critical Thought, 1810–1835* (Philadelphia, 1936), p. 18.

See Prescott's Diary (1817), Prescott Papers, MHS, pp. 48, 85; Farnham's *Parkman,* pp. 94–95; and Parkman's first European Notebook in *The Journals of Francis Parkman,* ed. Mason Wade (New York, 1947), I, *passim.*

4. Bancroft, *History,* III, 397–98; VIII, 118–19. Letter to Mrs. J. C. Bancroft Davis, December 27, 1867, Bancroft Papers, MHS.

5. Parkman, Diary, July 4, 1844, Parkman Papers, MHS. See *Jesuits,* p. 448. Motley, *United Netherlands,* III, 189, 208, 531; IV, 549 ff. Prescott, *Ferdinand and Isabella,* III, 32, 447. These are only a few among many examples. Motley, too, criticized the "singular vagaries of the German transcendentalists" (*Morton's Hope,* II, 97).

6. Motley, *United Netherlands,* III, 382, 513–14.

7. *Ibid.,* IV, 549.

8. *Ibid.,* III, 532.

9. Prescott, "Irving's Granada," in *Biographical Miscellanies,* pp. 91–92; "Bancroft's United States," *ibid.,* p. 284.

10. *United Netherlands,* I, 314.

11. *Jesuits,* p. 448; cf. *ibid.,* p. 329.

12. *History,* I, 261–62; cf. II, 155.

13. "Bancroft's United States," in *Biographical Miscellanies,* p. 275: "The atmosphere here seems as fatal to the arbitrary institutions of the Old World as that has been to the democratic forms of our own. It seems scarcely possible that any other organization than these latter should exist here."

14. "The Polity of the Puritans," *N.A.R.*, LXIX, 479; *United Netherlands*, III, 154; cf. *ibid.*, p. 383.

15. The image is Motley's, *ibid.*, pp. 382–83; letter to O. W. Holmes, February 26, 1862, in *Correspondence*, II, 65. Bancroft compared progress to the movement of the Mississippi River: "There are little eddies and side currents which seem to run up hill; but the onward course of the mighty mass of waters is as certain as the law of gravitation." Letter to the Barre Democratic Committee, July 10, 1840, Bancroft Papers, MHS.

16. Cf. Motley, *United Netherlands*, III, 121; 476–77.

17. *Ibid.*, pp. 382–83; *Dutch Republic*, I, 44; Prescott, *Ferdinand and Isabella*, III, 447; Bancroft, *History*, IV, 7.

18. *History*, VIII, 116–19. Cf. *The Heart of Emerson's Journals*, ed. Bliss Perry (New York, 1929), p. 56.

19. *History*, VIII, 119–20; I, 472; II, 333; III, 88.

20. *Ibid.*, I, 51, 312.

21. *Ibid.*, IV, 275; VI, 324; X, 86. Parkman made the same point in *Montcalm and Wolfe*, I, 9. After describing the "commonplace" morality and government of England during this period, he said: "The middle class, as yet almost voiceless, looked to him [Pitt] as its champion; but he was not the champion of a class . . . he was himself England incarnate." See below, Chapter III. Motley's English people were also wiser than Elizabeth in perceiving that Spain must be fought. *United Netherlands*, II, 281.

22. Bancroft, *History*, V, 4.

23. *Ibid.*, VII, 24.

24. *United Netherlands*, III, 155; see also I, 381, 492, 499; II, 281; and III, 187. Cf. Bancroft, *History*, III, 322.

25. *United Netherlands*, I, 486; IV, 543. In his final judgment of Philip (*United Netherlands*, III, 542) Motley also shows that the opposite of each of Philip's major aims was achieved.

26. "Macaulay's History," in *The American Scholar*, p. 344.

27. *Montcalm and Wolfe*, I, 2. *Ferdinand and Isabella*, III, 116. Prescott cited this result as evidence that Providence "still educes good from evil." *History*, VI, 526; and *ibid.*, IV, 389; cf. *ibid.*, p. 215. Cf. Motley's final essay on Philip II, *United Netherlands*, III, 512.

28. *Dutch Republic*, II, 424–25. Cf. *United Netherlands*, 539.

29. Prescott to Ticknor, January 21, 1824, in Ticknor, *Prescott*, p. 65.

30. Motley, "Historic Progress and American Democracy" (1868), in *John Lothrop Motley: Representative Selections* . . . , ed. C. P. Higby and B. T. Schantz (New York, 1939), p. 105.

31. Letter to George Bancroft, October 18, 1878, Bancroft Papers, MHS.

32. Motley, *United Netherlands*, III, 513–14.

33. Prescott, *Ferdinand and Isabella*, I, xl.

34. *Ibid.*, III, 107.

35. *Ibid.*, pp. 109–11. Cf. Macaulay, "The War of Succession in Spain," in *Works*, V, p. 642: "The Castilian of those times was to the Italian what the Roman, in the days of the greatness of Rome, was to the Greek. The conqueror had less ingenuity, less taste, less delicacy of perception than the conquered; but far more pride, firmness, and courage, a more solemn demeanour, a stronger sense of honour. The subject had more subtlety in speculation, the ruler more energy in action. The vices of the former were those of a coward; the vices of the latter were those of a tyrant."

36. *Ferdinand and Isabella*, III, 495–96.

37. *United Netherlands*, III, 121.

38. *Ferdinand and Isabella*, I, 297; and I, lxxxiii. Cf. III, 12.

39. *United Netherlands*, III, 20–21. The idea that the Dutch were trained to adversity is

reiterated throughout Motley's histories, most elaborately in his long introduction to *Dutch Republic*, I, 44.

40. *United Netherlands*, I, 382–83; and *ibid.*, II, 118.

41. Bancroft, *History*, I, 429. Motley, *United Netherlands*, III, 21, 529, 544.

42. At one low point in English fortunes "the profuse indulgence in falsehood which characterized southern statesmanship, was more than a match for English love of truth." *United Netherlands*, II, 355–56. For the descriptions of Elizabeth and Alexander Farnese, see *ibid.*, pp. 293, 300.

43. *Ibid.*, IV, 112–13.

44. *Ibid.*, II, 74–75; IV, 106–7.

45. *History*, II, 58.

46. See, for example, *Montcalm and Wolfe*, I, 8–16, 21–23. "Yet Canada had a vigor of her own. It was not in spiritual deference only that she differed from the country of her birth. Whatever she had caught of its corruptions, she had caught nothing of its effeminacy. . . . Even the French regular troops, sent out to defend the colony, caught its hardy spirit, and set an example of stubborn fighting which their comrades at home did not always emulate" (p. 23). Cf. *Conspiracy of Pontiac*, I, 112–13. Cf. Bancroft, II, 89; IV, 312. See Motley, *United Netherlands*, IV, 554.

47. *Pioneers of France in the New World*, 25th ed. (Boston, 1885), p. x. In this revised edition the original introduction of 1865 is unchanged. I have used this edition because Parkman said that its natural descriptions were more accurate, based as they were on a visit he made to Florida after the first edition had been published.

48. *Montcalm and Wolfe*, I, 26–27; and *ibid.*, p. 35.

49. *Ibid.*, pp. 5–6, 18. France, where the jaded aristocracy played with the newest radical ideas "as children play with fire" (p. 16), was worst of all.

50. *History*, VI, 138; II, 145, 155. Letter to Emerson, February 29, 1836, Bancroft Papers, MHS. Of his second volume Bancroft wrote: "I have gone largely into the spirit of Quakerism; & have had occasion to contrast George Fox & William Penn with John Locke. The view, I have taken, from what I know of your modes of thought, will not be new or disagreeable to you; the public at large may start at the truth. But what could I do? If Locke did actually embody his philosophy, political & moral, in an American Constitution, why not say so in all simplicity? And if the Quakers were wiser than he, why not say that too? Do you remember Locke's chapter on enthusiasm? Pennsylvania is the practical refutation of his argument." On May 13, 1837, Bancroft again wrote to Emerson, emphasizing his conviction that the contrast was accurate, but expressing some concern about its reception. Bancroft Papers, MHS. He received a letter from George Ripley (September 20, 1837, Bancroft Papers, MHS) praising him for attacking what Ripley called "the always ignorant and often petulant idolatry of Locke."

51. *History*, II, 343, 455.

52. *Ibid.*, VII, 260, 29; VIII, 346.

53. "Polity of the Puritans," *N.A.R.*, LXIX, 490; letter to his wife, January 15, 1858, in *Correspondence*, I, 209. Motley was convinced by Bancroft's criticism of Locke's plan for a Carolina government.

54. "Irving's Granada," in *Biographical Miscellanies*, pp. 91–92, 97.

55. "The Age of Schiller and Goethe," in *Literary and Historical Miscellanies* (New York, 1855), p. 189. Cf. his letter to Levi Frisbi, April 13, 1821, Bancroft Papers, MHS.

56. *History*, II, 338; VI, 399.

57. *Ibid.*, II, 58, 155, 211–12. "Western democracy," Turner said, "was no theorist's dream. It came stark and strong and full of life, from the American forest." *The Rise of the New West, 1819–29* (New York and London, 1906), pp. 68–69.

58. Bancroft, *History*, VII, 301. Cf. Motley, *United Netherlands*, II, 113–14; IV, 133.

59. *History*, VI, 323–24. Cf. Prescott, *Peru*, II, 467, discussed below, pp. 153–54. When Bancroft did praise learning, he emphasized the subject's character. Admitting that the philosopher Berkeley was learned and "disciplined by polished society," Bancroft emphasized his union of "innocence, humility, and extensive knowledge, with the sagacity and confidence of intuitive reason." Berkeley had "every virtue under heaven." *History*, III, 372.

60. From "Whiggism and Democracy," *Boston Statesman*, October 17, 1835; this quotation is from Bancroft's MS. copy, Bancroft Papers, MHS.

61. *Dutch Republic*, I, 145. *John of Barneveld*, I, 264; II, 10–11.

62. Motley, *United Netherlands*, I, 89; cf. III, 302.

63. *Ferdinand and Isabella*, III, 32.

64. *Montcalm and Wolfe*, I, chap. x.

65. Motley, *United Netherlands*, I, 314.

66. *History*, II, 214.

67. *Ibid.*, p. 345.

68. See, e.g., Motley, *United Netherlands*, I, 38, 48. Prescott, *Ferdinand and Isabella*, I, xxxviii, 236, 297; and *The Conquest of Mexico* (Philadelphia, 1860), I, 75, 312. Parkman, *Montcalm and Wolfe*, I, 12, 14. Parkman called Louis XV's immorality "effeminate libertinism" (*ibid.*, p. 14), and attacked Louis' "languor."

69. *History*, VIII, 67. *Ferdinand and Isabella*, III, 28–29, 32, 380.

70. *United Netherlands*, III, 208. *Dutch Republic*, I, 441, 502; II, 35; III, 340. Cooper makes the same inconsistent excuse for Natty Bumppo after condemning a priest for following the maxim. *The Prairie* (New York, 1851), pp. 258–65.

Prescott was regularly more lenient than Motley, for he said he believed that the Past should not be judged by the higher standards of the Present. (*Mexico*, II, 35–36.) He was inconsistent on this point, however, especially where there was a scoundrel to be chastised: his heroes' sins may have been the sins of the age, but his villains' sins were another matter. See, for example, *Peru*, II, 200.

71. *Dutch Republic*, II, 400. The idea and the word ("malignity") are William's, but Motley accepts both without criticism. *United Netherlands*, II, 310. Cf. *ibid.*, III, 186–87.

72. Farnham, *Parkman*, pp. 89–90. Cf. Parkman's letter to the *Boston Advertiser*, October 14, 1862, quoted in Howard Doughty, "Parkman's Dark Years: Letters to Mary Dwight Parkman," *Harvard Library Bulletin*, IV (Winter 1950), 81.

73. *United Netherlands*, IV, 242; I, 129.

74. See Parkman, *Pioneers*, pp. 90–92; Motley, *United Netherlands*, II, 100–101, 281; IV, 320–21. Motley also wrote a paragraph in praise of "enterprise" (*ibid.*, III, 26–27).

75. Parkman seems to be an exception. The Puritans, he said, had elevated thrift and hard work for gain to the position of religious duties—"in defiance of the Gospels." (*Pioneers*, xi. Cf. Bancroft, *History*, III, 312.) Neither Parkman nor Prescott had any Protestant heroes whose economic motives required evaluation. But in La Salle and Cortés, respectively, the economic motive is absorbed in the brilliant glare of more heroic and more pious motives. La Salle "was not a mere merchant; and no commercial profit could content his ambition." *La Salle*, p. 90. Cortés, Prescott says, "was not a vulgar conqueror. . . . His enterprises were not undertaken solely for mercenary objects." *Mexico*, III, 357–58.

76. *United Netherlands*, I, 382–83.

77. *Ibid.*, IV, 133, 242, 444, 482, 550–56.

78. *History*, I, 429–30; VI, 137; VII, 304.

79. *Ferdinand and Isabella*, I, 380.

80. *Dutch Republic*, II, 255–58. Consider his comment on Jacob van Heemskerk (*United Netherlands*, IV. 320): "Inspired only by the love of glory, he asked for no remuneration for

his services save thirteen per cent. of the booty, after half a million florins should have been paid into the public treasury."

81. *Ferdinand and Isabella*, III, 490–91. For the use of "success" as a test of virtue, see *ibid.*, p. 401.

82. *Ibid.*, 462; Parkman, *Pioneers*, p. xii. Parkman conjures "the shades," who "rise from their graves in strange, romantic guise."

83. *Ibid.*, p. 428.

84. *United Netherlands*, IV, 215–17.

85. II, 302–12.

86. *Ferdinand and Isabella*, III, 478–79. Cf. *Peru*, I, 468–69.

87. *United Netherlands*, IV, 556.

88. *History*, II, 468.

NOTES TO CHAPTER III

1. *United Netherlands*, II, 117; III, 31, 187.

2. See, for example, Parkman's conclusion to *Montcalm and Wolfe*, II, 413–14. Motley, "Balzac," *N.A.R.*, LXV, 91–92; *Four Questions for the People, at the Presidential Election* (Boston, 1868), pp. 52–53.

3. Bancroft, *History*, I, 397. Cf. Prescott, *Peru*, II, 467–68.

4. Ralph Waldo Emerson, *Representative Men*, in *The Works of Ralph Waldo Emerson*, 4 vols. in one (New York: Tudor, n.d.), II, 369. All further citations of Emerson refer to this edition.

5. *History*, II, 21. Cf. Prescott, *Peru*, II, 180.

6. Bancroft, *History*, VIII, 248–49; VI, 324. Motley, *Dutch Republic*, III, 126–27, 621. Bancroft, *History*, VIII, 463. Prescott, *Ferdinand and Isabella*, II, 65, 75–76; III, 439. Parkman, *Montcalm and Wolfe*, I, 8–9.

7. There are well over fifty examples of such phrases, with Prescott by far the leader in their use; examples of the idea are even more numerous. I cite only a few. *Ferdinand and Isabella*, III, 51, 78, 130, 162–63, 196. Motley, *Dutch Republic*, I, 178–79; II, 568–71. *United Netherlands*, I, 216, 218; IV, 31–32, 38–39. Parkman, *Montcalm and Wolfe*, II, 89–90, 266, 277. Bancroft, *History*, IV, 312; IX, 97–99, 120.

8. *United Netherlands*, I, 314.

9. *History*, VIII, 117.

10. *Ibid.*, VI, 302, n. 1; 300–301. Cf. Bancroft's letter to Samuel Eliot about his own experiences, October 12, 1821, Bancroft Papers, MHS. The best novel of Cooper's in which to find the explicit statement of all these virtues is, of course, *The Pioneers*.

11. *History*, VII, 369–70. Cf. Curtis P. Nettels, *The Roots of American Civilization* (New York, 1946), p. 682.

12. See Parkman, *The Oregon Trail: Sketches of Prairie and Rocky-Mountain Life* (Boston, 1894), pp. xi, 11–13. Châtillot, Parkman said, "was a proof of what unaided nature will sometimes do" (p. 13).

Henry Nash Smith, *Virgin Land: The American West as Symbol and Myth* (Cambridge, Mass., 1950), pp. 64–68.

13. *Conspiracy of Pontiac*, I, 158, 159; *Montcalm and Wolfe*, I, 431; *Conspiracy of Pontiac*, I, 161–62.

14. *History*, IV, 108; IX, 217; IV, 110–11. *Montcalm and Wolfe*, II, 132.

15. *Ferdinand and Isabella*, I, 83.

16. *United Netherlands*, I, 46–47, 48, 50.

17. *Dutch Republic*, II, 399; *Ferdinand and Isabella*, III, 185–86. For the leaders' willingness to share hardships with the men, see *Montcalm and Wolfe*, II, 90; *Ferdinand and Isabella*, III, 130; Bancroft, *History*, IX, 99; Motley, *United Netherlands*, IV, 31–32.

18. *Ferdinand and Isabella*, I, 85, 97–98.

19. *Ibid.*, II, 128. Cf. p. 132: Columbus' original reception at court was "such as naturally flowed from the benevolent spirit of Isabella."

20. *Ibid.*, I, 248.

21. *Ibid.*, II, 41–42.

22. *Ibid.*, pp. 64–65, 75.

23. *Ibid.*, III, 169–72, 181, 183–202.

24. *Ibid.*, II, 77.

25. *Ibid.*, p. 78.

26. *Ibid.*, III, 172.

27. *Ibid.*, pp. 397, 392, 398–99.

28. See Mario Praz, *The Romantic Agony*, trans. Angus Davidson, 2d ed. (New York, 1951), chap. iv.

29. *Ferdinand and Isabella*, III, 197–98.

30. *Ibid.*, pp. 198–202. Cf. Motley's portrait, above, p. 16.

31. *History*, VII, 396; IX, 217–18, 120.

32. *Ibid.*, V, 405; IV, 338; V, 437.

33. Bancroft recognized that Americans had a predilection for full-blown oratory. In 1820, he admitted that his German audience had been surprised when he declaimed his doctoral speech "in the American style"; some years later, he described an American lady's criticism that the language and manner of one of his speeches had been too restrained for good oratory. Letter to Andrews Norton, September 16, 1820; letter to his wife, December 31, 1842; both in Bancroft Papers, MHS.

34. *History*, VII, 274–75; V, 335, 391. Parkman, *Montcalm and Wolfe*, I, 8–9. Motley, *Dutch Republic*, III, 621.

35. The words are Parkman's, *Montcalm and Wolfe*, II, 188–89. See *ibid.*, pp. 79, 184–86, 216; Bancroft, *History*, IV, 316, 332, 296.

36. Motley, *Dutch Republic*, II, 244. Parkman, *Montcalm and Wolfe*, II, 89–90.

37. Bancroft, *History*, IV, 418; VIII, 462–68 (italics mine). Jefferson's letter to Adams (August 15, 1820) is quoted in Boorstin, *Lost World*, p. 129. Elsewhere (IX, 60) Bancroft remarks that the Declaration was "ratified not by congress only, but by the instincts and intuitions of the nation."

38. *Dutch Republic*, II, 248; Bancroft, *History*, IV, 314; Prescott, *Ferdinand and Isabella*, III, 192; *Dutch Republic*, I, 497–501.

39. III, 620, 623, 589, 622.

40. *United Netherlands*, II, 100.

41. Motley, *Dutch Republic*, I, 441–42; cf. *United Netherlands*, I, 50–51.

42. Bancroft, *History*, IX, 218; Motley, *Dutch Republic*, II, 40.

43. *Ibid.*, p. 242.

44. *Ibid.*, p. 245.

45. *Ibid.*, p. 457; III, 627, 454. Cf. Prescott, *Mexico*, II, 371–72, 374; *Ferdinand and Isabella*, III, 195.

46. *Dutch Republic*, II, 64–69; *Morton's Hope*, II, 62–65. In the novel, Vassall Deane, a silent, self-possessed man who looks down with contempt on the town's petty and tyrannical authorities, chivalrously protects them from the rabble at the risk of his own life. His "elo-

quence" has the same effect as William's, whereupon he reverts to his usual impressive silence.

47. Bancroft, *History*, III, 165, 166, 170, 173. Cf. Washington Irving, *A History of the Life and Voyages of Christopher Columbus* (New York, 1848), I, 24–27, 30; II, 292–93; Bancroft, *History*, I, 6–7. Prescott, *Ferdinand and Isabella*, III, 242–45. Cf. Emerson, *Works*, II, 374–75.

48. *La Salle and the Discovery of the Great West*, 11th ed. (Boston, 1894), pp. 75, 108, 143, 169–70, 174, 188, 263.

49. *Ibid.*, 290, 307, 310, 311. Cf. Prescott, *Ferdinand and Isabella*, III, 242–45, where Columbus' imagination "feeds too exclusively on this lofty theme."

50. *La Salle*, 319–20, 350, 360, 361, 385, 400, 392.

51. Motley, *John of Barneveld*, I, 50. See *United Netherlands*, IV, 38–39. The *Manfred* lines are from *The Works of Lord Byron*, ed. Thomas Moore (London and Boston, n.d.), I, 16.

52. *Montcalm and Wolfe*, II, 42, 46, 389; I, 19–20; II, 39; Motley, *United Netherlands*, I, 45–46. *Montcalm and Wolfe*, II, 39.

53. *History*, VI, 25, 61, 453; *Montcalm and Wolfe*, II, 406–7. Bancroft's Pitt is "the noblest representative and type" of England. IV, 247. Parkman says that George III "had begun to hate [Pitt] as a lion in his path." *Montcalm and Wolfe*, II, 392.

54. Parkman, *Frontenac*, pp. 14–15, 1, 208, 51, 186, 406, 426; *Montcalm and Wolfe*, II, 46.

55. *History*, IV, 314; X, 86.

56. Howard Doughty, "Parkman's Dark Years," in *Harvard Library Bulletin*, IV, pp. 82 ff.

57. *Vassal Morton*, pp. 292, 362. Cf. Motley, *Morton's Hope*, II, 183.

58. *Jesuits*, p. 98. See below, Chapter V.

59. *Ibid.*, p. 146.

60. *Ferdinand and Isabella*, III, 425–26, 301. Cf. Prescott's comment on Gonsalvo de Cordova, *ibid.*, p. 130.

61. *United Netherlands*, I, 170–71.

62. *Ibid.*, pp. 137–38.

63. Prescott thought the page headings in *The Rise of the Dutch Republic* were too dramatic. See his letter to Motley, April 28, 1856, in *Correspondence of . . . Motley*, I, 192; Motley, *United Netherlands*, I, 134.

64. *United Netherlands*, I, 135; cf. *ibid.*, p. 163. *Ibid.*, pp. 170–71.

65. *Dutch Republic*, III, 144–45. Cf. Prescott, *Ferdinand and Isabella*, III, 377–78.

66. *Montcalm and Wolfe*, II, 413–14. Cf. Emerson, *Works*, II, 400. Eric Goldman uses the phrase "happy sense of escape" when he says that the Brahmin historians found democratic America offensive. See "The Historians," in *Literary History of the United States*, ed. R. E. Spiller *et al.* (New York, 1948), I, 529.

67. *United Netherlands*, IV, 483; *John of Barneveld*, I, 12; II, 114–15, 165. Cf. *United Netherlands*, I, 314; IV, 50.

68. Motley to his mother, September 8, 1862, in *Correspondence*, II, 90. Cf. his letter to her on August 18, 1862, *ibid.*, p. 82.

69. Letter from Motley to O. W. Holmes the elder (November 14, 1861, *ibid.*, p. 42): "I do not regret that Wendell is with the army. It is a noble and healthy symptom that brilliant, intellectual, poetical spirits like his spring to arms when a noble cause like ours inspires them. The race of Philip Sidneys is not yet extinct, and I honestly believe that as much genuine chivalry exists in our Free States at this moment as there is or ever was in any part of the world, from the Crusaders down." Cf. letter from Parkman to the *Boston Daily Advertiser*, September 4, 1861, in which he defended the bravery of sons of "cultivated New England" families.

Motley, *Four Questions for the People*, pp. 67–69. He tried to combine the grandeur of Grant's accomplishment with his simplicity of character. For Motley's comments on Bismarck see "Historic Progress," in *Representative Selections,* p. 108. See below, p. 87.

70. Letter to his daughter Mary, June 22, 1862, in *Correspondence,* II, 78. In a letter to his mother (August 3, 1864), he characterized Lincoln in these terms: "I venerate Abraham Lincoln exactly because he is the true honest type of American Democracy. There is nothing of the shabby genteel, the would-be-but-couldn't-be fine gentleman; he is the great American Demos, honest, shrewd, homely, wise, humorous, cheerful, brave, blundering occasionally, but through blunders struggling onward toward what he believes the right" (*ibid.,* p. 170).

Motley's remark about Southern valor appears in "Historic Progress," in *Representative Selections,* p. 105; see also *Four Questions for the People,* pp. 21–22.

71. *Dutch Republic,* III, 616; I, 143–44. *John of Barneveld,* I, 31; II, 112–13. *Montcalm and Wolfe,* I, vi.

72. *Montcalm and Wolfe,* I, 198. Bancroft, *History,* III, 377, 378, 396. Bancroft praised Jared Sparks for firmly upholding Franklin's reputation. Letter to Sparks, March 13, 1853, Bancroft Papers, MHS. Franklin, Bancroft said, "discerned intuitively the identity of the laws of nature with those of which humanity is conscious." *History,* III, 378.

Prescott, *Ferdinand and Isabella,* III, 46–49. Motley, *United Netherlands,* I, 359. Bancroft, *History,* IV, 155.

NOTES TO CHAPTER IV

1. "Buckle's History of Civilization" (1858), in *The American Scholar,* p. 413.

2. *Dissertation on the Origin of the Scythians or Goths* (1787), quoted in Peardon, *Transition,* p. 115. Cf. Peardon's discussion of Gilbert Stuart, Mrs. Macaulay, and others who adopted similar ideas, chaps. iii–v.

3. "History can have neither value nor charm for those who are not impressed with a sense of its continuity." Motley, *United Netherlands,* IV, 549; cf. Bancroft, *History,* IV, 9. *Ibid.,* III, 397.

4. Prescott, in *Biographical Miscellanies,* p. 89. Sharon Turner, *History of the Anglo-Saxons* (1799–1805), quoted in Peardon, *Transition,* p. 219. Prescott, *Ferdinand and Isabella,* I, vi.

5. *Ferdinand and Isabella,* I, xxxii, xxxiii ff. Cf. "Irving's Granada," in *Biographical Miscellanies,* p. 104.

6. *Ferdinand and Isabella,* I, xxxii–xxxiii. See J. C. Levenson, *The Mind and Art of Henry Adams* (Boston, 1957), pp. 39–52.

7. *Ferdinand and Isabella,* I, xxxiii, xxxiv.

8. *Ibid.,* pp. xxxv, xxxvi-xxxvii, xxxviii.

9. *Mexico,* I, 476–77; cf. *ibid.,* II, 4; and *Peru,* I, 7.

10. *Ferdinand and Isabella,* I, xl–xli.

11. See Gooch, *History and Historians,* pp. 60–61. *Ferdinand and Isabella,* I, xli.

12. *Ibid.,* pp. xlv–xlviii. He was careful, here, to date the first record of "popular representation" in Castile.

13. *Philip II,* I, 379. *Ferdinand and Isabella,* I, xliv–xlv.

14. Motley, *United Netherlands,* III, 522. Parker, "Hildreth's United States," in *The American Scholar,* pp. 266, 277. Emerson, *Works,* II, 82; cf. III, 59–60. Motley, "Historic Progress and American Democracy," in *Representative Selections,* pp. 105–6.

15. *History,* X, 86; IV, 4. For relationships, see, for example, II, 452–64; IX, 499–501.

16. *Ibid.,* IV, 11. Cf. IV, 7; and "Office of the People," in *Literary Miscellanies,* pp. 411–13.

17. *History,* IV, 456–57, 74; VII, 22.

18. *Ibid.*, C, 63; VII, 295; II, 454 (cf. IV, 5); IV, 7. Prescott pointed out that the motto misquoted Berkeley's poem (*Biographical Miscellanies*, p. 272). Bancroft himself had a precedent, however, for John Quincy Adams misquoted it first (1802).

19. Bancroft, "The Necessity, the Reality, and the Promise of the Progress of the Human Race," in *Literary Miscellanies*, p. 508. (Cf. *History*, VII, 295, 355.) *History*, IV, 456; II 454. See II, 214, 451.

20. H. B. Adams, "The Germanic Origins of New England Towns," *Johns Hopkins Studies in Political Science*, I–II (Baltimore, 1882–83), 2. Bancroft, *History*, II, 59. Prescott also refers to "our Anglo-Saxon ancestors" (*Ferdinand and Isabella*, I, 274).

21. Bancroft, *History*, IV, 456 (cf. II, 74; IV, 13); X, 226–27; II, 225. Prescott said that simplicity was Dante's "most conspicuous quality," and he compared Dante to Homer on this basis. Letter to Ticknor (n.d.), quoted in Ticknor, *Prescott*, pp. 63–64.

22. Letter to Prescott, July 28, 1848, Bancroft Papers, MHS. *History*, IV, 456–57.

23. *History*, II, 458. Letter to Mrs. J. C. Bancroft Davis, September 4, 1870, quoted in Howe, *Bancroft*, II, 239–40. See *History*, IX, 2–3. Except for the Bancroft Papers in MHS, and for Howe's *Bancroft,* I have relied on Russel B. Nye, *George Bancroft: Brahmin Rebel* (New York, 1944), for biographical information on Bancroft.

24. *History*, X, 61, 62, 78.

25. *Ibid.*, pp. 79 (cf. II, 457–59), 81, 82.

26. Parkman, *Montcalm and Wolfe*, II, 38–39. Bancroft, *History*, X, 86, 97 (cf. *ibid.*, pp. 8–9), 110–14.

27. Bancroft, "The Age of Schiller and Goethe," in *Literary Miscellanies*, p. 189. *History*, X, 87, 87–92. Cf. *ibid.*, IX, 473–76.

28. *Ibid.*, IX, 499, 500–501. In his third volume (p. 396), Bancroft tried to show how naturally the colonies had grown toward "national freedom and independence." In America, he said, these two qualities "were not the offspring of deliberate forethought; they were not planted by the hand of man; they grew like the lilies, which neither toil nor spin." The contrast to the French Revolution is implicit.

29. Cf. Emerson, "Race," in *Works*, II, 47–50. Bancroft to Levi Frisbi, April 13, 1821, Bancroft Papers, MHS. Letter to Prescott, July 28, 1848. Letter to Polk, August 5, 1848. All in Bancroft Papers, MHS. Letter of February 4, 1849 (no addressee), in Howe, *Bancroft*, II, 96.

30. *Ibid.*, II, 170–71. Bancroft to Department of State, March 5, 1869, Bancroft Papers, MHS. Bismarck to Motley, September 19, 1869, in *Correspondence*, II, 313–14. Bancroft to Mrs. J. C. Bancroft Davis, September 4, 1870; and Bancroft to C. C. Perkins, June 12, 1869. Both in Howe, *Bancroft*, II, 235–40, 228.

31. Quoted in Nye, *Bancroft*, pp. 249, 257–59.

32. Thiers, whom he had once praised, now typified such "ignorance." Letter to Mrs. Hamilton Fish, December 11, 1870, in Howe, *Bancroft*, II, 249.

33. Letter to Bancroft, Bancroft Papers, MHS. Letters to his daughter, Lily: April 23, 1866, in *Correspondence*, II, 215–16; July 3, 1866, *ibid.*, pp. 224–25; and August 7, 1866, *ibid.*, p. 241. Letter to Holmes, August 17, 1872, *ibid.*, p. 351.

34. Letter to his wife, July 25, 1872, *ibid.*, p. 340. "Historic Progress," in *Representative Selections*, p. 108. *Four Questions for the People*, p. 12. "Slavery," he said, "had eaten out that respect for nationality which is the most noble and vital part of any organized form of associated humanity, and the leading characteristic of the present epoch in the world's history." *Ibid.*, p. 20.

35. "Historic Progress," in *Representative Selections*, p. 108; cf. *Correspondence*, II, 352.

36. Letter to his daughter Lily, August 7, 1866, *ibid.*, p. 242. *Morton's Hope*, II, 18.

37. *Dutch Republic*, I, 1–2, 3, 4, 5, 6, 11.

38. *Ibid.*, pp. 7, 11–12, 7–8, 9, 10, 10–11.

39. *Ibid.*, pp. 9, 10, 11.

40. J. C. F. Schiller, "History of the Revolt of the Netherlands," in Nathan H. Dole, ed., *The Works of Friederich Schiller*, trans. E. B. Eastwick and A. J. W. Morrison (Boston, 1901), pp. xxxviii–xxxix. Motley, *Dutch Republic*, I, 13–15, 17. Prescott, citing Livy, made the same comparison when describing a Spanish victory over the French, who "resembled their Gaulish ancestors in the facility with which they were discouraged by unexpected obstacles, and the difficulty with which they could be brought to rally." *Ferdinand and Isabella*, III, 163.

The best example of Motley's atavism in the narrative sections combines the very scene of a victory won by "Hermann, first of Teutonic heroes," and the racial traits of Louis of Nassau, "another German warrior," who fought to defend "not only the rights of man, but the rights of God." II, 190. In this battle, won by the Germanic forces, thé Spaniards are "very hot" (later, "fiery"); the Teutons, "very cool," pp. 192–93.

41. *Dutch Republic*, I, 19–20 (cf. *United Netherlands*, III, 17–18). Parkman, *Jesuits*, p. 88. *Dutch Republic*, I, 21.

42. *Ibid.*, pp. 39, 91.

43. *Ibid.*, pp. 91, 92, 143–44; II, 500.

44. *United Netherlands*, III, 270; II, 195, 281–82. *John of Barneveld*, I, 227, 230. *United Netherlands*, I, 362; III, 271; IV, 10–11; III, 26–27 (cf. Schiller, "Revolt of Netherlands," in *Works*, p. xxxi); II, 300, 448; III, 18, 20.

45. *Vassal Morton*, p. 301; *Pioneers*, p. 188; *Pontiac*, I, 158; *Half-Century*, I, 311–12; *Montcalm and Wolfe*, II, 411–12. Consider this comment on the Canadians: "The Canadians, though brave and patient, needed, like Frenchmen, the stimulus of success" (*Montcalm and Wolfe*, II, 171).

NOTES TO CHAPTER V

1. "War of the Succession in Spain," in *Works*, V, 639.

2. See Joseph Haroutunian, *Piety versus Moralism: the Passing of the New England Theology* (New York, 1932). Notebooks V (February 15, 1829), Prescott Papers, MHS, pp. 72–87.

3. Notebooks VIII (June 1837), pp. 12, 37, 39, 37, 43–44. *Ibid.* (July 1837), pp. 46–47, 48. Prescott Papers, MHS.

4. *Ibid.*, p. 49; *Ferdinand and Isabella*, I, lxx.

5. Letter to Samuel A. Eliot, November 23, 1823, Bancroft Papers, MHS.

6. Boorstin, *Lost World*, p. 111. Motley, *John of Barneveld*, I, 4, 339. Motley did emphasize (as I have shown in Chapter II) the religious motive for the Dutch rebellion, but he considered that motive as a passion for a religion which contained the germs of liberty. This kind of loyalty—an opposition to tyranny and the corruption of religion—he could understand, even though the Protestants were themselves dogmatic. In the volumes on Barneveld, however, he distorted the evidence to show that Maurice's motives were personal rather than religious. Listing contemporary charges against Maurice which were based on hearsay—and against which he had defended Maurice in the last volume of *United Netherlands*—he accepted them as fact in later explanations of Maurice's conduct toward Barneveld. See *United Netherlands*, IV, 294–95, 475–76. Cf. *John of Barneveld*, I, 45–46, 329–30; II, 51–53. Notice, too, that Motley attributes motives of social ambition to the masses who supported Maurice. They "found in membership of the oligarchy of Heaven a substitute for those democratic aspirations on earth which were effectively suppressed between the two millstones of burgher aristocracy and military discipline." *Ibid.*, II, 114–15.

7. *Ibid.*, I, 139 (cf. p. 264), 141, 334, 336, 337–38, 344, 355.

8. *United Netherlands*, II, 121; Parkman, *Pioneers*, p. 427.

9. Letter to George Ripley, September 12, 1857, Bancroft Papers, MHS. For his interpretation of Edwards, Bancroft was chosen by "several" of the Edwards "family connection" to write the chapter on Edwards for Appleton's new *Cyclopedia*. Bancroft, Mr. T. Edwards said, was the one man qualified to write such a study! T. Edwards to Bancroft, January 20, 1858, Bancroft Papers, MHS. *History*, IX, 499–501. Cf. Perry Miller, "Jonathan Edwards to Emerson," *New England Quarterly*, XIII (1940), 589–617.

10. *Half-Century*, II, 104, 130–31.

11. *Ibid.*, pp. 133, 154, 97–98, 153.

In *John of Barneveld* (I, 338–39), Motley summed up the popular interest in theology in one comic paragraph: "In burghers' mansions, peasants' cottages, mechanics' back-parlours, on board herring smacks, canal boats, and East Indiamen; . . . wherever and whenever human creatures met each other, there was ever to be found the fierce wrangle of Remonstrant and Contra-Remonstrant, the hissing of red-hot theological rhetoric, the pelting of hostile texts. The blacksmith's iron cooled on the anvil, the tinker dropped a kettle half-mended, the broker left a bargain unclinched, the Scheveningen fisherman in his wooden shoes forgot the cracks in his pinkie, while each paused to hold high converse with friend or foe on fate, free will, or absolute foreknowledge; losing himself in wandering mazes whence there was no issue. Province against province, city against city, family against family; it was one vast scene of bickering, denunciation, heartburnings, mutual excommunication and hatred."

12. Motley, *John of Barneveld*, I, 39; Bancroft, *History*, IV, 276–77. Bancroft said explicitly: "Protestantism is not humanity; its name implies a party struggling to throw off some burdens of the past, and ceasing to be a renovating principle when its protest shall have succeeded." *Ibid.*, 271. Cf. IV, 154.

13. Bancroft, Journal, Bancroft Papers, MHS. Prescott to Wm. Gardiner, March (n.d.) 1816; quoted in Ticknor, *Prescott*, p. 39. Wade, *Parkman's Journals*, I, 132.

14. Parkman, *Jesuits*, p. 207.

15. *Dutch Republic*, I, 188; II, 433–34, 450.

16. Parkman, *Pioneers*, pp. 14, 132, 150; Bancroft, *History*, I, 44–45, 37, 51, 34, 57. Prescott, *Ferdinand and Isabella*, II, 145.

17. *Dutch Republic*, I, 72; *United Netherlands*, III, 64–65, 65 n. 44, 264–65.

18. *Dutch Republic*, I, 553, 572. Cf. *United Netherlands*, II, 83–84.

19. Bancroft, *History*, X, 181–203. Cooper, *The Pioneers; or the Sources of the Susquehanna* (New York, 1859), pp. 344–46. Cooper, *The Prairie*, pp. 197–99.

20. *Mexico*, II, 88.

21. *Jesuits*, pp. 88–89.

22. *Ibid.*, p. 96.

23. *Ibid.*, pp. 114, 115, 120, 125.

24. *Ibid.*, p. 90.

25. *Ibid.*, pp. 96–97, 98, 117.

26. *Frontenac*, pp. 374–75 (cf. *Montcalm and Wolfe*, I, 101), 376, 376 n. 1, 377.

27. *Ibid.*, p. 405.

28. *History*, III, 291–92; I, 49, 51, 45–46, 47, 54–55. Cf. I, 73.

29. *United Netherlands*, IV, 358, 355, 358. Apparently Motley refers to the Immaculate Conception of *Mary*, not to her mother's "origin." The Immaculate Conception was defined as Catholic doctrine in 1854.

30. See, for example, Bancroft, *History*, X, 83; Parkman, *Montcalm and Wolfe*, I, 355; Prescott, *Ferdinand and Isabella*, I, lxx; and Motley, *United Netherlands*, I, iii–iv.

31. *Ibid.,* I, 38; *Dutch Republic,* I, 138–39.

32. *Ibid.,* III, 542–43.

33. *Ibid.,* p. 539.

34. *John of Barneveld,* I, 346, 340. Prescott to Bancroft, n.d. (endorsed "May 1840"), Bancroft Papers, MHS.

35. *Jesuits,* pp. 159–60.

36. *Ibid.,* pp. 99, 100, 109, 50, 176–77.

37. *Ibid.,* pp. 177, 178, 179.

38. *Ibid.,* p. 185.

39. *Ibid.,* pp. 201–2.

40. Schiller, "Revolt of the Netherlands," in *Works,* p. 40 (italics mine).

41. Prescott explicitly makes an exception of one monk: the chaplain who restrains Cortés on several occasions. *Mexico,* I, 479–81.

42. "Irving's Granada," in *Biographical Miscellanies,* p. 89; *Ferdinand and Isabella,* I, 247, 260 n. 46.

43. *Ferdinand and Isabella,* III, 419, 425–26.

44. *United Netherlands,* IV, 302–14; *Morton's Hope,* II, 216. *United Netherlands,* II, 422, 424; IV, 339, 13; I, 41. *Dutch Republic,* III, 599.

45. Praz, *Romantic Agony,* p. 190. On Machiavelli, see examples cited below, pp. 121, 123. Prescott's comment on the Neapolitans appears in his Diary (January 28, 1817), MHS, p. 85; cf. *Ferdinand and Isabella,* II, 258–59, 259 n. 1. See, for example, F. O. Matthiessen, *American Renaissance: Art and Expression in the Age of Emerson and Whitman* (New York, 1941).

46. Parkman, *Vassal Morton,* chap. xxxi, p. 170; cf. *ibid.,* p. 185. Prescott, *Ferdinand and Isabella,* I, 5, 6, 8, 24–25, 26. See, for example, Motley, "Peter the Great," in *Essays from the N.A.R.,* pp. 178–79; *United Netherlands,* III, 273.

47. *Dutch Republic,* I, 367, 367–68. Cf. *ibid.,* p. 366.

48. *Ibid.,* pp. 431, 438. *John of Barneveld,* I, 6–7; II, 262. For Motley's emphasis on Maurice's jealousy, see his use of the evidence in *ibid.,* I, 45–46. Prescott makes a slight effort to sustain a comparison of Gonzalo Pizarro and Macbeth. *Peru,* II, 324, 368.

49. *John of Barneveld,* I, 323; II, 152.

50. *United Netherlands,* III, 444–45. Motley claims that Champagny's request for more mendicant friars was intended as a "remedy" for the province's economic ills. Champagny did not ask for "more Jesuits." He asked for more mendicant friars to catechize the city's children; if not enough friars were available, he said, perhaps Jesuits could be sent to do the job. He then suggested that Jesuits from Antwerp be the first ones to be sent. (I have taken this version from Motley's own account, III, 23.)

51. Parkman, *Jesuits,* p. 97 (cf. Prescott, *Ferdinand and Isabella,* I, 245); *The Old Régime in Canada* (Boston, 1893), p. 8.

52. *Ibid.,* p. 35; *Jesuits,* p. 172; *Montcalm and Wolfe,* I, 68. Prescott, *Ferdinand and Isabella,* III, 336. Motley, *United Netherlands,* III, 443. *Montcalm and Wolfe,* I, 205. Prescott, *Peru,* I, 418. *Montcalm and Wolfe,* I, 101–4, 107. The name of the honorable priest was Girard.

53. Motley's statement that the "devilish arts of the Jesuits" changed the character of Philip William, son of William of Orange.

54. *Montcalm and Wolfe,* I, 114.

55. Prescott, *Ferdinand and Isabella,* II, 137–38. Parkman noted that priests, and especially French priests, had studied "the art of kindling the flames of zeal"—and controlling them—in the "female mind" (*Jesuits,* p. 198).

56. Prescott, *Ferdinand and Isabella,* I, 268–69. Parkman, *Jesuits,* pp. 146–47. Parkman

noted that the saints, "so human, yet so divine, in whom their faith impersonated and drama-tized the great principles of Christian truth . . . , hovered over them, and held before their raptured sight crowns of glory and garlands of immortal bliss." And as he described the Jesuits' departure "from out a living martyrdom" for "perils yet more appalling" in "the blood-stained dens of the Iroquois," he asked: "But, in this exaltation and tension of powers, was there no moment when the recoil of Nature claimed a temporary sway?" This question introduced a paragraph emphasizing the loneliness of suffering in the forest and expressing the hypothesis that the Jesuit sometimes thought nostalgically of the "ancient centre of his faith" and "rekindled [his] fervors to his stern apostleship" by experiencing an overpowering vision of the Virgin (pp. 147–48).

57. *Jesuits*, p. 351; *Montcalm and Wolfe*, I, 104, 116. Motley, *United Netherlands*, II, 30–32.

58. Prescott, *Ferdinand and Isabella*, I, 246. Parkman, *Frontenac*, p. 150.

59. Parkman, *La Salle*, pp. 28–29, 140–41; *Frontenac*, p. 25; *Half-Century*, I, 16–17; *Frontenac*, p. 374. Motley, *United Netherlands*, II, 424. Prescott, *Ferdinand and Isabella*, I, 336. *Frontenac*, p. 397; *Montcalm and Wolfe*, I, 16–17, 355. Motley, *John of Barneveld*, I, 54.

60. Parkman, *Half-Century*, I, 2; *Montcalm and Wolfe*, I, 355.

61. Prescott, *Philip II*, I, 74. Motley, *United Netherlands*, III, 531, 534, 531.

62. Letter to his father, March 3, 1855, in *Correspondence*, I, 172. *United Netherlands*, II, 356; III, 412; I, 439. *Dutch Republic*, II, 4. *United Netherlands*, III, 535.

63. "Maintaining over all Christendom a gigantic system of bribery, corruption, and espionage, keeping the noblest names of England and Scotland on his pension-list of traitors, and impoverishing his exchequer with the wages of iniquity paid in France to men of all degrees, from princes of blood like Guise and Mayenne down to the obscurest country squires, he ever felt that these base and bloody deeds were not crimes, but the simple will of the god-head of which he was a portion." *Ibid.*

64. *Ibid.*, pp. 534–35, 540–41.

65. *Ibid.*, p. 535 (italics mine).

66. Prescott (1847): "Yet whatever the vices of the Castilian cavalier, hypocrisy was not among the number" (*Peru*, I, 409). Parkman (1865): "Those who take this for hypocrisy do not know the Spaniard of the sixteenth century" (*Pioneers*, p. 99). Cf. *Dutch Republic*, II, 203; *United Netherlands*, IV, 443–44.

67. August 16, 1856, Prescott Papers, MHS.

68. *Ferdinand and Isabella*, II, 122. Letter to Motley, April 28, 1856, Prescott Papers, MHS. Letter to Bancroft, n.d. (endorsed "May 1840"), Bancroft Papers, MHS. See *Mexico*, III, 361–62.

69. Notebooks VII, Prescott Papers, MHS, pp. 109–10.

70. Letter to Motley, April 28, 1856, in *Correspondence of . . . Motley*, I, 192. Cf. Motley to his wife (May 28, 1858) criticizing Prescott's Philip. *Ibid.*, p. 228.

71. Motley, *Dutch Republic*, III, 137–40. See, for example, *ibid.*, I, 184. Prescott, *Philip II*, III, 447–48; I, 130. *Dutch Republic*, II, 4; I, 145: "Certainly if he had not possessed a feeling for art, he would have been a monster." *Ibid.*, I, 188; Prescott, *Philip II*, II, 248. *Dutch Republic*, I, 145; *United Netherlands*, I, 273. *Philip II*, I, 486–87.

72. "Peter the Great," in *Essays from the N.A.R.*, p. 192.

73. *Dutch Republic*, I, 124. Motley to his father, May 18, 1852, in *Correspondence*, I, 142: "It is a comfort, as I can't make speeches or write articles in the newspapers (if I wished) against General Haynau, or Emperor Nicholas, or President Bonaparte, to be able to pitch into the Duke of Alva and Philip the Second to my heart's content. It is quite satisfactory to express sentiments, which if I had the advantage of living three hundred years ago, and had had the audacity to express myself as freely, would have entitled me to be burned alive on an average

twice a day, and to know that the only martyrdom I am likely to experience is that of not finding a publisher for my treason, for fear that it won't pay; the only rack that of being roasted on the gridiron of some singeing, scorching, red-hot review."

74. *History,* IV, 278 (cf. X, 82); II, 453; III, 132–34, 138–39, 141, 149, 157–60; IX, 99–100.

75. See his letters to Samuel Osgood, February 21, 1868; to C. C. Perkins, June 12, 1869; to Mrs. J. C. Bancroft Davis, September 4, 1870—all in Howe, *Bancroft,* II, 203–41. See also his letter to Department of State, December 1, 1870, Bancroft Papers, MHS.

76. Letter to Professor Nippoli, March 5, 1869, Bancroft Papers, MHS. Bancroft recognized his diplomatic obligation to avoid meddling in German politics, but he told Nippoli that "my opinions as published belong to anyone who wishes to use them."

77. Parkman, *Jesuits,* p. 320.

78. Parkman, *Pioneers,* p. 97; Frontenac, p. 395.

NOTES TO CHAPTER VI

1. *History,* III, 266 (cf. Emerson, *Works,* IV, 20–22); II, 266.

2. *Ibid.,* III, 265, 266.

3. *Ibid.,* II, 266–69.

4. *Ibid.,* III, 291, 300, 285–88, 294, 278, 154, 190–91.

5. "Progress of the Race," in *Literary Miscellanies,* p. 413. *History,* III, 302, 305–6.

6. *Ibid.,* pp. 300, 304.

7. *Ibid.,* IV, 340–41, 342, 355.

8. *Ibid.,* p. 354. Cf. *William Gilmore Simms, The Yemassee: A Romance of Carolina* (New York: Lovell, Coryell and Co., n.d.), 1–20, 414–25.

9. *History,* II, 98; cf. Theodore Parker, "Prescott's Conquest of Mexico" (1849), in *The American Scholar,* p. 247: "The pilgrim and the puritan knew that the naked savages had no natural right adverse to the welfare of the human race"; but they also "knew," he said, that civilized men had to pay the full price. See Washington Irving, *A History of New York . . . , by Diedrich Knickerbocker* (London, 1820), pp. 68, 87.

10. *History,* V, 165. Parker, "Prescott's Mexico," in *The American Scholar,* pp. 246–47. See Julius W. Pratt, "John L. O'Sullivan and Manifest Destiny," *New York History,* XIV (July 1933), 214–34. Bancroft, *History,* IV, 425, 426.

11. *Ibid.,* II, 101.

12. *Ibid.,* VII, 398; VI, 505–6. For a discussion of the Indian in drama, see Albert Keiser, *The Indian in American Literature* (New York, 1933), pp. 65–101. This chapter was written before I had read Roy Harvey Pearce, *The Savages of America: A Study of the Indian and the Idea of Civilization* (Baltimore, 1953); his study is much more complex than Mr. Keiser's early work.

13. Otis Pease, for example, makes this error in *Parkman's History: The Historian as Literary Artist* (New Haven, 1953), p. 13; he says that Parkman, despite his prejudice, at least did better than previous writers by portraying the Indian as he really appeared to frontiersmen. But Prescott had criticized Charles Brockden Brown for excess in just this kind of portrayal, for emphasizing only "the rude and uncouth lineaments of the Indian character, its cunning, cruelty, and unmitigated ferocity, with no indications of a more generous nature." Preferring Cooper, Prescott admitted that Cooper's "portrait [was] not strictly that of the fierce son of the forest," but (like Cooper himself) he said that this portrait was "at least sufficiently true for poetical purposes." ("Brown," in *Biographical Miscellanies,* pp. 159–60.) Even in Cooper there are enough Indians with "uncouth lineaments" to justify his statement

in the Preface (1850) to the *Leatherstocking Tales* that he was taking a "poetic" view of his Indian heroes. His Sioux Mahtoree is as cunning and vicious as any of Parkman's savages. Simms and Robert Montgomery Bird, of course, are even more obvious predecessors of Parkman. See the portrayal of Ishiagaska in Simms's *The Yemassee*, pp. 45, 351–52; see Robert Montgomery Bird, *Nick of the Woods; or, the Jibbenainosay*, 2d ed. (New York, 1853), pp. iv–vii. See Cooper, *The Prairie*, pp. 59–65, 334. See also Keiser, *Indian in American Literature*, chap. x: "Stark Realism on Kentucky's Dark Ground." (See *ibid.*, pp. 142–43.)

14. *History*, VII, 118, 120.

15. Parkman to Bancroft, June 4 and July 30, 1882, Bancroft Papers, MHS.

16. Parkman, *Jesuits*, p. lxxxix; Bancroft, *History*, III, 305.

17. *Conspiracy of Pontiac*, I, 229, 237; *Jesuits*, p. 348. See Bird, *Nick of the Woods*, pp. iv–vii. Cf. Prescott, "Brown," in *Biographical Miscellanies*, p. 160.

18. *Frontenac*, pp. 402–3; cf. his use of an Indian's metaphor comparing the Iroquois to "wasps." *Ibid.*, p. 156. See, for example, *La Salle*, pp. 192–93; *Half-Century*, I, 250, 254. *Conspiracy of Pontiac*, I, 157; *Montcalm and Wolfe*, I, 335–36. Cf. *Jesuits*, p. 206.

19. Prescott, "Brown," in *Biographical Miscellanies*, pp. 126, 153–58. Parkman, *Half-Century*, I, 32 (cf. *Montcalm and Wolfe*, I, 208–9), 33. See Melville's description of "the cunning curtain of purpleness" under which Nature conceals the terrors around "Enceladus." *Pierre; or the Ambiguities* (New York, 1852), pp. 381–83. Cf. Parkman, *Jesuits*, p. 206.

20. Parkman, *Half-Century*, I, 33–34, 35–36.

21. *Jesuits*, p. 434; *Frontenac*, p. 286; *Jesuits*, p. 360; *La Salle*, pp. 203, 206; *Frontenac*, pp. 167, 286–87.

22. *La Salle*, pp. 212, 205, 211–12.

23. *Frontenac*, pp. 150, 211. ("It was one of those days when the trees stand white as spectres in the sheltered hollows of the forest, and bare and gray on the wind-swept ridges." *Ibid.*, p. 208.) *Half-Century*, I, 118; *Montcalm and Wolfe*, II, 281; *Half-Century*, I, 284–85, 276; *Frontenac*, p. 209; *Conspiracy of Pontiac*, I, 217. See Cotton Mather, "Decennium Luctuosum," in *Narratives of the Indian Wars*, ed. Charles H. Lincoln (New York, 1913), pp. 193, 201, 203 ("It is harder to Find than to Foil them"), 224, 238–39.

24. *La Salle*, pp. 201–25; *Montcalm and Wolfe*, I, 334–36, 506, 209.

25. Bancroft, *History*, III, 327; Parkman, *Half-Century*, I, 254; *Conspiracy of Pontiac*, I, 218.

26. Parkman, *Jesuits*, pp. xxxiv–xxxv, 112. Cf. William Byrd, *Histories of the Dividing Line betwixt Virginia and North Carolina*, ed. Wm. K. Boyd (Raleigh, 1929), p. 114. Cf. the descriptions of the same hags in Simms, *The Yemassee*, pp. 291–92, 296–300; and Cooper, *The Prairie*, p. 330: "withered crones."

27. *Half-Century*, I, 280. *Conspiracy of Pontiac*, I, 147. See *Jesuits*, p. 320, for Parkman's view of the inevitability of the Indian's decline.

28. *Jesuits*, pp. liii–lxvii. *Frontenac*, pp. 80, 107–10.

29. *Jesuits*, p. lx; *Montcalm and Wolfe*, I, 174, 175.

30. *Jesuits*, pp. 447, 448. *Conspiracy of Pontiac*, I, 146; cf. *Jesuits*, p. 434. Parkman made the same point in similar language in *Montcalm and Wolfe*, II, 146.

31. *Montcalm and Wolfe*, I, 172 (cf. *Conspiracy of Pontiac*, I, 186), 174.

32. *Jesuits*, pp. 336, 393, 398, 400–401, 423, 424, 432–33.

33. *Montcalm and Wolfe*, I, 258 (cf. *Half-Century*, II, 190–91, 196), 245, 265, 272–73, 277–79, 275, 283.

34. "Irving's Granada," in *Biographical Miscellanies*, p. 103. Letter to Obadiah Rich, Nov. 12, 1828, Prescott Papers, MHS. *Ferdinand and Isabella*, I, 236, 296, 306; II, 102–5; I, 313–15.

35. *Ibid.*, II, 105.

36. *Ibid.*, I, 346, 363, 365, 366, 367.

37. *Ibid.*, pp. 388, 400. The same imagery and the same traits prevail in the account of Ximenes' crusade against African Moslems. *Ibid.*, II, 305–6.

38. *Ibid.*, pp. 88, 31, 99.

39. *Ibid.*, pp. 99, 73, 99, 100.

40. *Philip II*, III, 293, 39, 49–50 (cf. *Conspiracy of Pontiac*, I, 202), 51, 76, 69, 71, 73, 77, 51–55, 53.

41. *Ibid.*, 164–65, 166, 168.

42. *Conspiracy of Pontiac*, I, 217, 229; *Philip II*, III, 285–88; cf. III, 103.

43. *Ferdinand and Isabella*, II, 41–42, 103–4; *Philip II*, III, 293, 295.

44. Motley, *Morton's Hope*, I, 198 (cf. I, 200).

45. *Philip II*, I, 181–82. *Morton's Hope*, I, 197; *United Netherlands*, III, 296. As support for this statement, Motley, who has conventionally referred to Dr. Lopez as "the Jew," quotes the following sentence from the sixteenth-century English account of Lopez' treason: "*And further to set him on, he was to be put in mind that he had daughters to marry,* for whom the king would provide, and what great honors and rewards he should have." Notice that in his text Motley has made Lopez the initiator of this part of the bargain.

46. *Ferdinand and Isabella*, I, 236; *Philip II*, I, 73; *Ferdinand and Isabella*, I, 235, 236, 237, 237 n. 8, 238, 237, 239 n. 13.

47. *Ibid.*, II, 137; I, 235, 251–52.

48. *Ibid.*, p. 253; II, 140, 142.

49. *Ibid.*, pp. 141, 143; III, 313; II, 146, 146–47.

50. It was published "while the Spanish sovereigns were still detained before Granada." *Ibid.*, II, 135.

51. *Ibid.*, pp. 135, 151–54, 152.

52. *Mexico*, I, 353. See, for example, *Peru*, II, 197–99.

53. Letter to Bancroft, October 27, 1839, Bancroft Papers, MHS.

54. *Mexico*, I, 13–14 (cf. I, 50), 125–31; II, 9–10, 51, 8; I, 73, 25. *Peru*, I, 410. (When he is first introduced, Atahuallpa is "seated on a low cushion, somewhat after the Morisco or Turkish fashion." (*Ibid.*, I, 396.) *Mexico*, I, 85.

55. *Peru*, I, 116–17, 171–72, 71 (cf. *Mexico*, I, 43), 143–44, 174, 173.

56. See, for example, *Mexico*, I, 28–33, 36, 48–49; *Peru*, I, 18, 46–47, 62–70. *Mexico*, II, 32–33, 33 n. 11, 177; *Peru*, I, 85.

57. *Mexico*, II, 34–35, 30–31, 35–36.

58. *Ibid.*, pp. 36, 33. See, for example, *Peru*, II, 196; *Philip II*, III, 293. *Mexico*, II, 36–37.

59. *Ibid.*, p. 38.

60. *Ibid.*, pp. 39, 350, 55. His picture of the two leaders is enlarged on pp. 57–58.

61. *Peru*, I, 462, 484, 439.

62. *Mexico*, I, 85–86; *Peru*, I, 40; *Mexico*, I, 107.

63. *Peru*, II, 198–99, 467–69, 469–70.

64. *Mexico*, II, 57–58; III, 18; I, 454. *Peru*, II, 273; cf. II, 41.

65. *Mexico*, II, 173, 173–74, 343–44. *Peru*, I, 485; II, 147–48.

66. *Mexico*, I, 421; II, 16–17. *Ibid.*, I, 461; II, 339; III, 35. *Peru*, II, 44, 44–45, 53, 238.

67. *Peru*, II, 66; I, 506, 504; II, 48, 50, 51, 238. *Mexico*, II, 339; III, 37. *Peru*, I, 254, 408, 419, 450. *Mexico*, I, 443, 450–51. *Peru*, I, 453.

68. *Mexico*, II, 149–50; I, 443; II, 325, 327, 328.

69. *Ibid.*, p. 319; *Peru*, I, 18, 77–80, 417.

70. *Mexico*, II, 24; cf. *Peru*, I, 420–21. *Mexico*, II, 66; *Peru*, II, 197–98. *Mexico*, II, 320, 343–44, 350–51. *Peru*, I, 485, 488.

71. *Mexico*, II, 349.

72. *Ibid.,* I, 291–92; cf. *ibid.,* p. 361. Parkman, *Jesuits,* pp. 73, 90, 118, 320, 35.

73. A major reason for the Huron's inability to understand Christianity was "the inert mass of pride, sensuality, and superstition." *Jesuits,* p. 135.

74. *Pioneers,* p. xii (italics mine); *Montcalm and Wolfe,* I, 478. Cf. *ibid.,* p. 491.

NOTES TO CHAPTER VII

1. Donald A. Rindge has used the analogy to dramatic acts, but his analysis of the history differs considerably from mine. See "The Artistry of Prescott's 'The Conquest of Mexico,'" *New England Quarterly,* XXVI (December 1953), 454–76.

2. Compare *La Salle,* p. 188, and Prescott, *Mexico,* II, 376.

3. Donald Rindge (*N.E.Q.,* XXVI, 456) gives a good argument for including such an epilogue in the history, but he fails to demonstrate that the epilogue which Prescott wrote actually achieves the formal balance for which he defends it. The epilogue does show the empire under Christian control, but its greatest emphasis is on the tireless activity of Cortés.

4. It is only recently that Maurice Collis, in *Cortés and Montezuma* (London: Faber & Faber. n.d.) has offered a hypothesis that reconciles Montezuma's unwavering belief in the prophecy with his inconsistent conduct.

5. Consider his rebuke of Cortés for insulting the Mexican gods, and his insistence on going alone to ask their forgiveness of this insult: *Conquest of Mexico,* II, 150. Consider, too, his warning to Cortés that building a chapel on the *teocalli* will be dangerous (*ibid.,* p. 209); and his conventional refusal to accept the Spaniards' God on his deathbed (*ibid.,* p. 344).

6. Admiral Morison praises Prescott's "vivid and spirited narrative style" but refuses to "analyze" it because "it is to be enjoyed and admired, not plucked apart." Samuel Eliot Morison, "Prescott: the American Thucydides," *The Atlantic Monthly* (November, 1957), p. 167. Donald Rindge (*N.E.Q.,* XXVI, 463) says that "Prescott is as careful an artist in the minutest details" as in "the larger elements," but in his discussion of Prescott's style (pp. 470 ff.) he overlooks faulty details.

7. *The Art of History* (London, 1926), 127–28.

8. See "Irving's Granada," in *Biographical Miscellanies,* pp. 91–92, 97.

9. "No *words, epithets,* that do not make it *clearer,* or *stronger. Figures* I dislike—unless they conduce highly to both these ends." Commonplace Book (1820–22), Prescott Papers, MHS.

10. See Ticknor, *Prescott,* pp. 148–50; and Prescott, Commonplace Book, p. 83.

11. In *Biographical Miscellanies,* p. 178.

12. See, for example, "a picturesque assemblage of water, woodland, and forest" (*Conquest of Mexico,* II, 51); *"terra firma"* (*ibid.,* p. 111); and "the pure element" (*ibid.,* p. 114).

13. See, for example, *ibid.,* p. 280. There, although Cortés and his troops have just returned to a rebellious city from which it is unlikely that they will be able to escape, Prescott concludes his account of their arrival by announcing that "both parties soon forgot the present in the interesting recapitulation of the past."

NOTES TO CHAPTER VIII

1. Chester Higby and Bradford Schantz use the analogy to drama (as Motley does) when discussing the *Dutch Republic,* but they include both Parts I and II in the "prologue." *Repre-*

sentative Selections, p. lxxxiii. For my discussion of Motley's "Historical Introduction," see above, Chapter IV.

2. See, for example, *Dutch Republic,* III, 239, 259.

3. Compare his treatment of the rebels' finances, *ibid.,* II, 375, 386. He says that the Dutch captured enough treasure to finance the war for two years, but soon he is once again lamenting William's lack of funds, and he does not explain the discrepancy.

4. *Ibid.,* I, 552, 553, 564, 565, 569, 571, 572. Cf. II, 103–4, 108, 166, 167; III, 620, 622.

5. She has promised Montigny's mother that she will intercede for him.

6. See above, Chapter II.

7. This entire section leads to Philip's own statement that the Spanish Inquisition was not needed in the Netherlands, because "the inquisition of the Netherlands is much more pitiless than that of Spain." Motley italicizes these words, *ibid.,* I, 341.

8. See, for example, the paragraphs on Charles V's treachery and niggardliness, *ibid.,* pp. 119–20.

9. See, for example, *ibid.,* II, 254–55, 542–44.

10. Motley, *Correspondence,* I, 225 (May 16, 1858).

11. "The weather-beaten Palinurus, as [Viglius] loved to call himself, had conducted his own argosy so warily that he saved his whole cargo and perished in port at last." *Dutch Republic,* III, 207–8. Cf. II, 49–50; III, 398.

12. See, for example, his detailed account of the torture of a naked bride on her wedding night, the night of the Spanish Fury, *ibid.,* pp. 114–15; cf. I, 68, for another among dozens of examples.

13. For pairs, see, for example, *ibid.,* p. 482: "boldly and bitterly"; II, 148: "clemency and forgiveness" and "distinguished and doomed seigniors." For rhetorical questions, see I, 53, 54, 66–67, 68, 72, 558.

NOTES TO CHAPTER IX

1. The phrase is Sir Henry Maine's. Quoted in Watt Stewart, "George Bancroft," *The Marcus W. Jernegan Essays in American Historiography* (Chicago, 1937), p. 23.

2. *A Half-Century of Conflict,* although written several years after *Montcalm and Wolfe,* covers the decades preceding the Seven Years' War.

3. The errors in Parkman's interpretation of Braddock's defeat have received considerable attention in recent years. The essential criticisms of earlier scholars are summarized conveniently in Otis Pease, *Parkman's History,* pp. 70–76.

4. Parkman assumes that "the Quakers" controlled the assembly, and he treats them consistently as a bloc.

5. R. W. B. Lewis, *The American Adam: Innocence, Tragedy, and Tradition in the Nineteenth Century* (Chicago, 1955), p. 170.

6. Bancroft himself had written of Louis XV, Madame de Pompadour, Newcastle, Pitt, Wolfe, Braddock, Amherst, Loudon, Townshend, Frederick, George III, Washington, and others.

7. Lewis, *The American Adam,* p. 166.

8. The French, for example, regarded the Acadians as mere "tools of policy, to be used, broken, and flung away," *Montcalm and Wolfe,* I, 245. "Shirley's grand scheme for cutting New France in twain had come to wreck," *ibid.,* p. 417. And autumn was "that festal evening of the year, when jocund Nature disrobes herself, to wake again refreshed in the joy of her undying spring," *ibid.,* p. 433.

9. See *La Salle*, p. 168; and Parkman's letter to the *Boston Advertiser*, September 4, 1861. In both passages trite metaphors seem the more ludicrously mixed because of the heroic rhythm and blunt emphasis.

10. *Correspondence*, I, 237 (May 30, 1858).

11. See, for example, *Montcalm and Wolfe*, I, 494–95; II, 53, 94–95, 200.

12. See above, pp. 134–35. See *Montcalm and Wolfe*, I, 321–22.

Index